Danish and German Silent Cinema

Danish and German Silent Cinema

Towards a Common Film Culture

Lars-Martin Sørensen and
Casper Tybjerg

EDINBURGH
University Press

Edinburgh University Press is one of the leading university presses in the UK. We publish academic books and journals in our selected subject areas across the humanities and social sciences, combining cutting-edge scholarship with high editorial and production values to produce academic works of lasting importance. For more information visit our website: edinburghuniversitypress.com

© editorial matter and organisation Lars-Martin Sørensen and Casper Tybjerg, 2023, 2025
© the chapters their several authors 2023, 2025

Grateful acknowledgement is made to the sources listed in the List of Illustrations for permission to reproduce material previously published elsewhere. Every effort has been made to trace the copyright holders, but if any have been inadvertently overlooked, the publisher will be pleased to make the necessary arrangements at the first opportunity.

Edinburgh University Press Ltd
13 Infirmary Street
Edinburgh EH1 1LT

First published in hardback by Edinburgh University Press 2018

Typeset in 11/13 Monotype Ehrhardt by
IDSUK (DataConnection) Ltd

A CIP record for this book is available from the British Library

ISBN 978 1 3995 0837 7 (hardback)
ISBN 978 1 3995 0838 4 (paperback)
ISBN 978 1 3995 0839 1 (webready PDF)
ISBN 978 1 3995 0840 7 (epub)

The right of Lars-Martin Sørensen and Casper Tybjerg to be identified as the editors of this work has been asserted in accordance with the Copyright, Designs and Patents Act 1988, and the Copyright and Related Rights Regulations 2003 (SI No. 2498).

Contents

Figures vi
Acknowledgements ix
List of contributors x

1. Introduction 1
   Lars-Martin Sørensen and Casper Tybjerg
2. Danish-German Cinematic Interconnections and the Prospects of an Entangled Film Historiography 24
   Casper Tybjerg
3. How 'Danish' were Danish Stars in Germany during the Silent Era? 51
   Alice A. Salamena and Stephan Michael Schröder
4. How 'German' was German Film in Denmark during the Silent Era? 79
   Lars-Martin Sørensen
5. Sherlock Holmes in Transit 106
   Palle Schantz Lauridsen
6. Female Stars of German Cinema in an Entangled Danish Film Culture 130
   Helle Kannik Haastrup
7. Same Frame, Different Lens? Exporting Danish Film Style 158
   Vito Adriaensens
8. 'Die Deutsch-Nordische-Film-Union marschiert!': the Entangled Relations between Nordisk Films Kompagni, UFA, and DNFU 1918–1928 183
   Isak Thorsen
9. Pat and Patachon as Transnational Film Stars 208
   Jannie Dahl Astrup

Index 238

Figures

Images

1.1 Same moment, different cameras. A and B cameras were used for domestic and export versions of Pat and Patachon films. Danish Film Institute.   14

3.1 Olaf Fønss on the cover of *Die Filmwoche* in 1923 shortly before the inflation reached its peak: The price of the issue was 3 billion marks! Danish Film Institute, Olaf Fønss collection, Scrapbook 1920–1924.   61

3.2 Asta Nielsen wearing a blond wig in *Die Kinder des Generals* (1912). Danish Film Institute.   64

3.3 The only still existing fan letter to Valdemar Psilander, written by Maria von Wallenstern in 1916, is typical for the utmost care and even display of splendour many of the fan letters show. Danish Film Institute.   67

3.4 The ardent fan Sophie Ruppert sent more than fifty letters to Olaf Fønss between 1914 and 1930. This is one of at least eight portraits she included with her letters. The writing reads 'in perpetual memory'. Danish Film Institute, Olaf Fønss collection.   69

3.5 Lotte Johanssen's fan letter to Olaf Fønss from 1916 is written in a very readable Kurrent, yet it takes familiarity with Kurrent to decipher the letter. Danish Film Institute.   70

4.1 'The Little Trumpeter' high on the fortifications fighting the Prussian invaders. Danish Film Institute.   81

4.2 Three Danes and a German shooting *Engelein* (1914). From the left: Axel Graatkjær, Asta Nielsen, Urban Gad and Karl Freund. Danish Film Institute.   83

4.3 German child actor Otto Reinwald in director Benjamin Christensen's striking framing. *Sealed Orders* (1914). Danish Film Institute.   91

FIGURES

4.4	Marketing film as fine art. Poster featuring the name and image of Nobel Prize winner Gerhard Hauptmann. Danish Film Institute.	95
4.5	A 'Germanised' Dane and an international celebrity from Germany. Asta Nielsen and Henny Porten cheek to cheek in *I.N.R.I.* (1923). Danish Film Institute.	102
5.1	The first issue in one of the Danish series based on the German penny dreadfuls shared its colourful front page drawing and its story with issue 20 in the German series.	111
5.2	Sherlock Holmes (Viggo Larsen) eavesdropping in *Droske 519 (Cab 519)*. Danish Film Institute.	118
5.3	Alwin Neuss as Sherlock Holmes in *Den stjaalne Millionobligation (The Stolen Legacy)*. Danish Film Institute.	121
5.4	Advertisements for *Baskervilles Hund* (*Politiken*, 2 November 1914). The dog looks quite good-natured as opposed to Conan Doyle's description in the novel: 'Never in the delirious dream of a disordered brain could anything more savage, more appalling, more hellish be conceived than that dark form and savage face which broke upon us out of the wall of fog' (Doyle 2017: 651).	123
5.5	When *Sherlock Holmes' Sejr* reached the Danish provinces, the advertisements on many occasions featured a drawing of Alwin Neuss' Sherlock (*Randers Amtsavis*, 17 March 1916).	126
6.1	The Asta Nielsen look in 1925: The Unique Asta 'Den Enestaaende Asta'. 1925. *Vore Damer* 13, no. 19. Royal Danish Library, Copenhagen.	134
6.2	Pola Negri with her signature turban: 'Vore Damers Filmsleksikon – Pola Negri'. 1925. *Vore Damer* 13, no. 47. Royal Danish Library, Copenhagen.	140
6.3	The high priestess of cinema Asta Nielsen: Asta Nielsen at home 'Asta Nielsen i sit hjem'. 1925. *Vore Damer* 13, no. 27. Royal Danish Library, Copenhagen.	144
6.4	Pola Negri and her European 'hygge': 'Pola Negri og hendes Hollywood Hjem'. 1925. *Vore Damer* 13, no. 7. Royal Danish Library, Copenhagen.	148
6.5	Brigitte Helm as the vamp in *Metropolis* on the cover of *Palads-Teatrets Films Nyheder. Sæson 1926–27*, no. 17. Danish Film Institute.	153
7.1	1914, Berlin Grunewald. From left to right: Karl Freund, Axel Graatkjær, Urban Gad. Danish Film Institute.	159

7.2 Axel Graatkjær and Johan Ankerstjerne on an August
Blom set at Nordisk's Valby studio. Danish Film Institute. 172
7.3 Screengrab from *Phantom* (F. W. Murnau, 1922). Courtesy
of Flicker Alley. 173
7.4 *Engelein* (Urban Gad, 1914). Axel Graatkjær (far left),
Karl Freund (to Axel's right) and Asta Nielsen. Danish
Film Institute. 176
7.5 Screengrab from *Algol. Tragödie der Macht* (Hans
Werckmeister, 1920). Courtesy of Filmmuseum München. 178
8.1 Ole Olsen in Nordisk Film's main office in Berlin. Danish
Film Institute. 188
8.2 'Die Deutsch-Nordische-Films-Union marschiert!' Full page
advertisement in *Der Kinematograph*, 6 November 1925, 39. 194
8.3 The trademarks of DAFU and DNFU. 196
8.4 The last feature produced by Nordisk Film in the silent era,
The Joker. Danish Film Institute. 203
9.1 *Schwiegersöhne* (1926, Hans Steinhoff). Danish poster
by Sven Brasch. Danish Film Institute. 211
9.2 Behind the scenes of *Zwei Vagabunden im Prater* in Vienna
(1925, Hans-Otto Löwenstein). Danish Film Institute. 214
9.3 Director Hans Steinhoff (middle) with Carl Schenstrøm
(left) and Harald Madsen (right) on the set of *Schwiegersöhne*
(1926). *Internationale Filmschau*, 5 February 1926. 216
9.4 Harald Madsen and Carl Schenstrøm as Pat and Patachon
on the cover of the Austrian film magazine *Mein Film*,
no. 52, 1926. 218
9.5 German distributor and producer Lothar Stark (seated)
with actors Harald Madsen and Carl Schenstrøm.
Year unknown. Danish Film Institute. 229

Tables

Table 8.1 Nordisk Film's film production 1918–1928 193
Table 8.2 Deutsch-Nordische-Film-Union's co-productions 197

Acknowledgements

The research for this volume would not have been possible without the generous support of the three private Danish foundations:

AUGUSTINUS FONDEN

AAGE OG JOHANNE
LOUIS-HANSENS FOND

DEN A.P. MØLLERSKE
STØTTEFOND

The authors wish to thank the foundations and The Danish Film Institute for hosting our project.

DANISH FILM INSTITUTE

Visit stumfilm.dk / Danish Silent Film:

Notes on the contributors

Lars-Martin Sørensen, PhD, is Head of Research at the Danish Film Institute. Sørensen has authored film historical monographs on Danish and Japanese film, numerous film scholarly articles; headed the four-year collective international project underlying this volume, and is the Editor-in-Chief of the academic online film journal *Kosmorama.org*.

Casper Tybjerg is Associate Professor of Film Studies at the Department of Communication, University of Copenhagen. He is a scholar of Danish and international silent film. He has recently completed a book on the theory and method of film historiography, focusing on the work of Carl Theodor Dreyer. He has also assisted in the Danish Film Institute's efforts to restore Danish silent films and has co-organised several retrospectives, including at the Pordenone Silent Film Festival.

Alice Alessandra Salamena works as research assistant at the Department of Scandinavian and Finnish Studies at the University of Cologne, where she is part of the research project *Fan mail to Danish Film Stars in the 1910s. Exploring the agency and practices of early film fans*, funded by the German Research Foundation (DFG). Currently, she is pursuing a Master's Degree in Scandinavian Studies and Comparative Literature. She is a blog writer and part of the editorial team of the online magazine *norroena.de*.

Stephan Michael Schröder is Professor of Scandinavian Studies at the University of Cologne. One of his main research topics is the relationship between Danish literature and cinema in the silent era, on which he has written numerous articles and a book (*Ideale Kommunikation, reale Filmproduktion. Zur Interaktion von Kino und dänischer Literatur 1909–1918*, 2011). At present, he is part of the research project *Fan mail to Danish Film Stars in the 1910s. Exploring the agency and practices of early* *film fans*, funded by the German Research Foundation (DFG). For more information and a complete bibliography, go to smschroeder.de.

Palle Schantz Lauridsen, dr. phil. is associate professor at the University of Copenhagen, Department of Nordic Studies and Linguistics, where he teaches media analysis, methodologies and media history. His philosophical doctoral thesis (2020) dealt with the multiple configurations of the Sherlock Holmes character in Danish popular culture from a media archaeological point of view.

Helle Kannik Haastrup is associate professor at the University of Copenhagen. Her main research topics include celebrity culture and social media, star studies in a cross-media perspective and digital film and media culture. She has written the first introduction to celebrity culture in Danish *Celebritykultur* (2020), and her current research focus is on the celebrity as role model, influencer and activist on social media. She has recently co-edited *Rethinking Cultural Criticism. New Voices in the Digital* Age (2021).

Vito Adriaensens (PhD, MFA) is a filmmaker and scholar. His experimental films have screened internationally and his first feature, inspired by the Metamorphoses, is *Ovid, New York*. He is the co-author of *Screening Statues. Sculpture and Cinema*, and the author of *Velvet Curtains and Gilded Frames. The Art of Early European Cinema*. He is currently an Adjunct Associate Professor of Film at Columbia University and a researcher at the Université libre de Bruxelles.

Isak Thorsen holds a doctorate in Film Studies from the University of Copenhagen and is the author of *Nordisk Films Kompagni 1906–1924. The Rise and Fall of the Polar Bear* (2017) and co-editor of *A History of Danish Cinema* (2021). He has contributed to several anthologies, among them *Dansk-tyske krige – kulturliv og kulturkampe* (2020) and has written for journals such as *Film History*, *Kintop*, *Porn Studies*, *Journal of Scandinavian Cinema* and *Kosmorama*.

Jannie Dahl Astrup holds a PhD in Film Studies from the University of Copenhagen, with a thesis about the history of the Danish production company Palladium and its transnational mode of distribution in the silent era. Her PhD was conducted at the Danish Film Institute as part of the research project *A Common Film Culture? Denmark and Germany in the Silent Film Era, 1910–1930*. She is a film archivist at Danish Film Institute, Copenhagen.

CHAPTER 1

Introduction

Lars-Martin Sørensen and Casper Tybjerg

This book is a study of the entanglement of Danish and German film cultures in the silent era, of Danish cinema in Germany and German cinema in Denmark. It covers the period from the emergence of the feature film around 1910 to the breakthrough of the talkies around 1930 (a few of the articles, to give proper scope to their topics, start a bit earlier or end a bit later). During this period, scores of Danish-born film professionals were active in Germany and numerous German-born film workers left their mark on Danish film. The stories of the two national cinemas have mostly been told according to narratives of rise and fall: in the years before 1914, Danish cinema, led by the dominant company, Nordisk, rose to international prominence, but declined rapidly when World War I cut off foreign markets; whereas German cinema was seen as artistically and commercially marginal until 1919 and the creative explosion of the early years of the Weimar Republic. Such narratives are simplifications; as first approximations and broad outlines, they are reasonable and accurate enough, but they tend to focus attention on particular aspects of cinema history and not others. We do not seek to overturn these established narratives, but we do want to highlight some new aspects.

Behind the book lies the collective research project 'A Common Film Culture? Denmark and Germany in the Silent Film Era, 1910–1930'. The first section of this introductory chapter will present the project and the current digitisation initiative at the Danish Film Institute from which new access, fresh insights and this study have all emerged. The second section gives a brief sketch of the overall landscape of Danish-German history leading up to the film-cultural entanglements in the silent era, followed by a third section on existing film-historical literature on German-Danish film relations. The fourth and fifth sections will list the most important archives and collections underlying the research for this volume and introduce the individual chapters of this book.

German film scholars have long taken an interest in the international relations of the German cinema before World War II, as the literature review section clearly shows, but while there was a surge of interest in the early 1990s in the connections with Danish cinema, German scholars have since largely turned their attention elsewhere. This fact has given our project a certain lop-sidedness, in that most of the contributors are Danish. In a way, however, this also reflects the lop-sidedness of the relationship between Denmark and Germany, where Denmark was, from Germany's perspective, only one among many neighbouring countries, while Germany's power and size loomed very large for Denmark.

From Data Collection to Research Project

An important impetus for our research project came from data collection. At the Danish Film Institute, work has been ongoing for two decades on writing up entries for what is now called the Danish Film Database, previously known as the National Filmography. This work made evident the limitations of a purely national perspective and the extent of border-crossing activity. To take one example: the Danish film pioneer Viggo Larsen, who managed (meaning 'directed' before an actual 'director' was introduced) the production of almost all films from Nordisk Films Kompagni in Copenhagen from 1906–1909, had an astonishing total of 162 German titles to his credit. Two Danish cinematographers, Axel Graatkjær and Frederik Fuglsang, worked in Germany from the early 1910s onwards, lensing sixty-nine and eighty German-made films, respectively. Indeed, more than thirty Danish-born film professionals did significant work in Germany during the silent period, including major figures like Asta Nielsen, Carl Th. Dreyer and Benjamin Christensen. During World War I, the Danish company Nordisk bought up German distributors and exhibitors, effectively aiming to establish a vertically integrated film corporation with Germany as its home market.

This also facilitated cross-border movement in the opposite direction: German scriptwriters submitted their scripts for Nordisk in Copenhagen in German and could count on a reply from Nordisk in the same language. Between 1907 and 1922, around fifty German writers were behind seventy-seven scripts for films made in Denmark (Sørensen 2020). While few Germans spoke Danish, Denmark was clearly part of a German-speaking cultural sphere. For Danish filmmakers who lost their jobs when the Danish film industry contracted at the end of the 1910s – Robert Dinesen, Holger-Madsen and even Dreyer – Germany was an obvious place to go. And while Denmark was on the periphery of this cultural sphere, it arguably exerted an outsize influence. The power of the giant combine Universum Film Aktien-Gesellschaft (UFA) was partly based on its incorporation of the distribution and exhibition network Nordisk had built, which was effectively nationalised when UFA was formed in 1917.

A very different but also long-lasting impact was that of the comic duo Pat and Patachon (Fyrtaarnet og Bivognen in Danish), produced and promoted by the Danish production company Palladium. Pat and Patachon not only managed the transition from silents to sound, but also made it big on the small television screens until the 1970s, especially in Germany (Astrup, Braae and Ruedel 2022).

The extensive exchange sketched here prompts the central research question that runs through the remainder of this volume's chapters: how and to what extent did Denmark and Germany constitute a common film culture during the silent era rather than two distinct cultural spaces, delimited by language, national regulations, borders and boundaries?

The answers to the question of commonality obviously vary over time and depend on what perspective one takes. There is no doubt that to the Danish film pioneers, the common film culture was first and foremost understood as a common market, whereas – as pointed out by Stephan Michael Schröder (2020) – common ground was understood as 'a deeply rooted cultural relationship, even kinship, which transcends the realm of cinema' in some of the writings of the German Cinema Reform Movement. This movement eagerly promoted cinema reform while battling the materialistic and amoral values allegedly promoted by moving images. Schröder's observation reveals a certain asymmetry in the way the relationship between the two countries was understood by each of them. In fact, asymmetries prevail in a number of respects, as we shall show in the following, not least in the 'big numbers' of the German-Danish film trade. No coherent statistical overviews of film imports and exports between the two nations exist, let alone calculated in a consistent manner throughout the period studied here. However, a few snapshots from secondary sources can shed at least some light on the overall landscape of film exchange in the 1910s and 1920s.

During the early 1910s, when Danish film was expanding rapidly on the international scene, Danish film accounted for around 3–4 per cent of the German market, according to Schröder (2020), whose calculation is based primarily on German trade press journals. In comparison, if we count the films approved by the Berlin censor's office in 1912, 35 per cent of the films were French, 29 per cent American, 23 per cent Italian and just 7 per cent German. Danish film and British film each made up 3 per cent of the total. These figures, of course, do not say anything about the actual number of screenings of the individual titles around the country. The cultural impact of those 3 per cent may have been disproportionate. Schröder therefore suggests operating with a loosely estimated 10 per cent share of Danish films on German screens, because Danish films were immensely popular in the early 1910s. Kristin Thompson's *Exporting Entertainment* (1985) noted the usefulness of the Trade Information Bulletins of the US Department of Commerce as a source for the international film business in the 1920s; these indicate that on the German market in 1926–1927, of all the films exhibited, only around 16–17 per cent were from countries other than Germany or the United States, who shared the bulk of the market more or less equally (Canty 1928, 4). Danish films would only have been a small part of those 16–17 per cent.

No comparable figures are available for the prevalence of German films on Danish screens in the 1910s, but we do have some figures for the 1920s. A report published in 1924 by a semi-private research group investigating state and private monopolies in Denmark refers to 'statistics' for 1922 indicating that German films accounted for 8 per cent of the films screened in Denmark, while 85 per cent were American; Danish and Swedish film together accounted for 3–4 per cent of screenings (Andersen 1924, 40). During the 1910s, the German share would likely have been lower; the boost to the popularity of German films given by international hits like Lubitsch's *Madame Dubarry* (1919) and *Anna Boleyn* (1920) would still have been felt in 1922. Certainly, the years after 1920 saw a huge increase in the coverage of German film in Danish newspapers and the trade press (see Sørensen, this volume). Figures from a Trade Information Bulletin indicated that out of a total number of 1168 films passed by the Danish censors in 1926 (637 features, 531 shorts), 72 (six per cent) were German, but the year before, only 18 films out of 939 were German (Bureau 1928, 7).

Between 1912 and 1922, Germany turned a film trade deficit into a large surplus. According to the *Jahrbuch der Filmindustrie* ('The Film Industry Yearbook'; Wolffsohn 1923, 148), Germany imported 35,850 metres of exposed and unexposed film stock in 1912. Ten years later, the number had risen nearly tenfold to 353,595 metres. Export figures for the same period are 22,110 metres in 1912; in 1922, German film export had risen sharply to 1,027,905 metres of exposed and unexposed film, implying a significant growth in the overall activity of the German film trade and resulting in export figures three times the size of imports. During the latter half of the 1920s, German censors approved between 183–243 German films per year (Wolffsohn 1930, 285). By the end of the silent era, in 1930, the share of German films on Danish screens had risen to 20 per cent, with American films making up 74 per cent, while British, French, Swedish and Soviet films accounted for 6 per cent together. In 1930, Danish film companies only produced three features, thus falling below one per cent of the 395 features screened in Denmark that year (Dinnesen and Kau 1983, 35).

While these figures certainly mirror the fact that relations between Germany and Denmark are in some respects similar to those between a giant and a dwarf, they say very little about the qualitative cultural exchange taking place across the Danish-German border during the silent era. Moreover, the 'dwarf-giant' relationship makes the very high profile of Nordisk Films Kompagni in Germany before World War I stand out as even more remarkable. The same goes for the significant roles played by Danish cinematographers and directors in the German film industry of the 1920s. We will have much more to say about this in the following chapters.

Matters of Culture and Identity

The lopsidedness of the Danish-German relationship was also apparent in the realm of culture and identity. During the nineteenth century, Germany came to be viewed in Denmark as the nation's arch-foe (Østergaard 1990), its influence resented, but inescapable. In Germany, on the other hand, when Denmark was thought of at all, it was generally viewed positively, as a 'Germanic' little brother of sorts. These diverging attitudes were shaped by the very different reactions to the Danish-German War of 1864, the Second Schleswig War, which for Denmark was a humiliating defeat and a national trauma, but for Germany merely a successful warm-up before the triumphantly victorious wars against Austria (1866) and France (1870–1871).

Before the nineteenth century, Danish and German culture were closely entangled in Denmark – and how could it have been otherwise? The Danish monarch ruled over both Danish-speaking and German-speaking populations (as well as Norwegians, Icelanders, Greenlanders, Faroese islanders and the inhabitants of the Danish tropic colonies). Copenhagen, the capital of the realm, was both bilingual and bicultural, a nodal point where Danish and German culture met and interacted (Detering, Gerecke and de Mylius 2001). At the beginning of the eighteenth century, around 20 per cent of the population of Copenhagen were German-speakers (Winge 1996, 51). To be sure, the perceived status of Danish and German culture was not equal; there were convictions of superiority among many 'Germans', and the Danish-German cultural exchange was mostly mono-directional from Germany to Denmark (Frandsen 1994, 7). Still, the relative ease of the relationship between the two largest population groups in the monarchy persisted a long time.

The lands subject to the Danish king formed a 'composite state' (Østergaard 2000); the Danish unified monarchy had a single ruler, but the legal terms under which the different parts of the realm were tied to it varied considerably. This composite state and its common culture would come apart entirely under the pressure produced by the advent of nationalism in the early nineteenth century. In literature, a surge of romantic nationalism contributed to an interest in aesthetically constructing a Danish or Nordic identity. One might still note, however, that romanticism reached Denmark as an import from Germany, that a romantic author like Adam Oehlenschläger (1779–1850) published his only novel in German and that the poet and clergyman N. F. S. Grundtvig (1783–1872), arguably the most vociferous spokesman for Danish nationalism, relied heavily on German thinkers like Herder or Fichte (Schröder 2001, 73–89).

While the importation of romantic nationalism invigorated Danish literature (and culture) in the nineteenth century, in the political realm it would prove fatal to the Danish bicultural state and its status as an important European power. The status of the duchies of Schleswig and Holstein became a source of conflict: these lands were ruled by the Danish king, but under knotty legal conditions that made Danish sovereignty subject to contentious dispute. The predominantly German-speaking middle classes and gentry began agitating for independence from Denmark and entry of Schleswig-Holstein into the German Confederation, while Danish nationalists argued that the Danish state should fully incorporate Schleswig and disengage from Holstein with its almost entirely German-speaking population. Tensions escalated, leading to what was effectively both a civil war and a Danish-German conflict, the First Schleswig War of 1848–1850. It ended in defeat for the army of the Schleswig-Holstein independence movement, but the settlement imposed by the great powers (which upheld the *status quo ante*) left the most important issues unresolved. When the Danish king died without issue in 1863, a succession crisis sparked the Second Schleswig War, known in Germany as the German-Danish War, and in Denmark as the War of 1864 (see Buk-Swienty 2015 for a popular account of the war in English). The war ended in a crushing defeat for Denmark; the whole of Schleswig-Holstein was lost. The large Danish-speaking population in Schleswig, approximately 200,000 people, came under Prussian rule.

As a result of these tensions in Schleswig and of the wars, Danish national identity, not to mention Danish nationalism, tended to have a strongly anti-German cast. The former arch enemy Sweden graduated to a Scandinavian brother during the nineteenth century, while Denmark was reinvented as a small, homogenous nation state (Frandsen 1994, 7) and the long period of a common Danish-German culture fell prey to amnesia. '"Danish national identity," writes historian Rasmus Glenthøj, 'was constructed in opposition to "the German," where symbols, language and history, among other things [. . .], worked as "border guards" separating the national community from "the others"' (Glenthøj 2012, 35). While revanchist sentiment in Denmark abated somewhat as the nineteenth century wore on, the heavy-handed Germanisation policies directed at the Danish minority in Schleswig continued to nourish anti-German sentiments and reinvoked the trauma of the lost war. The importance of this issue can be seen in a report concerning Danish attitudes to Germany entitled '*Bericht über die Presseverhältnisse und Pressebearbeitung in Dänemark*' submitted on 25 October 1914 by the German professor Anton Hollmann to the German Ministry of Foreign affairs. Hollmann quoted from a long conversation he had with the literary scholar Georg Brandes (1842–1927), probably the leading Danish public intellectual of his time and a confirmed internationalist, who already on earlier occasions had heavily criticised the Prussian oppression of the Danes in Schleswig (Schröder 2001, 89–94). According to Hollmann, Brandes said:

> The leading circles of Germany will have to finally come to face the reality that Germany is wholeheartedly hated by us here in Denmark. [. . .] But you already know the reason why the Danes hate Germany. Without your petty-mindedly obdurate *Landratspolitik* [policy of imposing Prussian administration] in North Schleswig, you could have not only the Danish-minded population of North Schleswig, but also, even despite 1864, Denmark and therewith Scandinavia in your pocket! (quoted in Düring Jørgensen 1982, 126; cf. Segelke 2014, 91)

To Brandes it was evident that Denmark was part of the German cultural sphere, and that only Germany's stoking of Danish hostility kept Danes from realising that.

During World War I, Denmark pursued a policy of strict neutrality towards the great powers. In Schleswig, the Danish minority was subject to German military draft; Danish-speaking soldiers constituted the third-largest minority contingent in the German army, after Poles and Alsatians: some 26,000 served, of which more than 4100 were killed (C. B. Christensen 2020, 57–9). The outcome of the war then led to a resolution of the 'Schleswig issue'. Plebiscites were held in North Schleswig (10 February 1920) and Central Schleswig (14 March 1920). In the North, large majorities (75 per cent) voted for reunification with Denmark, while

80 per cent of voters in the central zone wanted to remain part of Germany (Fink 2020). Schleswig was accordingly divided. The 1920 settlement was widely considered satisfactory, though border revision remained a live political issue until World War II. In Schleswig, German irredentism grew powerful during the depression of the 1930s, but never became a force at the national level (Rasmussen 2020, 50–1).

While the Danish relations towards Germany were heavily coloured by the aftermath of the 1864 war, the conflict had swiftly lost its significance in Germany. In 1909, the author Herman Bang (1857–1912), at that time living in Berlin, wrote that 'of the Danes is left the memory of a small nation, with which – oh, so long ago – one had to fight' (Bang 1909, 383). In contrast to the Danish perspective, the Danish-German relation has generally held only a peripheral significance in Germany. This was already true in the eighteenth century and it is still to the present day. But peripheral as it was, it was mostly thought of in positive terms. Major late-nineteenth-century writers like J. P. Jacobsen (1847–1885, greatly admired by Rainer Maria Rilke), the aforementioned Herman Bang, Henrik Pontoppidan (1857–1943), or Martin Andersen Nexø (1869–1954) were translated into German and widely read there, while they have remained largely unknown in the English-speaking world (see Schoolfield 2001; Sandberg 2011; Præstgaard Andersen 2017).

This positive image of Danish culture was often supported and enhanced by the notion of an alleged common ethnicity and origin. Within the kind of ethno-nationalist or even racialist frameworks of thought prevalent in the period, Danish people could be regarded by Germans as fellow 'Teutons' or 'Nordics'. A striking example can be found in the pioneering two-volume history of the German cinema by Oskar Kalbus, published in 1935–1936, *Vom Werden deutscher Filmkunst* ('How German Film Art Came Into Being'). A section entitled 'The Nordic Invasion' describes the impact of Danish films and particularly Danish film actors before and during World War I. Kalbus contrasts the performance of Danish actors with the gesticulating style of the French and Italians:

> the Danish film actors appeared controlled, restrained, without cant or posing, and yet with the strength of gesture demanded by the muteness of the film. They are not only Germanic, they also play in a Germanic manner. They are born movie actors [*Sie sind nicht bloß Germanen, sie spielen auch germanisch. Sie sind die geborenen Filmschauspieler*]. (Kalbus 1935, 21)

Historiography, with its focus on nation states or national cultures, tends to emphasise differences, the exceptional, the historically important singular event. The day-to-day normality, on the other hand, is easily overlooked. Despite the Schleswig issue and its importance for constructing Danish national identity, Germany was arguably the land and culture Denmark had the closest ties to in 1910–1930.

Film Historiography

The most important predecessor and inspiration for our book is the anthology *Schwarzer Traum und weisse Sklavin* (Behn 1994). This was a proceedings volume of papers presented at a conference organised by the film-historical research centre CineGraph in Hamburg in November 1993, the second in a series of conferences devoted to cross-border interactions between Germany and other filmmaking nations, primarily in the silent period (see also Tybjerg, this volume). The book includes contributions by one Italian, nine German and three Danish scholars.[1] In the years just before, many of the contributors had published important work on the relations between Danish and German cinema; interest in pre-1920 German cinema (where the impact of Danish filmmakers and companies was greatest) had been stimulated by the 1990 retrospective *Prima di Caligari* at the Pordenone Silent Film Festival (Cherchi Usai and Codelli 1990).

Marguerite Engberg had written the article 'The Influence of Danish Cinema on German Film, 1910–1920' (1990) for *Griffithiana*, the journal then published by the Pordenone festival, in a theme issue relating to the *Prima di Caligari* retrospective. The article does not really make explicit its notion of influence, but is largely devoted to enumerating the many Danish film people who went to work in Germany. It also points out the decisive role of Nordisk in promoting the *Autorenfilm*, a significant trend in German cinema in 1913–1915 to make 'literary' films, either adapted from or based on original scripts by established literary authors. Unlike earlier treatments (for instance, Diederichs 1990), the articles by Leonardo Quaresima and Deniz Göktürk in the *Schwarzer Traum* volume both emphasise the key role played by Nordisk in introducing and boosting this trend (Göktürk 1994; Quaresima 1994; see also Quaresima 1990, 1995). Manfred Behn, the volume's editor, had contributed important sections on UFA and the Nordisk company to the massive *Das Ufa-Buch* (Bock and Töteberg 1992, 28–37). Heide Schlüpmann's contribution on Asta Nielsen builds on her book *The Uncanny Gaze* (2010; first published in German in 1990) to argue for Nielsen's significance as an exemplar of female control, not only of the movie production process, but also through an aesthetics where the female gaze shapes the narrative (Schlüpmann 1994).

The 1990 Pordenone retrospective had been an attempt to remedy the neglect of pre-Weimar filmmaking caused to a considerable degree by

Siegfried Kracauer's high-handed dismissal: 'It was only after the first World War that the German cinema really came into being. Its history up to that time was prehistory, an archaic period insignificant in itself' (Kracauer [1947] 2004, 15). He made only the briefest of mentions of Nordisk, simply paraphrasing the nationalist-tinged condemnation of the company's hardnosed business methods in the 1933 volume *Der Film in Wirtschaft und Recht*: 'The Danish Nordisk went to the limit to ruin Davidson's Projektion-A.G. Union' (Kracauer [1947] 2004, 22; citing von Boehmer and Reitz 1933, 5). Kracauer also cites Kalbus' 1935 book, which actually gives Danish-German interrelations more space than most later German-language histories of world cinema.

An interesting exception is *Weltmacht Film* ['Cinema, a World Power'], a 1960 introduction to the movies as an art written in German by the Danish theatre historian Vagn Børge (in German: Börge), who became a professor at the University of Vienna in 1948. Børge's book has a very substantial historical section, divided into seven chapters focusing on eight 'major film nations': France, Denmark and Sweden, Russia, Germany, England, Italy and the United States (Börge 1960). This is old-fashioned and narrow, but not all that different from other older film histories – except for the prominence afforded the two Scandinavian countries, which would have been unlikely if Børge had not been Danish. Working from available Danish accounts (of which more in a moment), Børge succinctly describes both Nordisk's attempt to take over the German market during World War I and the power and importance of Asta Nielsen's art. However, Børge's interesting and original book is rarely cited and has vanished into obscurity. In the much more influential German-language history of film *Geschichte des Films* (Gregor and Patalas 1962), the interconnection of Danish and German cinema is barely mentioned. Nordisk's international reach before and during World War I is noted, but after that, 'Danish cinema sank to the provincial level above which it would rise only sporadically in the future' (Gregor and Patalas 1962, 28).

The first full history of the German cinema was the *Geschichte des deutschen Films* published in 1993. The cinema of the Wilhelmine period (ending with the fall of Kaiser Wilhelm II in 1918) is given its due in a section written by Wolfgang Jacobsen, but his account focuses on aesthetics, making no mention of the role of Nordisk. He gives Asta Nielsen and her films pride of place and treats them as the most important body of work in the whole period, but her Danish background is barely mentioned. The Danish entanglements become more visible with a more recent volume, *A New History of the German Cinema* (Kapczynski and Richardson 2012). The book is a mosaic; it is made up of a multitude of small chapters by different authors, each devoted to a particular film or personality. Two of the six chapters on the Wilhelmine period revisit chapters from the *Schwarzer Traum* anthology: Heide Schlüpmann writes on Asta Nielsen's power within the German film industry and Deniz Göktürk returns to August Blom's *Atlantis* (1913) and the *Autorenfilm* (Schlüpmann 2012; Göktürk 2012). In the Weimar section, Patrick Vonderau considers the importance of the Scandinavian theatre for the *Kammerspielfilm* (Vonderau 2012). While Vonderau's book *Bilder von Norden* (2007) is mainly concerned with the interconnections between the film cultures of Germany and Sweden in the 1914–1939 period, it occasionally touches on Denmark, for instance through the important role played by Nordisk in distributing major Swedish productions like *Terje Vigen* (1917) in Germany.

From a relatively early date, historians of Danish silent cinema have emphasised the importance of the German market to Danish film companies. Ebbe Neergaard made this point in his survey of Danish film history and Erik Ulrichsen stressed the international significance of *Atlantis* (Neergaard 1960; Ulrichsen 1956, 37–8). In her magisterial two-volume study of Danish silent cinema before 1914, *Dansk stumfilm. De store år*, Marguerite Engberg gives most attention to production and personnel, but also describes the focus on export of not just Nordisk, but other production companies as well. The most thoroughgoing study of Nordisk as a business is Isak Thorsen's *Nordisk Films Kompagni 1906–1924* (2017), which gives full attention to the importance of Germany for Nordisk, as do his contributions to *The Historical Dictionary of Scandinavian Cinema* (Sundholm et al. 2012). Jan Nielsen's massive study of the Danish film company Skandinavisk-Russisk Handelshus (later Filmfabriken Danmark) documents the German distribution of the company's films as exhaustively as the sources allow (Nielsen 2003). He refrains, however, from making any kind of inferences from the German inspirations for some of the company's most prestigious films like *Enhver* ('Everyman', 1915), inspired by Hugo von Hofmannsthal's play *Jedermann*, and the lost *De dødes Ø* (*The Isle of Death*, 1913), which recreated a large number of paintings by the symbolist artist Arnold Böcklin as tableaux.

German scholars, most of them with a background in Scandinavian studies, have also made a series of vital contributions to the historiography of the Danish cinema. While this is not their main focus, they tend to draw more extensively on German sources and stress more interrelations with Germany than do scholars from either Danish or other backgrounds. Stephan Michael Schröder's exhaustive two-volume study of all aspects of Danish authors' and other literary figures' relation to the cinema in the decade from 1908 to 1918, *Ideale Kommunikation, reale Filmproduktion*, is a clear example; Schröder discusses the German marketing and reception of films like *Atlantis* in detail, and relates the Danish debates around the cinema as an art form to the contemporary but more heated and moralistic debates in Germany sparked by the cinema reform movement (Schröder 2011). Constanze Gestrich's book *Die Macht der dunklen Kammern* (2008) examines how the Danish silent cinema depicted the lure of the Orient and other 'exotic' places; while the focus is clearly on Denmark, the account also examines the German discourse surrounding films like *Maharadjahens Yndlingshustru* (*A Prince of Bharata*, 1917) and its sequel *Maharadjahens Yndlingshustru II* (*A Daughter of Brahma*, 1919), which were popular enough to spawn a further German-made sequel, *Die Lieblingsfrau des Maharadscha, 3. Teil* ('The Maharajah's Favourite Wife, Part 3', 1921). Manfred Behn, who edited *Schwarzer Traum und weisse Sklavin*, presented a carefully researched paper on German policy towards the Danish cinema at a follow-up symposium to the CineGraph conference held in Copenhagen in 1995; the manuscript was circulated to other scholars, but has unfortunately remained unpublished (Behn 1995).

The careers of many film artists and film workers would span more than one country, particularly in the silent period. This is one of the most evident ways the history of film transcends national borders. A number of studies have been devoted to individual film artists active in both Denmark and Germany. The most significant figure here is undoubtedly Asta Nielsen. A very handsome two-volume set, consisting of an annotated filmography (with a subtitle meaning 'Asta Nielsen: Her Films') and an anthology of scholarly studies (subtitled 'Asta Nielsen: Her Cinema'), was published by Filmarchiv Austria in 2010 (Schlüpmann and Gramann 2010; Schlüpmann et al. 2010). The anthology *Importing Asta Nielsen* (Loiperdinger and Jung 2013) takes a very different approach, focusing on the worldwide distribution of Asta Nielsen's films and their role in changing the international film business as feature-length pictures became dominant. A special issue of *Early Popular Visual Culture* (vol. 19, no. 2–3) has extended and developed this work as well as publishing important new source material (see Zimmermann 2021). A third perspective is taken by Julie Allen, who is also a contributor to both the *Importing* anthology and the special issue as well as the translator of Nielsen's memoirs (Nielsen 2022). Allen has devoted a book-length study to Asta Nielsen as an icon of modernity and the role of national identity in her reception in both Germany and Denmark, as well as Australia and New Zealand (Allen 2013; see also Allen 2012a, 2012b, 2021a, 2021b, 2022).

After Asta Nielsen, the most popular Danish border-crossing stars were the comic duo Fyrtaarnet & Bivognen – Pat & Patachon. They have been the subject of book-length studies in both Denmark and Germany (Engberg 1980; Lange-Fuchs 1980; see Astrup, this volume). Among filmmakers, Carl Theodor Dreyer made two films in Germany, *Die Gezeichneten* (1922) and *Michael* (1924), examined, respectively, by Eisenschitz (2016) and Tybjerg (2004). Tybjerg has also discussed the border-crossing character of Dreyer's career in terms of entangled film history (2021). The reception and work of Benjamin Christensen in Germany has been the focus of several articles (Monty 1999; Tybjerg 1999, 2020), and while Urban Gad's career is closely tied to Asta Nielsen's, his life and work has been explored by Stephan Michael Schröder (2010) and Lisbeth Richter Larsen (2014, 2021).

Two of the articles cited were included in *A Common Film Culture?*, a theme issue (no. 276) of *Kosmorama.org*, the academic online journal of the Danish Film Institute; the theme of the issue was Danish-German film relations during the silent era (Sørensen 2020). This theme issue is a prequel of sorts to the present volume. They both present the results of the collective research project 'A Common Film Culture?'. Since 2019, the researchers behind the following chapters have met on a regular basis to discuss drafts for publications and cooperated on the collection of sources underlying project publications such as the *Kosmorama.org* 2020 theme issue and this book.

Digitisation, Research, Sources

The research project 'A Common Film Culture?' was financed by a grant that was part of a generous donation in 2018 from three private foundations to ensure the digitisation of the entire Danish silent film heritage. Of the approximately 2000 silent fiction films produced in Denmark from 1903–1929, around 170 short and 265 feature films, amounting to around 20 per cent of the entire production, survives (T. C. Christensen and Larsen 2021, 108). By the end of 2024, every extant film and fragment of Danish silent cinema will be online and free to watch at www.stumfilm.dk.

To early cinema research, a digitisation initiative like the current Danish one opens up new avenues of research. The vastly improved access to individual works and the possibilities afforded by digital analysis of groups of films are probably the most obvious advantages. In the Danish case, around fifty of the 435 films have only survived as unedited camera negatives. This means that 'digitisation' actually involves narrative reconstruction on the basis of written source material like souvenir programmes and preserved lists of intertitles, as well as the editing and trimming of individual clips to secure suitable pace of action. It also means we can safely assume that none of the fifty works in question have been watched by film historians writing on Danish cinema – or anybody else for the last hundred years for that matter. Therefore, the importance of these films to the history of Danish and international cinema has yet to be established.

The very concrete task of counting the works produced as compared to the works preserved and learning from archivists how many different film copies – for instance, foreign language versions, 35 mm negatives, A- and B-negatives, 16 mm positives – they sometimes use to piece together the best possible version of a film, also underscores the variable nature of 'a film'. The translations of intertitles were not the only changes wrought to foreign language versions of films. Consider, for instance, the difference between shots from different cameras (A- and B-negatives) when two cameras were used for shooting. Or the fact that export versions of popular films were often trimmed to considerably shorter duration than the original version of important works like the comedies of Pat and Patachon, which are instructive in this regard because of the long-lived and widely international circulation of those films (Astrup, Braae and

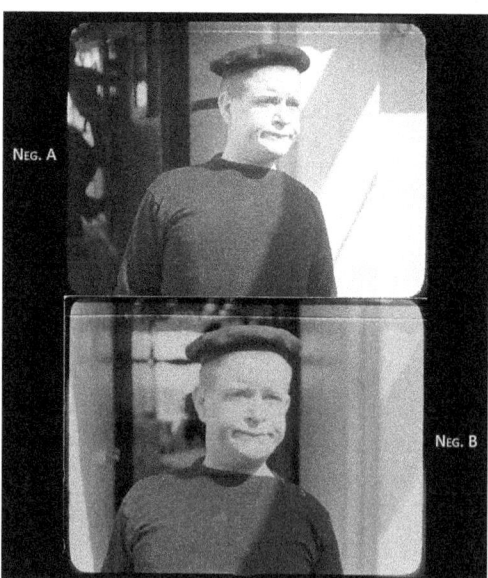

Figure 1.1 Same moment, different cameras. A and B cameras were used for domestic and export versions of Pat and Patachon films. Danish Film Institute.

Ruedel 2022). Add to this, the cuts made locally by censors and cinema owners, or the re-edited versions with sound added decades after the silent original premiered, or the televised version in a different format dubbed in German language. Suddenly the stable unit of 'a film' becomes a number of different versions based on the same material and situated in different contexts. Which one – or ones – eventually landed on the shelves of national film archives and were subsequently studied by film historians greatly influenced the film historical verdicts of posterity.

The handling and restoration of films draws attention to both the materiality and the unstable nature of a given film in an international context. Realising how difficult and limited access to the surviving Danish silent film heritage was in the past and how different alternate versions of the same film can be casts doubt on a number of film historical judgements. Take for instance the widely circulated notion that poor artistic quality caused Danish film's decline after World War I proposed by the *doyenne* of Danish silent film research, Marguerite Engberg, in her two-volume monograph on Danish silent cinema (Engberg 1977, 9). With only around 20 per cent of the total production surviving, Danish Film Institute curator Thomas C. Christensen has asked if such a verdict can plausibly be handed down at all (T. C. Christensen 1997; cf. Thorsen 2020, 215–16). Or take another verdict by Engberg, namely her rejection of film pioneer Viggo Larsen's capacity to develop artistically from film to film (Engberg 1977, 144; 1994, 8). In her critique, Engberg refers to Larsen's numerous works for Nordisk Films Kompagni, where – as mentioned above – he was leading director from 1906–1909. However, only a fraction of Larsen's films from the early years in Copenhagen survives and his list of 162 German productions goes unmentioned by Engberg even though the sheer number of productions seem to suggest that to some people, Viggo Larsen's contribution to silent cinema was anything but artistically uninteresting. Perhaps, in years to come, German digitisation drives will offer better access to Larsen's productions for German companies and pave the way for a re-evaluation of his legacy.

Taking the numbers into consideration – that is, the number of surviving films as compared to the total number of films produced – calls for caution and careful wording whenever making general statements on Danish silent cinema as such. The sources are incomplete even if access has improved vastly. This also applies to the non-filmic sources underlying this study. Documents from company archives, collections of fan mail and articles from newspapers, celebrity magazines and the trade press constitute the lion's share of sources for this volume. As far as Danish production companies are concerned, the supply of sources is relatively good. The Danish Film Institute offers access to substantial company archives from the two most important Danish players of the silent era: Nordisk Films Kompagni and Palladium. In Germany, the Federal Archive holds files on UFA, but the initial search undertaken by the research team failed to produce archives on important German companies and conglomerates such as PAGU and Westi. Private archives left by important individuals are again generously available in Denmark, where letter collections of stars like Asta Nielsen, Olaf Fønss and Clara Wieth are among the holdings of the Danish Film Institute. In fact, this project has uncovered that the fan letter collection of Olaf Fønss, with its approximately 2500 letters, turns out to be the largest collection of silent movie fan letters anywhere in the world. Also, the library at Lund University in Sweden has a collection of Asta Nielsen's letters. We found no similar private archives of important figures in Germany, where the aerial bombings during World War II presumably took their toll on archival holdings and the federal structure of the country complicates archival research, since the important institutions responsible for collections and access are decentralised like Germany herself.

Digitised newspapers and trade publications have been an important resource for many of the contributors. In Denmark, a large number of newspapers have been digitised and made searchable through 'Mediestream', the Royal Danish Library's digital media collections service. It offers access to 35 million full text searchable newspaper pages to registered users; everything more than 100 years old is freely available everywhere. The newspaper *Politiken* (traditionally the preferred source of Danish film historians because of its relatively extensive coverage of cinema) is unfortunately not included, but the complete archive is available to subscribers. In Germany, the German Digital Library (Deutsche Digitale Bibliothek) has undertaken to bring 'newspaper holdings and collections [. . .] from different institutions together in one portal'; it should eventually 'comprise all digitised historical newspapers which are stored in German cultural and scientific institutions' and make them searchable (*Deutsches Zeitungsportal* n. d.). At the time of writing, 4.5 million German newspaper pages are accessible, but this has happened so recently that we have not been able to take full advantage of it in our research. As part of our project, we had searchable scans of the trade publications *Erste Internationale Film-Zeitung, Der Kinematograph* and *Lichtbild-Bühne* made (unfortunately, a few years are missing), and we also had access to the most important Danish trade journal, the Copenhagen Cinema Owners Associations' *Filmen* (The Film) from 1912–1919; altogether, more than 100,000 digitally searchable pages.

The Plan of the Book

The book opens with a methodological chapter, 'Danish-German Entanglements' by Casper Tybjerg, who presents the concept of Entangled Film History and argues for its usefulness for a film historiography that crosses national borders. Two complementary chapters on reception follow: 'How "Danish" were Danish Stars in Germany during the Silent Era?' by Alice A. Salamena and Stephan Michael Schröder, and 'How "German" was German Film in Denmark during the Silent Era?' by Lars-Martin Sørensen. The former focuses particularly on the large trove of fan letters held by the Danish Film Institute and the limited degree to which the fans concerned themselves with the 'Danishness' of stars like Olaf Fønss and Clara Wieth. The latter chapter analyses how German film culture was perceived in Danish film trade journals and dailies and to what extent questions of nationality came into play there.

The remainder of the chapters provide a series of case studies that examine particular instances of reception as well as film distribution and production. The figure of Sherlock Holmes and the myriad border-crossing transmedia texts about him are a particularly apt subject for an entangled history, as Michelle Hilmes has pointed out (2017, 143), and Palle Schantz Lauridsen's chapter 'Sherlock Holmes in Transit' demonstrates the truth of this observation. Lauridsen investigates the entanglement of Danish-German film culture through the example of silent-era Danish and German Holmes films, but also looks at penny dreadfuls and stage plays to describe entanglements at the broader level of media culture.

Helle Kannik Haastrup's 'Female Stars of German Cinema in an Entangled Danish Film Culture' examines how three major female stars of the German cinema (Asta Nielsen, Pola Negri and Brigitte Helm) were an integral part of the 1920s Danish film culture, with a particular emphasis on their status as modern 'new women'. Haastrup works with transmedia theory as a framework for understanding how Danish film culture manifested itself in different types of media and media circuits.

Vito Adriaensens' 'Same Frame, Different Lens? Exporting Danish Film Style' examines the careers of Danish cameramen who found work in the German film industry, with a particular focus on Axel Graatkjær, who shot most of Nordisk's pictures before 1910, but subsequently worked in Germany until the end of the silent period, shooting a number of significant films and working with major directors like Lupu Pick, Murnau, Wiene and Paul Czinner.

The Danish production company Nordisk had been a major international force until World War I broke out in 1914, but despite subsequent setbacks, it remained thoroughly tied in with the German market, and by the late 1920s, the company's German subsidiary produced more films than the parent company in Copenhagen, as Isak Thorsen details in 'Die Deutsch-Nordische-Film-Union marschiert!': the Entangled Relations between Nordisk Films Kompagni, UFA, and DNFU 1918–1928.

The other major Danish production company of the 1920s was Palladium, whose biggest asset was the wildly popular comic duo Pat and Patachon. In 'Pat and Patachon as Transnational Film Stars', Jannie Dahl Astrup seeks to explain their popularity outside of Denmark through an examination both of the various entanglements of business partners, production companies, film consortiums and press discourse on Pat and Patachon in German-speaking countries, and of the eight films they made in Germany and Austria. Most of these were talkies, and the chapter therefore extends into the 1930s. While the overall project has been largely focused on the silent era, discussing Pat and Patachon's German-language talkies seemed highly pertinent, especially considering the significance of the duo to any discussion of an entangled German-Danish film culture.

Taken together, these studies clearly show that cinema in Denmark was deeply entangled with Germany; and while the German cinema was much bigger and had many other transnational entanglements, the number and significance of its links with Denmark underscore how important it is for film historians to keep the transnational perspective in mind.

Note

1. In a regrettable lapse in an otherwise well-edited volume, one of the latter, Carl Nørrested, had his last name misspelled as Nørrestedt.

References

Allen, Julie K. 2012a. 'Tea with Goebbels and Hitler: Asta Nielsen in Nazi Germany.' *Journal of Scandinavian Cinema* 2, no. 3: 333–41.
———. 2012b. 'Where Does "die Asta" Belong? The Role of National Identity in Asta Nielsen's German and Danish Reception in the Early 1920s.' *Journal of Scandinavian Cinema* 2, no. 1: 13–26.
———. 2013. *Icons of Danish Modernity: Georg Brandes and Asta Nielsen*. Seattle: University of Washington Press.
———. 2021a. 'Between Stage and Screen: Female European Stars of Early Feature Films in Australasia.' *Early Popular Visual Culture*, 19, no. 2–3: 175–200.
———. 2021b. 'Tracing the Australasian Asta Nielsen Boom in Trove and Papers Past: A Tool for Recreating the Circulation Histories of Silent Films.' *Early Popular Visual Culture* 19, no. 2–3: 261–74.

———. 2022. *Screening Europe in Australasia: Transnational Silent Film Before and After the Rise of Hollywood*. Exeter Studies in Film History. Exeter: University of Exeter Press.

Andersen, H. 1924. *Filmen i social og økonomisk Belysning*. Copenhagen: Komiteen til Belysning af Statsmonopoler.

Astrup, Jannie Dahl, Mikael Braae and Ulrich Ruedel. 2022. 'Towards Preserving a Transnational Comedy Phenomenon: The World of Pat and Patachon.' *Kosmorama* no. 281. Accessed 6 February 2023. https://www.kosmorama.org/artikler/pat-and-patachon

Bang, Herman. 1909. 'Tyskerne og vi. En Betragtning rettet til Fredsværnssagens Forkæmpere.' *Gads danske Magasin*, 15 April, 381–4.

Behn, Manfred, ed. 1994. *Schwarzer Traum und Weisse Sklavin: Deutsch-dänische Filmbeziehungen 1910–1930*. München: edition text+kritik.

———. 1995. 'Reaktionen auf die Nordisk in Deutschland zwischen 1914 und 1917.' Paper presented at the international symposium Dansk-tyske forhold og vekselvirkninger i film, Copenhagen, 3–4 November.

Bock, Hans-Michael and Michael Töteberg, eds. 1992. *Das Ufa-Buch: Kunst und Krisen, Stars und Regisseure, Wirtschaft und Politik*. Frankfurt a.M.: Tweitausendeins.

Börge, Vagn. 1960. *Weltmacht Film. Das geistige Gesicht einer neuen Kunst*. Wien: Austria-Edition.

Buk-Swienty, Tom. 2015. *1864. The Forgotten War That Shaped Modern Europe*. Translated by Annette Buk-Swienty. London: Profile Books.

Bureau of Foreign and Domestic Commerce, Motion Picture Section. 1928. *Market for Motion Pictures in Scandinavia and the Baltic States*. Trade Information Bulletin no. 553. Washington, DC: United States Department of Commerce.

Canty, George R. 1928. *The European Motion-Picture Industry in 1927*. Trade Information Bulletin no. 542. Washington, DC: United States Department of Commerce.

Cherchi Usai, Paolo and Lorenzo Codelli, eds. 1990. *Before Caligari. German Cinema, 1895–1920*. Pordenone: Biblioteca dell'Imagine.

Christensen, Claus Bundgård. 2020. 'National Identity and Veteran Culture in a Border Region: The Danish Minority in the German Army during the First World War.' *War in History* 27, no. 1: 57–80.

Christensen, Thomas C. 1997. 'Isbjørnens fald.' In *Filmæstetik & Billedhistorie*, edited by Helle Kannik Haastrup and Torben Grodal, *Sekvens. Filmvidenskabelig årbog*. Copenhagen: Institut for Film- og Medievidenskab.

Christensen, Thomas C. and Lisbeth Richter Larsen. 2021. 'Film Heritage Streaming at the Danish Film Institute.' *Journal of Film Preservation* no. 104: 105–12.

Detering, Heinrich, Anne-Britt Gerecke and Johan de Mylius, eds. 2001. *Dänisch-deutsche Doppelgänger. Transnationale und bikulturelle Literatur zwischen Barock und Moderne*. Göttingen: Wallstein.

Deutsches Zeitungsportal. n. d. 'About Us.' Accessed 27 May 2022. https://www.deutsche-digitale-bibliothek.de/content/newspaper/ueber-uns.
Diederichs, Helmut H. 1990. 'The Origins of the *Autorenfilm*.' In *Before Caligari: German Cinema, 1895–1920*, edited by Paolo Cherchi Usai and Lorenzo Codelli, 380–400. Pordenone: Biblioteca dell'Imagine.
Dinnesen, Niels Jørgen and Edvin Kau. 1983. *Filmen i Danmark*. Copenhagen: Akademisk Forlag.
Düring Jørgensen, Jesper. 1982. 'Tyske forsøg på kulturpropaganda i Danmark under den første verdenskrig.' *Fund og forskning i det Kongelige Biblioteks samlinger* 26: 125–52.
Eisenschitz, Bernard. 2016. 'Aimez-vous les uns les autres / Les Déshérités.' *Trafic* no. 99: 125–37.
Engberg, Marguerite. 1977. *Dansk stumfilm: De store år*. 2 vols. Copenhagen: Rhodos.
———. 1980. *Fy & Bi*. Copenhagen: Gyldendal.
———. 1990. 'The Influence of Danish Cinema on German Film, 1910–1920'. *Griffithiana* no. 38/39: 127–33.
———. 1994. 'Zwischen Kopenhagen und Berlin. Ein Überblick'. In *Schwarzer Traum und Weisse Sklavin: Deutsch-dänische Filmbeziehungen 1910–1930*, edited by Manfred Behn, *CineGraph Buch*, 7–14. München: edition text+kritik.
Frandsen, Steen Bo. 1994. *Dänemark – der kleine Nachbar im Norden. Aspekte der deutsch-dänischen Beziehungen im 19. und 20. Jahrhundert*. Darmstadt: Wissenschaftliche Buchgesellschaft.
———. 2011. 'På vej mod en ny normalitet? Et signalement af det dansk-tyske naboskab i 1908.' In *1908 – et snapshot af de kulturelle relationer mellem Tyskland og Danmark*, edited by Stephan Michael Schröder and Martin Zerlang, 20–35. Hellerup: Spring.
Gestrich, Constanze. 2008. *Die Macht der dunklen Kammern. Die Faszination des Fremden im frühen dänischen Kino*. Berliner Beiträge zur Skandinavistik, vol. 15. Berlin: Nordeuropa-Institut der Humboldt-Universität.
Glenthøj, Rasmus. 2012. *Skilsmissen: dansk og norsk identitet før og efter 1814*. Odense: Syddansk Universitetsforlag.
Gregor, Ulrich and Enno Patalas. 1962. *Geschichte des Films*. [Gütersloh]: Sigbert Mohn.
Göktürk, Deniz. 1994. '*Atlantis* oder: vom Sinken der Kultur.' In *Schwarzer Traum und Weisse Sklavin: Deutsch-dänische Filmbeziehungen 1910–1930*, edited by Manfred Behn, 73–86. München: edition text+kritik.
———. 2012. '18 December 1913: *Atlantis* Triggers Controversy about Sinking of Culture.' In *A New History of German Cinema*, edited by Jennifer M. Kapczynski and Michael D. Richardson, 51–6. Rochester: Camden House.
Hilmes, Michèle. 2017. 'Entangled Media Histories: A Response.' *Media History* 23: 142–4.
Kalbus, Oskar. 1935. *Vom Werden deutscher Filmkunst*. 2 vols. Vol. 1: *Der stumme Film*. Altona-Bahrenfeld: Cigaretten-Bilderdienst.

Kapczynski, Jennifer M. and Michael D. Richardson, eds. 2012. *A New History of German Cinema*. Rochester: Camden House.

Kracauer, Siegfried. 2004. *From Caligari to Hitler: A Psychological History of the German Film*. Rev ed. Princeton: Princeton University Press. 1947.

Lange-Fuchs, Hauke. 1980. *Pat und Patachon. Eine Dokumentation*. Berlin: Roloff & Seeßlen.

Loiperdinger, Martin and Uli Jung, eds. 2013. *Importing Asta Nielsen: The International Film Star in the Making 1910–1914*. New Barnet: John Libbey.

Monty, Ib. 1999. 'Benjamin Christensen in Germany: The Critical Reception of his Films in the 1910s and 1920s.' In *Nordic Explorations: Film Before 1930*, edited by John Fullerton and Jan Olsson, 41–55. Sydney: John Libbey.

Neergaard, Ebbe. 1960. *Historien om dansk Film*. Copenhagen: Gyldendal.

Nielsen, Asta. 2022. *The Silent Muse: The Memoirs of Asta Nielsen*, edited and translated by Julie K. Allen. Rochester: Camden House.

Nielsen, Jan. 2003. *A/S Filmfabriken Danmark: SRH/Filmfabriken Danmarks historie og produktion*. Copenhagen: Multivers.

Præstgaard Andersen, Lise. 2017. 'Pontoppidan på tysk.' *Nordica* 34: 227–42.

Quaresima, Leonardo. 1990. 'Dichter, heraus! The Autorenfilm and German Cinema of the 1910s.' *Griffithiana* no. 38/39: 101–20.

———. 1994. 'Wien – Kopenhagen – Wien. Schnitzlers *Liebelei* und die Nordisk'. In *Schwarzer Traum und Weisse Sklavin. Deutsch-dänische Filmbeziehungen 1910–1930*, edited by Manfred Behn, 87–104. München: edition text+kritik.

———. 1995. 'L'Autorenfilm allemand: Un cinéma national produit par des sociétés étrangères (1913–1915).' In *Cinéma sans frontières/Images Across Borders, 1896–1918. Internationality in World Cinema. Represensations, Markets, Influences and Reception*, edited by Roland Cosandey and François Albera, 237–48. Lausanne: Editions Payot.

Rasmussen, René. 2020. 'Slesvig mellem dansk og tysk – et historisk blik på det dansk-tyske venskabsår.' In *Medgang & Modgang: Udvekslinger mellem dansk og tysk kunst: Før/Nu*, edited by Amalie Marie Laustsen and Søs Bech Ladefoged, 38–53. Tønder/Aabenraa: Museum Sønderjylland.

Richter Larsen, Lisbeth. 2014. 'Flugten fra Berlin – Urban Gads øjenvidneberetning fra krigsudbruddet i 1914.' *Kosmorama* no. 256. Accessed 6 February 2023. https://www.kosmorama.org/kosmorama/artikler/flugten-fra-berlin-urban-gads-oejenvidneberetning-fra-krigsudbruddet-i-1914

———. 2021. 'Overlooked, Untold and Almost Forgotten: Urban Gad, Film Pioneer.' *Kosmorama* no. 276. Accessed 6 February 2023. https://www.kosmorama.org/en/kosmorama/en/overlooked-untold-and-almost-forgotten-urban-gad-film-pioneer

Sandberg, Anna. 2011. 'Herman Bang 1908: Mellem Danmark og Tyskland.' In *1908 – et snapshot af de kulturelle relationer mellem Tyskland og Danmark*, edited by Stephan Michael Schröder and Martin Zerlang, 196–220. Hellerup: Spring.

Schlüpmann, Heide. 1990. *Unheimlichkeit des Blicks. Das Drama des frühen deutschen Kinos*. Berlin: Stroemfeld/Roter Stern.

———. 1994. 'Ohne Worte. Asta Nielsen als Erzählering im Kinodrama.' In *Schwarzer Traum und Weisse Sklavin. Deutsch-dänische Filmbeziehungen 1910–1930*, edited by Manfred Behn, 125–35. München: edition text+kritik.
———. 2010. *The Uncanny Gaze: The Drama of Early German Cinema*. Urbana: University of Illinois Press.
———. 2012. '27 May 1911: Asta Nielsen Secures Unprecedented Artistic Control.' In *A New History of German Cinema*, edited by Jennifer M. Kapczynski and Michael D. Richardson, 44–50. Rochester: Camden House.
Schlüpmann, Heide and Karola Gramann, eds. 2010. *Asta Nielsen*. Vol. 2: *Nachtfalter. Asta Nielsen, ihre Filme*. Wien: Verlag Filmarchiv Austria.
Schlüpmann, Heide, Eric de Kuyper, Karola Gramann, Sabine Nessel and Michael Wedel, eds. 2010. *Asta Nielsen*. Vol. 1: *Unmögliche Liebe. Asta Nielsen, ihr Kino*. Wien: Verlag Filmarchiv Austria.
Schoolfield, George C. 2001. '*Die Aufzeichnungen des Malte Laurids Brigge*.' In *A Companion to the Works of Rainer Maria Rilke*, edited by Erika A. Metzger and Michael M. Metzger, 154–87. Rochester: Camden House.
Schröder, Stephan Michael. 2001. 'Zum Begründungszusammenhang von Sprache und nationaler Identität bei N.F.S. Grundtvig und Georg Brandes.' In *Aneignung – Abgrenzung – Auflösung. Zur Funktion von Literatur in den skandinavischen Identitätsdiskursen*, edited by Wolfgang Behschnitt. Würzburg: Ergon.
———. 2010. 'Und Urban Gad? Zur Frage der Autorschaft in den Filmen bis 1914.' In *Asta Nielsen*, edited by Heide Schlüpmann, Eric de Kuyper, Karola Gramann, Sabine Nessel and Michael Wedel, 194–210. Wien: Verlag Filmarchiv Austria.
———. 2011. *Ideale Kommunikation, reale Filmproduktion. Zur Interaktion von Kino und dänischer Literatur in den Erfolgsjahren des dänischen Stummfilms 1909–1918*. 2 vols. Berliner Beiträge zur Skandinavistik, vol. 18/1–2. Berlin: Nordeuropa-Institut der Humboldt-Universität.
———. 2020. 'On the "Danishness" of Danish Films in Germany until 1918.' *Kosmorama* no. 276. Accessed 6 February 2023. https://www.kosmorama.org/en/articles/danish-films-in-germany
Segelke, Arne. 2014. 'Brockdorff-Rantzau und die "Schleswig-Holsteinische Frage".' *Demokratische Geschichte* 25: 81–102.
Sundholm, John, Isak Thorsen, Lars Gustaf Andersson, Olof Hedling, Gunnar Iversen and Birgir Thor Møller, eds. 2012. *Historical Dictionary of Scandinavian Cinema*. Metuchen: Scarecrow Press.
Sørensen, Lars-Martin. 2020. 'A Common Film Culture? – Theme Issue on Danish-German Film Relations during the Silent Era.' *Kosmorama* no. 276. Accessed 6 February 2023. https://www.kosmorama.org/en/articles/common-film-culture
Thompson, Kristin. 1985. *Exporting Entertainment. America in the World Film Market 1907–1935*. London: BFI Publishing.
Thorsen, Isak. 2017. *Nordisk Films Kompagni 1906–1924. The Rise and Fall of the Polar Bear*. East Barnet: John Libbey.

———. 2020. 'Schreckgespenst aus Dänemark.' In *Dansk-tyske krige. Kulturliv og kulturkampe*, edited by Torben Jelsbak and Anna L. Sandberg. Copenhagen: U Press.

Tybjerg, Casper. 1999. 'Images of the Master: Benjamin Christensen's Career in Denmark and Germany.' In *Benjamin Christensen. An International Dane*, edited by Jytte Jensen, 8–21. New York: Danish Wave '99 / Museum of Modern Art.

———. 2004. 'Sandhedens masker: Herman Bang, Stiller, Dreyer.' *Kosmorama* no. 234 (winter): 39–64. Accessed 6 February 2023. https://www.kosmorama.org/kosmorama/arkiv/234/sandhedens-masker

———. 2020. 'Benjamin Christensen's Wonderful Adventure: Film History and Practitioner's Agency.' *Kosmorama* no. 276. Accessed 6 February 2023. https://www.kosmorama.org/en/articles/benjamin-christensen

———. 2021. 'The European Principle: Art and Border Crossings in Carl Theodor Dreyer's Career.' In *A History of Danish Cinema*, edited by Isak Thorsen, C. Claire Thomson and Pei-Sze Chow, 41–50. Edinburgh: Edinburgh University Press.

Ulrichsen, Erik. 1956. 'La belle époque.' In *50 aar i dansk film*, edited by Erik Balling, Svend Kragh-Jacobsen and Ole Sevel, 29–39. Copenhagen: Nordisk Films Kompagni.

von Boehmer, Henning and Helmut Reitz. 1933. *Der Film in Wirtschaft und Recht. Seine Herstellung und Verwertung.*

Vonderau, Patrick. 2007. *Bilder vom Norden. Schwedisch-deutsche Filmbeziehungen 1914–1939*. Marburg: Schüren.

———. 2012. '27 May 1921: *Scherben* Seeks Cinematic Equivalent of Theatrical Intimacy.' In *A New History of German Cinema*, edited by Jennifer M. Kapczynski and Michael D. Richardson, 105–10. Rochester: Camden House.

Winge, Vibeke. 1996. 'Dänemark – ein fortgesetztes Teutschland? Sprachliche Grenzgänger in Kopenhagen.' In *Grenzgänge. Skandinavisch-deutsche Nachbarschaften*, edited by Heinrich Detering. Göttingen: Wallstein.

Wolffsohn, Karl, ed. 1923. *Jahrbuch der Filmindustrie. 1. Jahrgang*. Berlin: Verlag der Lichtbildbühne.

———, ed. 1930. *Jahrbuch der Filmindustrie. 4. Jahrgang*. Berlin: Verlag der Lichtbildbühne.

Zimmermann, Yvonne. 2021. 'Asta Nielsen, the Film Star System and the Introduction of the Long Feature Film.' *Early Popular Visual Culture* 19, no. 2–3: 107–20.

Østergaard, Uffe. 1990. *De hæslige tyskere? fjendebilleder og fordomme i den danske offentlighed*. Aarhus: Center for Kulturforskning, Aarhus University.

———. 2000. 'Danmark er en multinational helstat.' *Information*, 2 February 2000.

CHAPTER 2

Danish-German Cinematic Interconnections and the Prospects of an Entangled Film Historiography
Casper Tybjerg

In July 1924, the German film trade journal *Lichtbild-Bühne* published an article on the program of releases the UFA Studio had scheduled for the 1924–1925 season. The article begins by praising its line-up of a dozen great German directors, 'whose names already have resonance and renown far beyond the borders of the homeland', but before discussing who they are, it adds in three non-German directors working for UFA, who had all previously directed one made-in-Germany film and had another slated for release in the coming season: 'And Herbert Wilcox and the two Danish directors Benjamin Christensen and Carl Th. Dreyer can already be counted among our own [*zu den unseren zählen*]' ('Das neue Ufaprogramm' 1924). The writer from *Lichtbild-Bühne* may have been motivated simply by nationalist impulses – because they contributed to the 'great deed [*Großtat*]' of UFA's prodigious 1924–1925 production slate, they could count as honorary Germans of sorts ('Das neue Ufaprogramm' 1924). But what if we decided to take the claim more in earnest?

For a Danish reader, it's hard not to feel an involuntary jolt of annoyance at this blatant attempt to appropriate two of Denmark's greatest filmmakers, yet the fact that they could so easily be integrated into the most prestigious and ambitious German production line-up perhaps reflects a deeper connection. Despite two nineteenth-century wars (the First [1848–1850] and Second [1864] Schleswig Wars) and a Danish nationalism marked by opposition to 'the German' (see Chapter 1), Danish cultural life was – at least until World War II – strongly marked by Germany. Perhaps the insistence of Danish film historians on a distinctly Danish film history was an artefact of a certain degree of nationalist myopia?

In this chapter, I will discuss a methodological framework I think is highly suitable for exploring the interactions between Danish and German cinema in the silent period: that of *entangled film historiography*. In an earlier article, I have argued that it makes sense to look at Dreyer's career through this lens (Tybjerg 2021). 'Entangled history' in this context translates the French term *histoire croisée*, a research approach formulated in the early 2000s by Michael Werner, a German-born French historian and Germanist, and Bénédicte Zimmermann, a French sociologist (Werner and Zimmermann 2002, 2003, 2004, 2006). *Histoire croisée* is an explicitly transnational approach. In the usage I will be following here, I take 'transnational history' to be an umbrella term, covering a variety of different approaches, of which *histoire croisée* or entangled history is one (Haupt and Kocka 2009, 19) – though as we shall see, some scholars use 'transnational film history' in a more specific sense.

Werner and Zimmermann have themselves preferred to either leave *histoire croisée* untranslated in English-language texts or to speak of 'crossed history'; 'entangled history' has been introduced as a translation by others. One reason that they have chosen not to adopt it may be that they were aware it had been used previously by others, at least in the plural form of 'entangled histories'. It appears in the title of the article '"Crossed Destinies": The Entangled Histories of West African Ethnic and National Identities' by anthropologist Richard Fardon (1996). Fardon here refers to a short novel by the Italian author Italo Calvino, *Il castello dei destini incrociati* (1973), translated as *The Castle of Crossed Destinies* (1976), in which a group of travellers, having magically lost the power of speech, tell each other their stories with a deck of tarot cards, each story seemingly linked to the next. The characters are united by 'the compulsion to tell their stories' (Fardon 1996, 124) as well as by having a constrained vocabulary for doing so – that of the pictures on the cards, supplemented by gestures. Fardon draws a parallel to ways in which people in West Africa construct their ethnic and national identities. Bénédicte Zimmermann was likely aware of this work; it is described by Heike Schmidt in her contribution, 'Entangled Memories', to a research project on social ties to which Zimmermann was also a contributor (Schmidt 2002; Zimmermann 2002). In a third contribution to the research project, Shalini Randeria also speaks of 'entangled histories' (in the plural), though without reference to either Fardon or Calvino (Randeria 2002).

The notions of 'crossed' and 'entangled' are thus very close to each other. In their first, German-language article, Werner and Zimmermann use the term *Verflechtung* to describe the core issue of their approach, although they still use the French term *histoire croisée* to name it (2002). *Verflechtung* means 'entanglement', but can also be translated as 'interweaving', 'intertwining' or 'interlacing'. While the latter words, suggestive of fibres and patterns, are perhaps closer to the French term, I find the almost tactile metaphorical suggestiveness of 'entangled history' both useful and appropriate. When I refer specifically to Werner and Zimmermann's writings, I will speak of *histoire croisée*, but otherwise I will use 'entangled history' as a synonym for it.

The very nature of the film medium, some scholars have argued, makes this approach highly suitable for investigating cinema's 'intensively entangled history':

> It is entangled in terms of films, of course – film crossing from one city, country or continent to another. Cinema history was entangled in terms of people like filmmakers, stars, camera personnel, businessmen and women being active in different spatial or temporal entities. There was an intensive entanglement in terms of money, strategies, power, public diplomacy [. . .]. And it was entangled also in cinema reception with audiences consuming foreign pictures, reading non-domestic magazines, dreaming of worlds they could (probably) never (physically) reach. So, entanglement was always at the heart of cinema – in terms of business, flows, content, labour, stories and phantasies. (Biltereyst and Meers 2020, 6)

Furthermore, the entangled history approach is a self-consciously reflexive one. It insists on acknowledging that both the objects of our study – nations and cultures, industries, styles, individuals – and the concepts we use to describe and understand them, are subject to change over time; they are themselves historical, not fixed. As historians, we too are part of history, and we are ourselves entangled with the matters we study. An entangled history approach acknowledges the *partiality* of what a research project like ours can explore, in both senses of the word: it can only examine a small part of the great overlapping networks of European cinema and World cinema, and it has necessarily been shaped by the situatedness, nationally and institutionally, of the participating scholars. Still, while the entangled approach has this strongly reflexive dimension, it rejects relativism and affirms its ability to arrive at 'specific forms of knowledge' (Werner and Zimmermann 2006, 50 n55).

In what follows, I will first discuss in greater detail the specifics of Werner and Zimmermann's *histoire croisée* approach. The second and third sections will then look at some of the ways this or other transnational approaches have been applied in film and media historiography, focusing on 'transnational' approaches in the second and 'entangled' in the third. Although there is a great deal of overlap, I argue that the entangled approach has some distinct advantages; I will discuss these, and address some misgivings to which the approach might give rise, in the fourth and final section.

From *histoires croisées* to Entangled History

Werner and Zimmermann laid out their approach in two programmatic articles; one in German (2002), the other in French, published in two slightly different versions (2003, 2004) and then reworked into English (2006). They observe that some scholars had spoken of *histories croisées* in the plural in the years before, to refer, 'in a vague manner, to one or a group of histories associated with the idea of an unspecified crossing or intersection' (Werner and Zimmermann 2006, 31). An example of this usage is provided by the 2004 special issue of the Canadian film studies journal *CiNéMAS* (vol. 14, no. 2–3) entitled 'Histoires croisées des images' (in the plural), of which more in the third section. Werner and Zimmermann, however, deliberately choose to speak of *histoire croisée* in the singular to denote a particular approach.

Before moving on to this, we should note in passing another, specifically film-related usage of the term 'histoires croisées' (in the plural). Films of the kind David Bordwell has called *network narratives* (Bordwell 2006, 99), in which the stories of characters living entirely separate lives come to fatefully intersect, are sometimes described in French as 'histoires croisées'. Thus, a reviewer has used the label 'Cinéaste des histoires croisées et complexes' to describe Alejandro González Iñárritu, director of *Amores perros* (2000), *21 Grams* (2003) and *Babel* (2006), which one might well translate as 'A director of complex network narratives' (Delgado 2015, 10). I think it is worth stressing this use of the phrase, which may also remind us of the Calvino novel mentioned earlier. Even if entangled historiography is clearly something quite different from such network narratives, the notion that we are tied together with other people, often in unexpected and unpredictable ways, is certainly part of *histoire croisée*.

Werner and Zimmermann argue that their concept of *histoire croisée* addresses the shortcomings of two other approaches to transnational history: the comparative approach and the cultural transfer approach. In a comparative analysis, one would try to isolate some relevant unit within the areas being compared and then look for similarities and differences. For instance, a recent international research project in New Cinema History has examined film programming data from the year 1952 in three European cities of roughly similar size, all of them ports but none of them capital cities: Gothenburg/Göteborg in Sweden, Antwerp in Belgium and Rotterdam in the Netherlands (Pafort-Overduin et al. 2020). The results from the research into each city could then be assembled into an agreed-upon format, allowing comparisons to be made. The method depends, obviously, on being able to identify relevant units and establishing that they are similar enough for a comparison to be meaningful.

The *histoire croisée* approach stresses the difficulty of finding such units and their contingent nature. If one were to make a comparison between

Denmark and Germany, it is difficult to say that one is comparing like with like, even if one focuses on a particular area like the film industry.

What is more, we are not dealing with stable units; even on a basic territorial level, the nations changed during the 1910–1930 period: a part of Schleswig that had been conquered by Prussia in 1864 was detached from the German Reich following a plebiscite in 1920 and integrated into Denmark. Werner and Zimmermann warn: 'The comparative approach assumes a synchronic cross-section' (2006, 35), and the Gothenburg/Antwerp/Rotterdam study does indeed focus on a particular year, 1952. Furthermore, because of its local scale, that study does not need to worry that what happens in one place will affect what happens in another; but that is always an issue when dealing with larger-scale units like neighbouring countries: 'the objects and practices are not only in a state of interrelationship but also modify one another reciprocally as a result of their relationship' (Werner and Zimmermann 2006, 35). In other words, the units being compared are not detached and independent, but tied together by reciprocal relationships where each influences and changes in response to the other.

The second approach to which Werner and Zimmermann contrast their *histoire croisée* is cultural transfer history, an approach Werner had himself pioneered in the 1980s. In our original description of the research project *A Common Film Culture?*, we envisioned using the cultural transfer approach ourselves. This approach sought to move beyond the reliance on the notion of 'influence' to explain how philosophical, scholarly, artistic or other kinds of ideas passed from one nation or cultural grouping to another: 'Until now the problems of cultural transfer in Europe have generally been studied according to the schema of the history of influences' (Espagne and Werner 1987, 970). The notion of influence, as art historian Michael Baxandall has pointed out, assumes that the originators are the active agents, *exerting their influence* upon recipients across time and space. Baxandall argues that this gets the historical process back to front; later figures *decide* what to appropriate from their predecessors (Baxandall 1985, 58–62).

Transfer history is more concerned with transfers across space, from one national or cultural area to another, but similarly emphasises the interpretive process at the receiving end, which inevitably would change the original idea – 'productive misinterpretations', as it were (Espagne and Werner 1987, 988). This emphasis contrasts with another traditional model for thinking about cultural transfers – that of translation, where there is a tendency to think of translations as ancillary and inferior to the original texts, stressing the ways they get things wrong. For transfer historians, such fault-finding is much less interesting than looking at the ways the transferred object was taken up by the receiving society.

It is not difficult to see that this approach could yield new insights compared to an influence-based one. Still, the emergence of the *histoire croisée* model shows that Werner had become dissatisfied with the way the transfer study approach tended to take for granted that intellectual ideas (a typical subject of investigation) go *from* one place *to* another, where both places and the direction of travel are assumed to be evident. Zimmermann explains in a recent article why this was dissatisfying:

> With their focus on transactions between two poles, transfers imply a fixed frame of reference that includes a point of departure and a point of arrival. In the case of transnational exchanges these points are generally located within national societies and cultures that are in contact with each other. Consequently the initial situation and that resulting from the transfer are apprehended through stable national frames of reference assumed to be well known, for instance 'German' or 'French' historiography. (Zimmermann 2020, 8)

Here, the proponents of the *histoire croisée* approach again stress that large-scale units like nations and cultures are not stable over time and are more imbricated with each other than one might assume, making it difficult or impossible to draw neat boundaries. The historian must therefore be conscious of and reflective about how such boundaries are drawn. In particular, the way historians go about this affects what kind of boundaries are drawn, and where. Rather than being able to work from a neatly drawn map that can be examined at arm's length, historians find themselves having to navigate and survey a landscape already covered with a bewildering variety of features, markers and criss-crossing tracks.

Now, this emphasis on the historically shifting and contingent character of the objects historians investigate, the concepts they use to describe and understand them, and the position they themselves occupy in relation to either, may seem a bit vertigo-inducing. But Werner and Zimmermann are quite willing to acknowledge that one has to start somewhere. It is hard to escape the pull of the concept of a national culture, for instance, but one should be willing to adjust 'objects, categories, and analytical schemes' in the course of one's research (2006, 46). Werner and Zimmermann call this *pragmatic induction*:

> Pragmatic induction thus implies starting from the object of study and the situations in which it is embedded, according to one or more points of view – previously defined, it is true, but subject to continual readjustments in the course of empirical investigation.' (Werner and Zimmermann 2006, 47)

The important thing is not to assume a one-size-fits-all model.

As an example, Werner and Zimmermann refer to an anthology co-edited by Werner, studying the development of the classical concert in Europe from the eighteenth to the early twentieth century. Werner and his colleagues stress the importance of studying the institutions and venues where classical music was played, arguing that musicological histories exclusively devoted to composers and works ignore such social, economic and practical frameworks at their peril (Bödeker, Veit and Werner 2002, §1). On the other hand, Werner also cautions against simply imposing a sociological framework imputing a general process of *embourgeoisement*, a shift in the musicians' role from being servants of noble patrons to being salaried or self-employed professionals, and of the audience from being the guests and entourages of the nobility to being a paying public. To do so would be to ignore the very different paths taken in different locales, their mutual influences and interconnections, and the specific character and social place of the musical art itself, Werner argues (Werner 2002, §§1–2).

Pragmatic induction thus implies an analysis of 'the manner in which individuals actually connect themselves to the world, the specific construction of the world and the elements of context produced by this activity in each particular case, and finally the uses arising from such construction' (Werner and Zimmermann 2006, 47). It suggests beginning at a small scale and observing the patterns that emerge, while recognising that one already begins with a set of large-scale concepts that affect the framing and may require modification. This, I would argue, is where we find the particular advantage of using the concept of Entangled Film History rather than the related one of Transnational Film History, but before going into more detail about that, it is worth looking at the ways these concepts have been used in practice.

The Aspirations of Transnational Film History

An interest in the *transnational* has marked a number of scholarly fields in both the Humanities and the Social Sciences; one introduction mentions 'Migration Studies, Anthropology, Sociology, Political Science, Geography, International Relations, History, Cultural Studies and Film Studies' (Villazana 2013, 25), to which one should add various Area Studies fields. A fascinating history of the uses of the term and its cognates from the nineteenth century onwards can be found in the entry on 'transnational' in *The Palgrave Dictionary of Transnational History* (Saunier 2009), but I shall not attempt to survey this whole landscape. After touching briefly on transnational history, I will focus on the transnational in film studies.

'Transnational history' as the name for a general approach or research program appears to come into vogue in the early 1990s in the US; in the early 2000s it is enthusiastically taken up in Germany as well (Sørensen 2009; Tyrell 2009). The Latin prefix *trans-* means 'beyond'; while in some contexts it has been used more or less interchangeably with 'inter-', 'multi-', or 'supra-', the general trend has been to use 'transnational' to indicate a rejection of methodological nationalism (see Chernilo 2006 for a discussion of the development of this concept), but not a global scope. Thus, a transnational historiography studies phenomena that a historiography focused on particular nation-states tends to elide, but does not necessarily move up to a much more distant perspective comprehending entire cultures or the world as a whole. In his book *Global History*, Sebastian Conrad offers the following characterisation:

> While many comparative studies with a global scope are large in scale, encompassing whole empires and civilizations, transnational history focuses on phenomena that are geographically much more limited. In contrast to the comparative framework, the 'transnational' focuses on the fluid and interwoven dimensions of the historical process, studying societies in the context of the entanglements that have shaped them, and to which they have contributed in turn. To what extent did processes that transcended state borders impact social dynamics? In addressing such issues, transnational history gives particular attention to the role of mobility, circulation and transfers. (Conrad 2016, 44)

Given this understanding of the term, transfer studies and *histoire croisée* both fit comfortably under the umbrella of transnational history, although it should of course be remembered that these historiographical approaches developed before or in parallel to transnational history. Still, they are less widespread and have remained more specific in their methodological assumptions and recommendations, which is why I think it makes most sense to treat them as special cases of a broader paradigm.

In Film Studies, the article 'Transnational Cinema: Mapping a Field of Study' offers a useful survey. Here, Deborah Shaw (one of the founding editors of *Transnational Cinemas*, a scholarly journal founded in 2010 and renamed *Transnational Screens* in 2019) divides the field's development into two phases. In the first phase, there were 'four key areas of focus' for scholarship in the field: 'migration and cinema and exilic and diasporic filmmaking; transnationalising readings of national and regional cinema; historical readings of transnational cinema; and film festival studies' (Shaw 2017, 290). In the second phase, 'we have moved away from privileging some areas as "proper" objects of study in transnational film studies'; transnational cinema has become a 'conceptual framework' and there are now 'few areas within Film Studies on which [it] had not left its imprint' (Shaw 2017, 297). The question is, however, whether 'transnational film history' exists as a distinct sub-field, and whether it is the best label for a research project such as the one presented in this anthology.

One reason for using the term might be to acknowledge the 'intrinsic transnational characteristics of film' (Brizuela 2009, 393). As Shaw notes, scholars of early cinema have emphasised how it 'benefitted from a coproduction landscape and circulated freely across borders without the linguistic restrictions faced with the introduction of sound' (Shaw 2017, 293; citing Bean, Kapse and Horak 2014; see also Abel, Bertellini and King 2008). Shaw mentions two historical studies that explicitly take a transnational perspective: Andrew Higson's article on the 'Film Europe' production initiatives of the 1920s, and Tim Bergfelder, Sue Harris and Sarah Street's study of European production design of the late 1920s and 1930s (Higson 2010; Bergfelder, Harris and Street 2007). A third work that might have been mentioned is the anthology *Global Neorealism. The Transnational History of a Film Style* (Sklar and Giovacchini 2012).

Shaw's 'critical review of the field' is, as she herself stresses, 'principally limited to English language publications' (Shaw 2017, 296). However, in an article offering an outline of what a transnational film history that focuses on Germany might entail, Ralf Heiner Heinke and Cristoph Ziener have given a brief rundown of relevant work written in German. This includes works on race and representation in Weimar cinema (Nagl 2009), multiple-language film versions (Wahl 2009), the Nazi regime's attempts to court and later dominate an international market (Offermanns 2001) and relations with the Hollywood industry (Saekel 2011; Spieker 1999). One might add Joseph Garncarz's examination of the supposed takeover of German screens by Hollywood movies following World War I; Garncarz demonstrates that that in terms of popularity with audiences, German films were in fact dominant in their home market from at least 1925 (when German cinemas began collecting popularity figures) until the mid-1960s, challenging the conventional story of US hegemony (Garncarz 2013).

Heinke and Ziener give particular praise to the series of anthologies released by CineGraph, the Hamburg-based centre for film-historical research, based on the annual conferences they have hosted since 1988. CineGraph's initial series of conferences sought to remedy the excessive focus on 'Expressionism' in historical studies of filmmaking in Weimar Germany by focusing on four popular, commercial filmmakers of the period: Reinhold Schünzel, Richard Oswald, Joe May and E. A. Dupont (Schöning 1989; Belach and Jacobsen 1990; Bock and Lenssen

1991; Bretschneider 1992). All four became exiles during the Nazi period, though Dupont began working abroad before 1933. Subsequent conferences and publications turned to examining German cinema's interconnections with other countries (Schöning 1993; Behn 1994; Schöning 1995; Sturm and Wolgemuth 1996; Roschlau 2008; Bono and Roschlau 2011; Bock, Distelmeyer and Schöning 2022b), producers and companies with transnational profiles (Wottrich 2001, 2002; Distelmeyer 2003, 2004) and topics such as films with multiple-language versions (Distelmeyer 2006), European Westerns (Roschlau 2012) and filmmakers in exile (Wottrich and Schiemann 2017; Bock, Distelmeyer and Schöning 2022a).

These CineGraph publications do not explicitly identify themselves as 'transnational film history'. In fact, the yearly festival held alongside the conference, CineFest, calls itself 'International Festival of the German Film Heritage', elegantly suggesting that the German film heritage is a border-crossing one. The same non-explicit transnationalism characterises the anthology *Ufa international* (Stiasny, Kasten and Lang 2021), which also grew out of a film retrospective, held at the German Historical Museum in Berlin in 2019: one of the contributors, Wolfgang Fuhrman, has elsewhere described his studies of the interaction between the interwar German film industry and Latin America as '*histoire croisée*', but such explicit methodological framings have been left out of the contributions to the anthology (Fuhrmann 2020, 3–5; 2021). Patrick Vonderau's work on the reception of Swedish cinema in Germany and other German-Swedish cinematic interconnections also does not claim adherence to a specific theoretical principle, even if they are clearly explorations of transnational issues (Vonderau 2000, 2007, 2012; Florin and Vonderau 2019).

Much of this work focuses on the 1918–1945 period, and this is quite appropriate, Heinke and Ziener write:

> The interwar period is an object lesson in approaching polycentric historiographical concepts (entangled history/*histoire croisée*) in a film-historical way. In order to do justice to a transnational perspective, it is necessary to re-question traditional film-historical caesuras and historiographical narratives (e.g. the introduction of the sound film or the Nazi party's seizure of power) and to deconstruct them diachronically. (Heinke and Ziener 2016, 410)

We may note in passing that this quote indicates that Heinke and Ziener do not see any significant distinction between taking a transnational perspective and using an entangled-history approach.

Heinke and Ziener provide an example: an examination of two 1934 films, *Der verlorene Sohn*, directed by Luis Trenker, and *Redes*, directed by Fred Zinnemann in collaboration with Emilio Gómez Muriel. These films are both transnational along numerous dimensions, in terms of their makers, the circumstances of their production and their themes. Both directors were born in the Austro-Hungarian Empire, Zinnemann in a city now in Poland and Trenker in a town now in Italy. Zinnemann emigrated to the US in 1929 to pursue a filmmaking career there, while Trenker became a successful figure in German cinema and later television, though he remained an Italian citizen. *Der verlorene Sohn* was produced by Paul Kohner for Deutsche Universal and partly shot on location in New York, while *Redes*, a film sponsored by the progressive Mexican government, was shot in Mexico with American photographer Paul Strand behind the camera. *Redes* is a Flaherty-inspired documentary-like drama about poor Mexican fishermen and their struggles against exploitation by greedy capitalists. *Der verlorene Sohn* is about a Tyrolean mountain guide who travels to the US in pursuit of a beautiful heiress but ends up destitute amid the grim reality of the Depression; although his luck turns and he reconnects with the heiress, he rejects her and joyously returns to his Alpine home. As Heinke and Ziener point out, migration is a key theme in both films, and from very different perspectives, both films offer critiques of the misery American capitalism wreaks upon others (Heinke and Ziener 2016, 421). *Redes* describes the desperate living conditions that often cause people to migrate, while *Der verlorene Sohn* shows the misery and nostalgia affecting many emigrants.

Redes and *Der verlorene Sohn* are thus films whose transnational character is both *strong* and *marked*, using the terminology proposed by Mette Hjort in her essay 'On the Plurality of Cinematic Transnationalism', identified by Shaw as a key effort in conceptualising the field (Hjort 2010; Shaw 2017, 293). In her essay, Hjort advises scholars to recognise two dimensions of transnationality: one a scale going from weak to strong transnationality and the other a distinction between marked and unmarked transnationality. On the first dimension, 'a given cinematic case would qualify as strongly transnational, rather than only weakly so, if it could be shown to involve a number of specific transnational elements related to levels of production, distribution, reception, and the cinematic works themselves' (Hjort 2010, 13). On the second, 'marked transnationality' describes cases where filmmakers 'intentionally direct the attention of viewers towards various transnational properties that encourage thinking about transnationality' (Hjort 2010, 14).

In her work on Nordic cinema, Hjort has emphasised the importance of a transnational approach. In the editors' introduction to their *Companion to Nordic Cinema*, she and Ursula Lindqvist write: 'It is our view that a transnational approach provides the necessary framework for pinpointing the specificities of Nordic cinema, from its manifest achievements to its cultural and institutional conditions' (Hjort and Lindqvist 2016, 6). The contributors' articles (including my own) and the work of other scholars whose efforts she has encouraged and organised testifies to the fruitfulness of Hjort's transnational approach. However, she has also warned about difficulties that marching under the banner of transnationalism could potentially cause.

Hjort's admonitions arise from the status of the word 'transnational' as a 'virtue term', an aspirational concept that 'picks out processes and features that necessarily warrant affirmation as signs, among other things, of a welcome demise of ideologically suspect nation-states and the cinematic arrangements to which they gave rise' (Hjort 2010, 14). But transnationalism is not 'inherently virtuous', she insists; 'there may even be reason to object to some forms of transnationalism' (Hjort 2010, 15). However, the normative implications of the term 'transnational' are not so easily evaded: 'Its success clearly relies heavily on this inherent value dimension that endows it with a new perspective and vision', as the leading scholar of historical memory Aleida Assmann has written, continuing:

> This normative stance is often underpinned by a cosmopolitan ethos that betrays a general dissatisfaction with the dated nineteenth-century ideal of the autonomous, free, coherent and bounded nation and the desire to move forward towards a new national imaginary stimulated by ongoing local and global reconfigurations. (Assmann 2014, 546–7)

Hjort argues that it is possible to distinguish between more and less valuable forms of cinematic transnationalism: the *more valuable* forms are characterised by qualities such as 'a resistance to globalization as cultural homogenization' (Hjort 2010, 15), which fits well with the kind of ethos Assmann describes. Today's big Hollywood franchise spectaculars evidently *promote* cultural homogenisation and therefore present a *less valuable* form of transnationalism, if using this criterion of value. From a *heuristic* standpoint, however, it is not so evident that 'more transnational' does not mean 'more valuable': if researchers identify their stance as 'transnational' from the outset, their attention is likely to gravitate towards cinema whose transnational character is both *strong* and *marked* – as we saw Heinke and Ziener do.

Perhaps I am being overly fussy here, but I do see a risk that assuming the marque of 'transnational film history' may oblige the researcher to follow certain paths and not others, rather than having the evidence lead the way. I believe that if we adopt the methodological framework (and the label) of 'entangled film history', we can avoid some of these issues.

The Varieties of Entanglement

There is a second issue with the term 'transnational' that the Danish historian Ulrich Langen has pointed out in an essay written with characteristic brio:

> One of the weaknesses of transnational history lies in the term itself. Transnational history seeks to free itself from a narrowly national way of seeing that has typified a great deal of historiography. But is it not something of a semantic sticky wicket that precisely the word 'national' forms part of the term? It comes inescapably to mind that the very perspective problematized by transnational historiography – the perspective of the nation-state, nation and frontiers – is thus inadvertently given an indirect but defining significance. In the attempt to escape the national straitjacket one has perhaps just made space for it. (Langen 2009, 251–2)

In some contexts, it makes sense to use a term with 'national' right in the middle; but in many others, Langen argues, the greater flexibility afforded by the term *histoire croisée* is prefereable: 'The French term offers the possibility of stressing that it is not just national borders that are crossed, but both visible and invisible boundaries – cultural boundaries, social boundaries, mental boundaries, and so on' (Langen 2009, 252).

Such boundary-crossings are certainly in evidence in the previous-mentioned 2004 special issue of the journal *CiNéMAS* entitled 'Histoires croisées des images'. This terminology is actually at best tangential to Werner and Zimmermann's *histoire croisée*; the plural form (*histoires*) differs from their singular term (*histoire*), and none of the articles refer to their work. What is more, the term 'histoires croisées' does not appear in any of the articles, only in the editor's introduction (Arnoldy 2004). The articles deal with a very diverse set of cases where the history of cinema can be said to intersect or be intertwined with that of other image media, or – in some cases – modes of thought. One article thus explores the intersection of psychoanalysis and cinema, while another looks at the use of lecturers to provide commentary for silent films in the cinemas of Soviet Russia (Berton 2004; Pozner 2004). Several articles look at the intersections between the histories of film and photography, while Thomas Elsaesser gives an early account of his media archaeology, his framework for connecting the insights of early cinema studies and of film theory with the study of the emerging digital media (Elsaesser 2004; see also Elsaesser 2016).

The notion of exploring sites where the histories of different media intersect has also been central to the researchers affiliated with the Entangled Media Histories (EMHIS) research and teaching network set up in 2013 and based at Lund University in Sweden.[1] In a position paper on the theoretical and methodological framework tying together the network, Maria Cronqvist and Christoph Hilgert refer to *histoire croisée* as one important component, but the framework also draws on transfer theory, transnational history and global history (Cronqvist and Hilgert 2017, 131). In a response article, Australian media scholar Bridget Griffen-Foley comments that 'reminding English-speaking historians' of approaches like *histoire croisée* is an important service in and of itself (Griffen-Foley 2017, 146).

Although Cronqvist and Hilgert do not comment on the fact, they speak of 'histories' in the plural, probably to signal the diversity and catholicity of the approaches involved. While transnationality is central to their framework, another goal is to examine *transmedial* issues: 'the ambition is to raise awareness of the traditional blind spots in media-historical scholarship and challenge its common methodological nationalism and mono-medial tendencies' (Cronqvist and Hilgert 2017, 131). They want researchers to go beyond the historical study of particular media and think about 'the role of one medium or several media in a wider communicative context, their role within the media ensemble in general' (Cronqvist and Hilgert 2017, 133).

In her response to Cronqvist and Hilgert's position paper, Michelle Hilmes, a leading American scholar of broadcasting, recommends three research strategies for entangled media historiography: the first is 'to look for key individuals, people whose careers make them 'cultural translators' as they actively move from one national setting to another or migrate from one media industry to the next' (Hilmes 2017, 142). The second strategy is to focus on specific 'texts' that have been 'particularly significant in crossing media platforms and national contexts', mentioning Sherlock Holmes as a pertinent example (Hilmes 2017, 143). The third strategy is to look for organisations, 'usually somewhat hidden and marginal ones, devoted to trespassing in 'foreign' territory' (Hilmes 2017, 143). I would be somewhat wary of the notion of a 'cultural translator', which I think shares some of the issues affecting the notion of cultural transfer; it suggests that cultures are more-or-less closed and complete systems, like languages. Still, Hilmes' advice seems quite sensible and relevant to an entangled film history as well.

The EMHIS network's participants, already working along these lines, have produced a number of focused case studies, of which a representative cross-section has been assembled in a special issue of the journal *Media History*. The editors' introduction stresses the variety of media examined: 'The empirical examples are taken from both written and audiovisual news journalism, television documentaries, radio programming, and weekly magazines' (Hilgert, Cronqvist and Chignell 2020, 3). However, the emphasis throughout is on journalistic media, on reportage and its role in the political process. Most of the papers focus on state-owned media, their activities and employees, and art and entertainment are conspicuous by their absence. Five scholars associated with EMHIS have collaborated on a chapter for *The Handbook of European Communication History* on media in the immediate post-war period, where the cinema, supposedly 'omnipresent', gets less than one page (Wagner et al. 2019, 193, 194). It is of course not entirely fair to pick on a fifteen-page handbook entry where space is at a premium and it is necessary to prioritise strictly; but when the authors write of Italian Neorealism only that it 'became famous in the late 1940s and early 1950s' as part of an 'emerging trend' towards 'the depiction of everyday life in films', it is evident that their priorities lie with other parts of the media ensemble (Wagner et al. 2019, 194).

The lack of interest in Neorealism is striking because it has been discussed by film scholars as an example of a topic where an entangled approach has proven particularly productive: the manner in which the debates of the 1920s in several European countries on cinematic modernism were taken up in 1930s Italy, along with the surprisingly multifarious cinematic interconnections between Mussolini's regime and Soviet Russia, were crucial parts of the background from which the Neorealist movement drew its sustenance; and subsequently, it became a touchstone for filmmakers across the globe, including the partisans of 'Third Cinema' (see Salazkina 2012; Sklar and Giovacchini 2012). This account of Neorealism is used as an example of entangled historiography in the Film Studies publication that most explicitly adopts an entangled approach: the anthology *The Emergence of Film Culture*, edited by Malte Hagener. In his introduction, Hagener describes the anthology as 'a collaborative attempt to begin writing a *histoire croisée* (entangled history) of the avant-garde, its legacy and aftermath', citing Werner and Zimmermann's article (Hagener 2014, 3). The anthology covers not only the international film avant-garde of the interwar years, but also the related topics of the development of film study and theory and of institutions devoted to the cinema, like archives, film schools and festivals.

In Hagener's eyes, the key advantage of the entangled approach is its concern 'to multiply perspectives in order to shatter any one dominant reading, and to open up historiography to the potential limitless infinity of empirical reality' (Hagener 2014, 4). The phrasing here is perhaps a bit melodramatic; speaking of the need to 'shatter' a 'dominant reading' makes it sound like established film historiography forms a heavy and despotic burden, which is hardly the case. Still, inertia and inattention make it difficult to dislodge well-established historiographical frameworks, and the impetus provided by entangled film historiography is an important one.

On a purely practical level, a multiplicity of perspectives is the inevitable consequence of the scholarly anthology as a format. This is often seen as a disadvantage, because anthologies tend to lack a consistent line of argument with a concluding synthesis; but the entangled history approach encourages us to look at the strengths of the format, where the juxtaposition of the work of scholars with different backgrounds, emphases and styles can cause patterns and interconnections to become visible that would not have been apparent to any individual participant. This is made explicit by the editors of the anthology *Nordic Film Cultures and Cinemas of Elsewhere*, where they describe how they have organised the book in 'thematic constellations' in order 'to generate dialogue between chapters that – even when based in different periods, places, and languages – echo each other in surprising ways' (Ellis, Lunde and Stenport 2019, 4). Arguably, the advantages of the format are particularly apparent when the anthology is a very tightly focused one, like *Importing Asta Nielsen*, a collection of articles about the worldwide distribution and reception of Asta Nielsen's films in the 1910–1914 period (Loiperdinger and Jung 2013). The carefully restricted focus makes both repeated patterns, dialogic interconnections and differences in perspective all the more visible. While neither *Importing Asta Nielsen* or the *Cinemas of Elsewhere* identify themselves as entangled film history, their transnational scope, shifts in scale and sophisticated conceptualisation show enough affinity with the entangled approach to allow us to say that, like Hagener's anthology, they testify to the usefulness and practicability of entangled film history as a methodological framework.

Objectivity, Agency, Readability

Entangled historiography's disinclination towards single perspectives and 'dominant readings' has drawn some criticism from scholars who look for synthesis and explanation. In a survey article about cultural transfers, Matthias Middell, a prominent scholar in the field of transnational history, claims that *histoire croisée* does not provide 'a fully developed theory or a coherent methodical program', but only offers suggestions about how a series of different perspectives could be adopted and combined, given a certain degree of scholarly virtuosity. He continues:

> While the theoretical considerations are convincing, the operationalization of a *histoire croisée* proves to be extraordinarily difficult, which is why it is easier to find commitments to the points of the programme than convincing examples of their implementation. (Middell 2016, 11)

Part of the issue here, I think, is that Werner and Zimmermann seek to emphasise that 'operationalization' is itself if not chimerical, then at least much more difficult than social-science-inspired historiography has generally allowed for, and they reject the temptation to use 'operational' definitions to allow comparisons if it carries the cost of eliding actual historical complexity. *Histoire croisée*'s insistence on complexity and the way categories and terms change their meaning in the course of history is linked to another claim made by Werner and Zimmermann in favour of their approach, one that has met with resistance from at least some historians.

Werner and Zimmermann argue that because comparative history predefines the units that are compared to each other, whereas *histoire croisée* lets them shift and transform according to what historians find in the sources, *histoire croisée* is more empirical and less subjective than comparative history – it respects what Hagener calls the 'limitless infinity of empirical reality'. Historians strongly committed to constructivist views and a problem-based historiography reject this. One example is Alessandro Stanziani, a global historian whom Zimmermann herself refers to in a note for his 'general discussion' of related approaches like 'entangled, shared or connected histories' (Zimmermann 2020, 7, 12 note 1). Stanziani writes that 'it seems useless to oppose *l'histoire croisée* and connected history to comparative history. [. . .] The connections found in archives are just as subjective as the comparisons made by a historian' (Stanziani 2018, 12).

One should note the rhetorical sleight-of-hand of the words 'just as', because no evidence for that is actually offered. Instead, we get constructivist pabulum about the many ways documents are skewed to reflect the perspectives of those who made them and those who later make use of them:

> Archives and documents are never ready-made, lying in wait of discovery; they are produced first by the historical actors in administrations or companies that originally provided them, then by the archivists who classified them, and finally by historians who select a given document and present it in an equally individual manner. (Stanziani 2018, 12)

Werner and Zimmermann, with their consistent emphasis on the way historians are themselves entangled with their object of study, would not deny any of this. The point that they make – and support with arguments and evidence – is that *even so*, even given all the problems entailed by the uneven shape of the historical record, the *histoire croisée* approach is more objective and source-based.

To show this, they refer to Zimmermann's research on unemployment in late nineteenth and early twentieth-century Germany and France, pointing out how the 'öffentliche Arbeitsvermittlung' and *'placement public*', seemingly similar terms for public job placement services, are actually significantly different in terms of both their historical development, their social role and even their conception of what 'public' means (Werner and Zimmermann 2002, 625). Direct comparison was ruled out, both by this fact and by the way the systems in one country would change because of the other's example.

Historians in my experience often proceed from rather loose and vague research questions that identify a topic but not much else. Only by immersing themselves in the sources do they acquire the knowledge that allows them to identify the right avenue of research. The historian of exploitation cinema Eric Schaefer has spoken half-jokingly of '"critical mess historiography"', based on assembling 'a large pile of information – a "critical mess"', and only when the pile is big enough 'looking for patterns in order to be able to draw conclusions' (Schaefer 2012, 151; citing Singer 2001, 66). A common experience among historians is to have felt compelled to shift the direction of one's research after finding something unexpected in the documents. *Historie croisée* explicitly takes this as a methodological condition, which I think is a clear advantage of the entangled approach.

I have had my own concerns about the practicability of an entangled history framework. They have been of two kinds: concerns about the role of the historical individual, and concerns about the place of self-reflexive methodological ruminations. As to the first, I have repeatedly stressed the importance of regarding filmmakers as historical agents (Tybjerg 2005, 2020). It was as a framework for approaching the career of Carl Th. Dreyer, which spanned a number of countries and film industries, that I was initially attracted to the concept of entangled history (Tybjerg 2021). There already exists a number of studies of individuals with boundary-crossing careers, testifying to the importance of this kind of research frame (Matthews 2006; Hodgin 2016; Terkanian and Chignell 2020). However, in Werner and Zimmermann's programmatic article on *histoire croisée*, they explain the consequences of placing the figure of crossing, of points of intersection, at the very heart of their approach, and it is possible to read this section as ruling out the possibility of taking the life and career of an individual as the focal point of one's research:

> First, the notion of intersection precludes reasoning in terms of individual entities, considered exclusively in themselves, with no external reference point. *Histoire croisée* breaks with a one-dimensional perspective that simplifies and homogenizes, in favor of a multidimensional approach that acknowledges plurality and the complex configurations that result from it. (Werner and Zimmermann 2006, 38)

This is somewhat difficult to parse; on an initial reading, the phrase 'precludes reasoning in terms of individual entities', would appear to go against a biographical approach. If we read on a bit further, however, Werner and Zimmermann mention 'persons' as something that can be examined from the perspective they advocate.

Moreover, Zimmermann has recently published a short restatement of the main points of *histoire croisée* which specifically suggests making 'a fulcrum of people's agency' when pursuing empirical historical inquiry:

> Paying attention to agency does not mean shrinking the analysis back down to short-term and micro dimensions to the detriment of long-term and macro features; rather it calls for combining the long-term character of structures with the short-term character of what is happening in a given situation. The aim is to grasp the dynamic interplay between the structuring activity of people and the structuring power of existing frameworks that may constrain or sustain individual agency, and in turn be changed by people's activity. (Zimmermann 2020, 9)

When Werner and Zimmermann rejected 'reasoning in terms of individual entities, considered exclusively in themselves', they were not rejecting the agency of individual people, but rather making the philosophical point that interactions with others may mean that a person does not stay the same: 'the entities, persons, practices, or objects that are intertwined with, or affected by, the crossing process, do not necessarily remain intact and identical in form' (Werner and Zimmermann 2006, 38). Judging from their references, their position is one that insists a human being, at the most abstract philosophical level, is formed and transformed by such interactive processes. They cite the German philosopher Michael Theunissen's book *Der Andere* (1977 [1965]; Eng. 1986); Theunissen's project has been summarised as the attempt to construct 'a theory of mutual recognition and relational intersubjectivity that could ground a critical theory of modernity' (Sinnerbrink 2019, 3). I cannot claim any expertise in such matters of First Philosophy, but in practical terms, the important thing here is that this philosophical foundation does not rule out thinking in terms of individual agency.

In my article looking at Dreyer from an entangled history perspective, I voiced another concern: that the emphasis on reflexivity could risk surrounding the historiographical account with self-reflective disquisitions and methodological hedges to the degree that the ostensible subject was blocked from view. I have come to the conclusion, however, that this need not be an issue. Film historians, I would argue, do not need to include an explicit accounting for the whole process of reflexion in their written accounts. Sometimes they will be addressing readers who can be assumed to be interested mainly in the historical topic, while at other times they will be dealing with readers who are concerned with the intellectual process underlying the research as much or more as with the results. Where the emphasis should lie is fundamentally a rhetorical choice. Historians addressing a popular audience will frequently eschew the inclusion of explicit theoretical and methodological reflections, but a careful writer can make those reflections apparent to professional readers anyway, as long as the latter are willing to read between the lines. An entangled historiography, then, can be both accessible and engaging.

Conclusion: The Pragmatics of Entangled Film History

In this article, I have tried to explain why I believe entangled film history is a useful framework for a research project like ours. We have found it to be a more appropriate theoretical framework than the cultural transfer theory on which we had originally intended to rely. For a number of the border-crossing film people we have been examining, the notion of 'cultural translators' seemed a bad fit, and their doings were ill suited to being described in terms of 'productive misunderstandings' or 'conjunctures of reception'.

More generally, I hope to have shown that there are at least four reasons why entangled film history is a useful research framework.

First, while entangled film history is clearly related to transnational film history, I believe that it is easier to fall into the trap of equating 'more transnational' with 'more valuable' when marching under the banner of transnationalism. Cases of 'strong' and 'marked' transnationality (in Mette Hjort's terms) are likely to attract most attention. While an entangled film historiography will always take transnational issues into consideration, I think it can more readily accommodate weaker and less marked cases, taking in misunderstandings, misappropriations and disappointments as well as more successful border-crossings.

Second, entangled film history can deal with the crossing of other boundaries than national ones, including the boundary between film and other media and art forms. Entanglements with other forms of culture and entertainment have been significant throughout film history, and an entangled film historiography, even if it is definitionally centred on the cinema, will take account of their importance.

Third, entangled film history is grounded in a critique of approaches that take nations or other large-scale units to be stable and easily demarcated. I have long believed this critique to be warranted and important. The first academic conference paper I ever gave was presented at the 1993 CineGraph conference on the interconnections between

German and Danish cinema in the silent period (Tybjerg 1994), a conference premised on the need to escape the boundaries set by methodological nationalism in film historiography. I regard the entangled approach as a particularly effective way of enabling this escape without turning it into an exclusive concern.

Fourth and last, the entangled approach proceeds from pragmatic induction. As described by Werner and Zimmermann, it is a notion I find very attractive. It allows the entangled approach to respect individual agency while paying attention to its dynamic interplay with social structures. Pragmatic induction also acknowledges the need evidently felt by many historians to immerse themselves in the sources before being able to see where the significant research questions might lie, and to adjust their conceptual framework in light of their archival research. Pragmatic induction ensures the continuous methodological reflections that the entangled film historian undertakes will remain firmly anchored in the empirical reality of the historical record.

Note

1. https://emhis.blogg.lu.se

References

Abel, Richard, Giorgio Bertellini and Rob King, eds. 2008. *Early Cinema and the 'National'*. Eastleigh: John Libbey.

Arnoldy, Édouard. 2004. 'Présentation.' *CiNéMAS: Revue d'études cinématographiques* 14, no 2–3: 7–18.

Assmann, Aleida. 2014. 'Transnational Memories.' *European Review* 22, no. 4: 546–56.

Baxandall, Michael. 1985. *Patterns of Intention: On the Historical Explanation of Pictures*. New Haven: Yale Univerisity Press.

Bean, Jennifer M., Anupama Kapse and Laura Horak, eds. 2014. *Silent Cinema and the Politics of Space*. Bloomington: Indiana University Press.

Behn, Manfred, ed. 1994. *Schwarzer Traum und Weisse Sklavin: Deutsch-dänische Filmbeziehungen 1910–1930*. München: edition text+kritik.

Belach, Helga and Wolfgang Jacobsen, eds. 1990. *Richard Oswald: Regisseur und Produzent, CineGraph Buch*. München: edition text+kritik.

Bergfelder, Tim, Sue Harris and Sarah Street. 2007. *Film Architecture and the Transnational Imagination: Set Design in 1930s European Cinema*. Amsterdam: Amsterdam University Press.

Berton, Mireille. 2004. 'Freud et l'« intuition cinégraphique » : psychanalyse, cinéma et épistémologie.' *CiNéMAS: Revue d'études cinématographiques* 14, no. 2–3: 53–73.

Biltereyst, Daniël and Philippe Meers. 2020. 'Comparative, Entangled, Parallel and 'other' Cinema Histories. Another Reflection on the Comparative Mode Within New Cinema History.' *TMG Journal for Media History* 23, no. 1–2: 1–9.
Bock, Hans-Michael, Jan Distelmeyer and Jörg Schöning, eds. 2022a. *Fluchtlinien: Filmkarrieren zwischen Ost- und Westeuropa*, CineGraph Buch. München: edition text+kritik.
———, eds. 2022b. *Grenzüberschreitende Licht-Spiele: Deutsch-Niederländische Filmbeziehungen*, CineGraph Buch. München: edition text+kritik.
Bock, Hans-Michael and Claudia Lenssen, eds. 1991. *Joe May: Regisseur und Produzent*, CineGraph Buch. München: edition text+kritik.
Bono, Francesco and Johannes Roschlau, eds. 2011. *Tenöre, Touristen, Gastarbeiter: Deutsch-Italienische Filmbeziehungen*, CineGraph Buch. München: edition text+kritik.
Bordwell, David. 2006. *The Way Hollywood Tells It: Story and Style in Modern Movies*. Berkeley & Los Angeles: University of California Press.
Bretschneider, Jürgen, ed. 1992. *Ewald André Dupont: Autor und Regisseur*, CineGraph Buch. München: edition text+kritik.
Brizuela, Natalia. 2009. 'Film.' In *The Palgrave Dictionary of Transnational History: From the Mid-19th Century to the Present Day*, edited by Akira Iriye and Pierre-Yves Saunier, 392–7. Basingstoke: Palgrave Macmillan.
Bödeker, Hans Erich, Patrice Veit and Michael Werner. 2002. 'Présentation.' In *Le concert et son public: mutations de la vie musicale en Europe de 1780 à 1914 (France, Allemagne, Angleterre)*, edited by Hans Erich Bödeker, Patrice Veit and Michael Werner, xiii–xvii. Paris: Éditions de la Maison des sciences de l'homme.
Calvino, Italo. 1973. *Il castello dei destini incrociati*. Torino: Einaudi.
———. 1976. *The Castle of Crossed Destinies*. Translated by William Weaver. New York: Harcourt Brace.
Chernilo, Daniel. 2006. 'Social Theory's Methodological Nationalism: Myth and Reality.' *European Journal of Social Theory* 9, no. 1: 5–22.
Conrad, Sebastian. 2016. *What is Global History?* Princeton: Princeton University Press.
Cronqvist, Marie and Christoph Hilgert. 2017. 'Entangled Media Histories: The Value of Transnational and Transmedial Approaches in Media Historiography.' *Media History* 23, no. 1: 130–41.
'Das neue Ufaprogramm.' 1924. *Lichtbild-Bühne* 17, no. 82: 1.
Delgado, Jérôme. 2015. '*Birdman*: Le tournant d'une carrière.' *Séquences: la revue de cinéma*, no. 294: 10–11.
Distelmeyer, Jan, ed. 2003. *Tonfilmfrieden/Tonfilmkrieg: Die Geschichte der Tobis vom Technik-Syndikat zum Staatskonzern*. München: edition text+kritik.
———, ed. 2004. *Alliierte für den Film: Arnold Pressburger, Gregor Rabinowitsch und die Cine-Allianz*. München: edition text+kritik.
———, ed. 2006. *Babylon in FilmEuropa: Mehrsprachen-Versionen der 1930er Jahre*. München: edition text+kritik.

Ellis, Patrick, Arne Lunde and Anna Westerstahl Stenport. 2019. 'Introduction: Nordic Film Cultures and Cinemas of Elsewhere.' In *Nordic Film Cultures and Cinemas of Elsewhere*, edited by Arne Lunde and Anna Westerstahl Stenport, 1–22. Edinburgh University Press.

Elsaesser, Thomas. 2004. 'The New Film History as Media Archaeology.' *CiNéMAS: Revue d'études cinématographiques* 14, no. 2–3: 75–117.

———. 2016. *Film History as Media Archaeology: Tracking Digital Cinema*. Amsterdam: Amsterdam University Press.

Espagne, Michel and Michael Werner. 1987. 'La construction d'une référence culturelle allemande en France: genèse et histoire (1750–1914).' *Annales* 42, no. 4: 969–92.

Fardon, Richard. 1996. '"Crossed Destinies": The Entangled Histories of West African Ethnic and National Identities.' In *Ethnicity in Africa: Roots, Meanings and Implications*, edited by Louise de la Gorgendière, Kenneth King and Sarah Vaughan, 117–46. Edinburgh: Centre of African Studies, University of Edinburgh.

Florin, Bo and Patrick Vonderau. 2019. *A Tale from Constantinople: The History of a Film that Never Was*. Höör: Brutus Östlings Bokförlag Symposion.

Fuhrmann, Wolfgang. 2020. 'Der Weg nach Rio in Brazil: Histoire Croisée, Public Diplomacy and Film-Historical Research.' *TMG Journal for Media History* 23, no. 1–2.

———. 2021. 'Guter Ruf und Große Pläne. Die Ufa in Lateinamerika 1919–1942.' In *Ufa international: Ein deutscher Filmkonzern mit globalen Ambitionen*, edited by Philipp Stiasny, Jürgen Kasten and Frederik Lang, 72–90. München: edition text+kritik.

Garncarz, Joseph. 2013. *Hollywood in Deutschland: Zur Internationalisierung der Kinokultur 1925–1990*. Frankfurt am Main: Stroemfeld.

Griffen-Foley, Bridget. 2017. 'Entangled Media Histories: A Response.' *Media History* 23, no. 1: 145–7.

Hagener, Malte. 2014. 'Introduction: The Emergence of Film Culture.' In *The Emergence of Film Culture: Knowledge Production, Institution Building, and the Fate of the Avant-Garde in Europe, 1919–1945*, edited by Malte Hagener, 1–18. New York: Berghahn Books.

Haupt, Heinz-Gerhard, and Jürgen Kocka. 2009. 'Comparison and Beyond: Traditions, Scope, and Perspectives of Comparative History.' In *Comparative and Transnational History: Central European Approaches and New Perspectives*, edited by Heinz-Gerhard Haupt and Jürgen Kocka, 1–30. New York: Berghahn Books.

Heinke, Ralf Heiner and Christoph Ziener. 2016. 'Globale Kinoexpansionen: Transnationale Filmgeschichte der Zwischenkriegszeit.' *MEDIENwissenschaft* 4: 409–24.

Higson, Andrew. 2010. 'Transnational Developments in European Cinema in the 1920s.' *Transnational Cinemas* 1, no. 1: 69–82.

Hilgert, Christoph, Marie Cronqvist and Hugh Chignell. 2020. 'Introduction: "Tracing Entanglements in Media History".' *Media History* 26, no. 1: 1–5.

Hilmes, Michèle. 2017. 'Entangled Media Histories: A Response.' *Media History* 23: 142–4.
Hjort, Mette. 2010. 'On the Plurality of Cinematic Transnationalism.' In *World Cinemas: Transnational Perspectives*, edited by Nataša Ďurovičová and Kathleen Newman, 12–33. New York: Routledge.
Hjort, Mette and Ursula Lindqvist. 2016. 'Introduction: Nordic Cinema: Breaking New Waves since the Dawn of Film.' In *A Companion to Nordic Cinema*, edited by Mette Hjort and Ursula Lindqvist, 1–12. Chichester: Wiley-Blackwell.
Hodgin, Nick. 2016. 'The Cosmopolitan Communist: Joris Ivens, Transnational Film-Maker before Transnationalism?' *Transnational Cinemas* 7, no. 1: 34–49.
Langen, Ulrik. 2009. 'På kryds og tværs: franske revolutionsemigranter 1789–1814 og *histoire croisée*.' In *Transnationale historier*, edited by Sissel Bjerrum Fossat, Anne Magnussen, Klaus Petersen and Niels Arne Sørensen, 251–66. Odense: Syddansk Universitetsforlag.
Loiperdinger, Martin and Uli Jung, eds. 2013. *Importing Asta Nielsen: The International Film Star in the Making 1910–1914*. New Barnet: John Libbey.
Matthews, Jill Julius. 2006. 'Modern Nomads and National Film History: The Multi-Continental Career of J. D. Williams.' In *Connected Worlds: History in Transnational Perspective*, edited by Ann Curthoys and Marilyn Lake, 157–69. Canberra: ANU Press.
Middell, Matthias. 2016. 'Kulturtransfer, Transferts culturels.' *zeitgeschichte-digital.de*. https://doi.org/10.14765/zzf.dok.2.702.v1.
Nagl, Tobias. 2009. *Die unheimliche Maschine: Rasse und Repräsentation im Weimarer Kino*. München: edition text+kritik.
Offermanns, Ernst. 2001. *Internationalität und europäischer Hegemonialanspruch des Spielfilms der NS-Zeit*. Hamburg: Kovač.
Pafort-Overduin, Clara, Kathleen Lotze, Åsa Jernudd and Thunnis van Oort. 2020. 'Moving Films: Visualising Film Flow in Three European Cities in 1952.' *TMG Journal for Media History* 23, no. 1–2: 1–49.
Pozner, Valérie. 2004. 'Le bonimenteur « rouge » : retour sur la question de l'oralité à propos du cas soviétique.' *CiNéMAS: Revue d'études cinématographiques* 14, no. 2–3: 143–78.
Randeria, Shalini. 2002. 'Entangled Histories of Uneven Modernities: Civil Society, Caste Solidarities and Legal Pluralism in Post-Colonial India.' In *Unraveling Ties: From Social Cohesion to New Practices of Connectedness*, edited by Yehuda Elkana, Ivan Krastev, Elísio Macamo and Shalini Randeria, 284–311. Frankfurt: Campus Verlag.
Roschlau, Johannes, ed. 2008. *Zwischen Barrandov und Babelsberg: deutsch-tschechische Filmbeziehungen im 20. Jahrhundert*. München: edition text+kritik.
———, ed. 2012. *Europa im Sattel: Western zwischen Sibirien und Atlantik*, CineGraph Buch. München: edition text+kritik.
Saekel, Ursula. 2011. *Der US-Film in der Weimarer Republik – ein Medium der "Amerikanisierung"? Deutsche Filmwirtschaft, Kulturpolitik und mediale Globalisierung im Fokus transatlantischer Interessen*. Paderborn: Ferdinand Schöningh.

Salazkina, Masha. 2012. 'Moscow-Rome-Havana: A Film-Theory Road Map.' *October* 139: 97–116.
Saunier, Pierre-Yves. 2009. 'Transnational.' In *The Palgrave Dictionary of Transnational History: From the Mid-19th Century to the Present Day*, edited by Akira Iriye and Pierre-Yves Saunier, 1047–55. Basingstoke: Palgrave Macmillan.
Schaefer, Eric. 2012. 'The Problem with Sexploitation Movies.' *Iluminace* 24, no. 3: 148–52.
Schmidt, Heike. 2002. 'Entangled Memories: *Bindung* and Identity.' In *Unraveling Ties: From Social Cohesion to New Practices of Connectedness*, edited by Yehuda Elkana, Ivan Krastev, Elísio Macamo and Shalini Randeria, 199–212. Frankfurt: Campus Verlag.
Schöning, Jörg, ed. 1989. *Reinhold Schünzel: Schauspieler und Regisseur*. München: edition text+kritik.
———, ed. 1993. *London Calling: Deutsche im britischen Film der dreissiger Jahre*. München: edition text+kritik.
———, ed. 1995. *Fantaisies russes: russische Filmmacher in Berlin und Paris 1920–1930*. München: edition text+kritik.
Shaw, Deborah. 2017. 'Transnational Cinema: Mapping a Field of Study.' In *The Routledge Companion to World Cinema*, edited by Stephanie Dennison, Rob Stone, Alex Marlow-Mann and Paul Cooke, 290–8. London: Taylor and Francis.
Singer, Mark. 2001. 'The Book Eater: Michael Zinman, Obsessive Bibliophile, and the Critical-Mess Theory of Collecting.' *The New Yorker* 76, no. 45: 62–71.
Sinnerbrink, Robert. 2019. 'Michael Theunissen and Recognition.' In *Handbuch Anerkennung*, edited by Ludwig Siep, Heikki Ikaheimo and Michael Quante, 1–4. Wiesbaden: Springer.
Sklar, Robert and Saverio Giovacchini, eds. 2012. *Global Neorealism: The Transnational History of a Film Style*. Jackson: University Press of Mississippi.
Spieker, Markus. 1999. *Hollywood unterm Hakenkreuz: der amerikanische Spielfilm im Dritten Reich*. Trier: WVT.
Stanziani, Alessandro. 2018. *Eurocentrism and the Politics of Global History*. Cham: Springer International Publishing.
Stiasny, Philipp, Jürgen Kasten and Frederik Lang, eds. 2021. *Ufa international: Ein deutscher Filmkonzern mit globalen Ambitionen*. München: edition text+kritik.
Sturm, Sibylle M., and Arthur Wolgemuth, eds. 1996. *Hallo? Berlin? Ici Paris!: deutsch-französische Filmbeziehungen 1918–1939*. München: edition text+kritik.
Sørensen, Nils Arne. 2009. 'Den transnationale vending?' *Historisk tidsskrift* 109, no. 2: 459–72.
Terkanian, Kate and Hugh Chignell. 2020. 'Nesta Pain: The Entangled Media Producer.' *Media History* 26, no. 1: 20–33.
Theunissen, Michael. 1977. *Der Andere: Studien zur Sozialontologie der Gegenwart*. 2nd ed. Berlin: De Gruyter.
———. 1986. *The Other: Studies in the Social Ontology of Husserl, Heidegger, Sartre and Buber*. Cambridge: MIT Press.

Tybjerg, Casper. 1994. 'Schatten vom Meister: Benjamin Christensen in Deutschland.' In *Schwarzer Traum und Weisse Sklavin: Deutsch-dänische Filmbeziehungen 1910–1930*, edited by Manfred Behn, *CineGraph Buch*, 105–15. München: edition text+kritik.
——. 2005. 'The Makers of Movies: Authors, Subjects, Personalities, Agents?' In *Visual Authorship: Creativity and Intentionality in Media*, edited by Torben Grodal, Bente Larsen and Iben Thorvig Laursen, *Northern Lights: Film and Media Studies Yearbook*, 37–65. Copenhagen: Museum Tusculanum.
——. 2020. 'Benjamin Christensen's Wonderful Adventure: Film History and Practitioner's Agency.' *Kosmorama*, no. 276. Accessed 7 February 2023. https://www.kosmorama.org/en/articles/benjamin-christensen.
——. 2021. 'The European Principle: Art and Border Crossings in Carl Theodor Dreyer's Career.' In *A History of Danish Cinema*, edited by Isak Thorsen, C. Claire Thomson and Pei-Sze Chow, 41–50. Edinburgh: Edinburgh University Press.
Tyrell, Ian. 2009. 'History.' In *The Palgrave Dictionary of Transnational History: From the Mid-19th Century to the Present Day*, edited by Akira Iriye and Pierre-Yves Saunier, 493–6. Basingstoke: Palgrave Macmillan.
Villazana, Libia. 2013. 'Redefining Transnational Cinemas: A Transdisciplinary Perspective.' In *Contemporary Hispanic Cinema*, edited by Stephanie Dennison, *Interrogating the Transnational in Spanish and Latin American Film*, 25–46. Boydell & Brewer.
Vonderau, Patrick. 2000. 'Geheime Verwandschaften? Der "Schwedenfilm" und die Geschichte des Weimarer Kinos.' *Montage/AV* 9, no. 2: 65–99.
——. 2007. *Bilder vom Norden. Schwedisch-deutsche Filmbeziehungen 1914–1939*. Marburg: Schüren.
——. 2012. '27 May 1921: *Scherben* Seeks Cinematic Equivalent of Theatrical Intimacy.' In *A New History of German Cinema*, edited by Jennifer M. Kapczynski and Michael D. Richardson, 105–10. Rochester: Camden House.
Wagner, Hans-Ulrich, Hugh Chignell, Marie Cronqvist, Christoph Hilgert and Kristin Skoog. 2019. 'Media After 1945.' In *The Handbook of European Communication History*, edited by Klaus Arnold, Paschal Preston and Susanne Kinnebrock, 189–204. Hoboken: John Wiley & Sons.
Wahl, Chris. 2009. *Sprachversionsfilme aus Babelsberg: die internationale Strategie der Ufa, 1929–1939*. München: edition text+kritik.
Werner, Michael. 2002. 'Introduction: II. Agents et promoteurs.' In *Le concert et son public: mutations de la vie musicale en Europe de 1780 à 1914 (France, Allemagne, Angleterre)*, edited by Hans Erich Bödeker, Patrice Veit and Michael Werner, 65–69. Paris: Éditions de la Maison des sciences de l'homme.
Werner, Michael and Bénédicte Zimmermann. 2002. 'Vergleich, Transfer, Verflechtung. Der Ansatz der Histoire croisée und die Herausforderung des Transnationalen.' *Geschichte und Gesellschaft* 28, no. 4: 607–36.
——. 2003. 'Penser l'histoire croisée: entre empirie et réflexivité.' *Annales: Histoire, sciences sociales* 58, no. 1: 7–36.

———. 2004. 'Penser l'histoire croisée: entre empirie et réflexivité.' In *De la comparaison à l'histoire croisée*, edited by Michael Werner and Bénédicte Zimmermann, 15–49. Paris: Seuil.

———. 2006. 'Beyond Comparison: Histoire Croisée and the Challenge of Reflexivity.' *History and Theory* 45, no. 1: 30–50.

Wottrich, Erika, ed. 2001. *Deutsche Universal: transatlantische Verleih- und Produktionsstrategien eines Hollywood-Studios in den 20er und 30er Jahren*. München: edition text+kritik.

———, ed. 2002. *M wie Nebenzahl: Nero-Filmproduktion zwischen Europa und Hollywood*. München: edition text+kritik.

Wottrich, Erika and Swenja Schiemann, eds. 2017. *Ach, sie haben ihre Sprache verloren: Filmautoren im Exil*. München: edition text+kritik.

Zimmermann, Bénédicte. 2002. '*Bindung* and Unemployment in Late Nineteenth-Century Germany.' In *Unraveling Ties: From Social Cohesion to New Practices of Connectedness*, edited by Yehuda Elkana, Ivan Krastev, Elísio Macamo and Shalini Randeria, 227–47. Frankfurt: Campus Verlag.

———. 2020. 'Histoire Croisée: A Relational Process-Based Approach'. *Footprint: Delft School of Design Journal* 14, no. 1: 7–13.

CHAPTER 3

How 'Danish' Were Danish Film Stars in Germany During the Silent Era?

Alice A. Salamena and Stephan Michael Schröder

This chapter examines how the 'Danishness' of border-crossing Danish silent screen stars was received in the German language area. Special focus is put on the examination of various publications on Danish celebrities in (fan) magazines and on several collections of fan letters which show how differently Danish stars and their 'Danish-ness' were constructed and negotiated by the press and by individual fans. The aim is to illuminate how differently Danish silent film stars were semanticised by German-speaking audiences, placing them at the node between Danish and German film, entangling the two into a Danish-German film culture.

Stars from Denmark like Olaf Fønss or Clara Wieth, but also others like Asta Nielsen, Robert Dinesen, Ebba Thomsen, Betty Nansen or Carl Schenstrøm and Harald Madsen, were celebrities whose fame and influence crossed and transcended national borders. It was not only Asta Nielsen's name that 'shone out in massive neon ads around the world' (Nielsen 2022, 148). Danish silent film stars were revered and adored abroad as stars of a media – to quote Fønss himself – not 'bound by the language of any nationality' (Fønss 1913, 7), but as heralds of 'the only common world language', as Béla Balázs appraised the semiotic capacity of the film (Balázs 2001, 22). Accordingly, many stars of the silent screen considered themselves 'citizens of every country in the world', as the US star Mary Pickford wrote in her memoirs (Pickford 1955, 127). Also, Danish celebrities living and working abroad like Dinesen, Fønss or Nansen, and in particular Asta Nielsen, more often than not cultivated a cosmopolitan self-representation, emphasising an identity not limited by the star's national origin. This play with national identity was made possible by the 'celebrity identity' constantly being subjected to semiotic negotiation (Marshall 2014). However, such (linguistic, cultural, biographical, territorial) transgressions of national boundaries did not always go smoothly in the early decades of the twentieth century marked by the high tide of nationalism – and not the least with regard to the relationship between Denmark and Germany. By projecting an identity that toyed with and/or collided with national discourses, the stars refused a firm nationalistic claiming (Lee 2016).

In a way this chapter supplements an earlier article on how Danish films were marketed in Germany and the press discourse on Danish films in the 1910s (Schröder 2020). However, the focus here will be a different one. Taking our cue mainly from New Cinema History, Celebrity Studies, Fandom Studies and Benedict Anderson's reflections on imagined communities, we will conduct an inquiry into if and how silent film stars from Denmark were perceived as 'Danish', and in what way we might frame their celebrity within Werner and Zimmermann's notion of *histoire croisée* (2006). Tybjerg's methodological introduction to this volume (see Chapter 1) rightly dismisses the notion of a 'cultural translator', as this lends itself too much to the interpretation of culture as a static object that is transmitted between two static entities. So rather than looking at silent screen stars as cultural translators, this article aims to situate the 'celebrity' in accordance with Richard Dyer's pioneering work *Stars* on cinema celebrity, understanding the function of star images as 'crucially in relation to contradictions within and between ideologies' (Dyer 1998, 34). Thus, the aim will be to show how the star as a 'border-crossing individual' (Tybjerg) might be a point of intercrossing her- or himself, actively contributing to cultural entanglement.

First, we will explore how – in which discourses – stars from Denmark were generally presented in German fan magazines. Then we will try to place Danish celebrities at, and also as, the intersection between Danish and German film culture, mainly taking up two of the most popular Danish stars during the 1910s and 1920s: the well-remembered Asta Nielsen and the less well-remembered Olaf Fønss, with a few comparative side glances at Clara Wieth. Finally, we will take a look at the way their Danish origin is (not) treated in fan mail from the German language area.

Magazines and Mail: Our Material

Placing fan magazines and fan mail at the centre of investigation allows us to approach the reception of stars from Denmark among the actual people in the audience, whereas 'audience' otherwise is more often than not only a fictional entity in the press. This claim seems self-evident with regard to fan mail, but how about fan and film magazines, which were obviously determined by an economic logic and not created and composed by the fans themselves? However, these magazines were not only an important source of information for cinemagoers, but also mediated between the industry and the audience, thus constantly negotiating the star's status and meaning. As Kathryn Fuller already wrote in 1996 in her seminal book *At the Picture Show. Small-town Audiences and the Creation of Movie Fan Culture*: 'Movie fan magazines of the 1910s and 1920s were mediating forces between the movie fan and the screen, fleshing out the movie star's character beyond his or her screen roles and contributing to the creation of movie fan culture' (Fuller 1996, 166). Interactivity with the fannish readers was explicitly aimed for, for instance by providing space for letters from the readers, by competitions or by answering readers' questions in special columns (Fuller 1996, 166, Orgeron 2009, Fee 2015, 128–31). In order to survive, the fan magazines addressed readers' preferences – or at least what they thought to be their preferences – and what they assumed would resonate most and best with the fans' perception of a celebrity.

In the German language area, however, explicit fan magazines emerged comparatively late. *Illustrierte Kino-Woche* (1913–1916, 'Illustrated Cinema-Week') and its successor, *Illustrierte Film-Woche* (1916–1922, 'Illustrated Film-Week'), remained the only ones until the end of World War I (Haller 2010, 327) and first abandoned its last features of a trade journal in 1919. A ladies' journal like *Elegante Welt* ('Elegant World') did not completely abstain from covering the glittering cosmos of the silent screen business, beginning in 1912. But a programmatic declaration to cover films and film stars first followed in 1918, maintaining 'that the majority of the readers will welcome it joyfully, if from now on the 'Elegante Welt' will deal with the film to an even greater extent' ('Kino und Elegante Welt' 1918, 17).

While fan magazines – at least in the US and England – are a commonly used source for research, the same cannot be said about fan mail. Fan mail swelled to a veritable flood during the 1910s, albeit the reported bombastic figures in the press and in memoirs should be read primarily as (self) advertising statements. But as noted in New Cinema History, fan mail is incontrovertibly one of the 'previously underused sources' (Biltereyst, Maltby and Meers 2019, 8) and 'remains a largely neglected element of celebrity and fan history' (Orgeron 2009, 20). The reason for this negligence is more empirical than methodological, as authentic fan mail from the silent era is simply seldom preserved. Fortunately, the Danish Film Institute houses two collections of fan mail to Danish stars, namely to Clara Wieth and to Olaf Fønss. While Wieth's collection encompasses 168 mail items, Fønss' impressive collection contains approximately 2500 mail items. The difference in numbers is caused by the fact that Wieth's collection seems to be a rigorous selection of the mail she received, while the rather conceited Fønss appears to have stored every mail item sent to him as a film star. These collections include letters from all over the world, but mostly from the German language area, and provide a rare opportunity to examine the 'Danishness' of Danish stars from the fans' perspective. These two collections can be supplemented by a single letter written to Valdemar Psilander (see Danish Film Institute 2021) plus fan mail from other (regrettably also quite selective) collections outside the Danish Film Institute, including 136 fan mail items written to Asta Nielsen, stored in the Lund University Library.

Obviously, one should keep in mind that fans are not ordinary cinemagoers, but rather dedicated ones. Hence, the reception of emotionally engaged fannish spectators is not congruent with the general public's (Ryan and Johanningsmeier 2013, 4–5). That being said, one has to acknowledge that the reception of the 'general public' during the silent era (and later) is a problematic notion in the first place, as it implicitly suggests a homogeneity with regard to gender, class, age, nationality and so forth, which never existed. It is impossible to make valid statements about the 'general public's' reception, but fan magazines and fan mail not only allow for a reconstruction of the perspective of individuals in the cinema, but also for valuable insights regarding the reception of Danish film stars among an important and impactful part of the audience. It is arguably the closest we get to the ordinary cinemagoers' reception.

Constructing the 'Danishness' of Stars in German Fan Magazines

When it was announced in *Elegante Welt* in 1918 that in the future the magazine would cover the sparkling world of cinema and its stars more extensively, this declaration was significantly illustrated with pictures showing 'The Stars of the Great Northern' with a large picture of Gunnar Tolnæs in the centre. Generally, stars from Denmark – including non-Danes made famous in Danish films, like the Norwegian Tolnæs and the Italo-German Rita Sacchetto – figured very prominently in the early German fan magazines. Already the first issue of *Illustrierte Kino-Woche* was illustrated with Asta Nielsen on the front page, and from 1913 to 1918, Danish stars appeared another eighteen times on the cover of *Illustrierte Kino-Woche/Illustrierte Film-Woche*, to which one could add the two covers with Tolnæs and Sacchetto as 'honorary Danes' of sorts. In a survey in 1913, Psilander was voted the most popular film star among the readers, followed by Asta Nielsen in second place, and even Clara Wieth figured in the list ('Das Resultat unserer Rundfrage' 1914). Taking into account that the survey was based on only 1648 votes, one may rightly question its representativeness. Still, Psilander and Nielsen were without a doubt extremely popular in the German language area, and the magazine concluded: 'Mr. Waldemar Psylander, Copenhagen is thus the winner of our survey'.

Generally, media coverage of stars from Denmark almost always mentioned their Danish origin, at times even emphasised it. Although the Danish names tended to get Germanised in the German press (Olaf Fønss becoming Olaf Fönss, even Olaf Fönß; Gunnar Tolnæs turning into Tolnäs; Valdemar Psilander appearing as Waldemar Psylander), the press clearly marked actors and actresses as 'Danish', not least by commenting on their accents (see for instance Jacobsohn 1915, 8 about Asta Nielsen's or Lewandowski 1921, 2 and 'S.W.' 1924, 144 about Olaf Fønss'). This flagging of the stars as 'Danish' is even further corroborated by the practice that Danish film stars appearing in the German language area were paid homage by laurel wreaths with red and white silk ribbons (Fønss 1932, 118) or by playing the Danish anthem when they arrived (Schenstrøm 1943, 93, 137; Fønss 1932, 116–17).

In accordance with the theoretical framework of *histoire croisée*, we understand this 'Danishness' of stars as a performative, not as an essential category. It has to be borne in mind that conceptions of 'Danishness' are semantic categories: produced discursively and subject to changes over time. Accordingly, one has to pay attention to why and in what context the 'Danishness' of stars was framed in media coverage and especially in fan magazines. Two main discourses are discernible: one referring to film history and one referring to Germany's ideological history.

The first one aims at the narrative that Danish films were influential, even decisive for overcoming cinema's primitive (French) beginnings and becoming a media with cultural ambitions, if not an art form. In a typical article on 'The Peoples and the Film' in the popular magazine *Berliner Illustrierte Zeitung* from 1925, the early dominance of French and Italian films was reportedly broken by the ambitious Danish films:

> There appeared on the canvas boards [. . .] a polar bear, which moved artfully bowing on a globe. What one then saw behind him in play was more careful, better, more believable, prettier [. . .]. That was the beginning of the Nordic invasion. From Denmark came Asta Nielsen, the first international film star, [and] Urban Gad, the first film director of world fame, gradually displaced with his clean works the Italians, who were too burlesque, and the Parisians, who were too pathetic and bloodthirsty. Berlin [. . .] now laid down its arms before Copenhagen. ('Die Völker und der Film' 1925)

When writing about stars from Denmark, this widespread narrative about Danish film's contribution to film becoming a serious artistic medium was either evoked directly (for example in the context of presenting Ebba Thomsen, 'H.S.' 1914) or by suggesting parallels between Danish films and the 'Führerrolle' ascribed to the progressive, much-discussed literature of the so-called Scandinavian Modern Breakthrough by authors like Ibsen, Strindberg or Bjørnson ('Gunnar Tolnæs' 1917, 7; Borchardt 1919b, 13). In a way, one might argue that this understanding of stars from Denmark as representatives for a development towards 'quality films' implies a discursive bridging between Danish and German film culture and is thus an indicator for a common film culture, as the Danish film is defined as the paragon for the German film.

A German tendency towards an inclusive look at stars from Denmark becomes much more obvious when examining how these were 'Nordified' in accordance with traditional discourses on 'Northernness', supplemented by contemporary race theory (see Zernack 1997 and Schröder 2020 for more detailed information on Wilhelminian discourses on 'Northernness'). Significantly, German journalists were sometimes wrong about the national origins of Scandinavian stars: for instance, the Norwegian Tolnæs became a Swede ('Gunnar Tolnäs' 1917, 8). However, these misstatements seemed not to matter, since the important point was that the actors came from the 'North'. In Wilhelminian discourse, this strongly suggested a link to the medieval ages in Scandinavia. Gunnar Tolnæs was thus revered for his 'Vikingness' (Droop 1918b). Such characterisations predictably went hand in glove with descriptions moulded by contemporary race theory. As an 'enviable feature of the Scandinavian race', the 'magnificent appearance' of Scandinavian actors – especially the male ones – was praised ('Gunnar Tolnäs' 1917, 7), and Carlo Wieth was referred to as 'the type of a Scandinavian, slim, blond with blue eyes' ('H.G.' 1914).

Sometimes the 'Northernness' of the actor was potentially on a collision course with his role, for instance when the 'Viking' Gunnar Tolnæs played a maharaja in the box-office successes *Maharadjahens Yndlingshustru I* and *II* (1917, *A Prince of Barata*; 1919, *A Daughter of Brahma*). The films paved his way to stardom in the German language area and were jokingly made responsible for a new disease called 'Gunnaritis' ('Gert' 1920). Tolnæs' ascent to full-blown star status was strongly supported by a cross-media campaign, orchestrated by Marie Luise Droop, who not only was the head of Nordisk's story department in Berlin, but also the company's always-on-the-go public relations manager in the German language area between 1916 and 1919/20 (see Jacobsen and Klapdor 1997 and DanLitStummFilm, n.d.). Moreover, Droop was a die-hard fan of Tolnæs, publishing articles on him and interviews with him, providing Nordisk (together with a co-author) with the draft for the second maharaja-film as well as writing a German novelisation of the films (Droop 1918a). However, such an eroticising of an 'oriental' played by the 'Northern' idol Tolnæs was not without problems. *Illustrierte Film-Woche* deemed it necessary to point out that the story takes place 'in the India of the Hindus, not of the Mohammedans', where:

> the remnants of Aryan mankind [. . .] have preserved themselves free until today. To those who approach the film with racial prejudices, it should be said at this point that these Aryan Brahmins with pedigrees going back to the grey prehistoric times, from the racial-theoretical point of view of a Gobineau, for example, can rightly count themselves among the master race ["Herrenmenschen"].

– a reference to the French godfather of race theory which was, however, partly modified in the following by the addendum 'if such ethnographic concepts exist at all' ('Gunnar Tolnæs in Berlin' 1919). The explicit need to justify the maharaja's race as Aryan might have been debatable in the contemporary discourse, as the addendum demonstrates. However, the de-orientalisation of the maharaja was not: Gestrich has shown how strategies of Whiteness are employed in these films to justify the potentially scandalous relationship between an Oriental man and a white woman (cf. Gestrich 2008, 131, 142) – and Tolnæs playing an Oriental, one might add.

According to our findings, in the German language area the Viking topos and references to a 'Nordic' race were used exclusively to describe men. Only in the USA was Betty Nansen marketed as a 'Vikingess' (Kvam 1997, 154). One might wonder why female stars from Denmark were generally less likely to be described in such terms in the German language area, although blonde stars like Clara Wieth or Else Frølich would have easily invited similar categorisations. One possible explanation is that referring to physical beauty in accordance with race ideals allowed male as well as female journalists to write freely about the beauty of men, which otherwise would have had suspicious overtones. At first glance, this Nordification of stars from Denmark rather seems to distance them from German culture. However, starting with Johann Gottfried Herder and culminating in Wilhelminian and Weimarian discourse, there was a strong conviction in Germany about a common (pan-)German(ic) culture and, beginning in the second half of the nineteenth century, even a common racial heritage with the 'countries close to the midnight sun' (Borchardt 1919b, 13).

The discourse on Danish stars in fan magazines and similar publications is ambiguous. On the one hand, stars from Denmark were pronouncedly marked as non-German; on the other hand, the commonalities between Denmark and Germany were oftentimes highlighted, both in a film-historiographical as well as in an ideological perspective. At the same time, it is worth noting that these two perspectives evoke contradictory discourses on 'Danishness': one epitomising 'Danishness' as a paragon of modernity (Allen 2012), the other one stereotyping 'Danishness' (as part of 'Northernness') by referring to allegedly common cultural and/or racial roots.

Negotiating the 'Danish' Celebrity Terrain: Asta Nielsen and Olaf Fønss

Although seemingly contradictory, this semanticising of Danish silent film celebrities can plausibly be examined on the background of P. David Marshall's conception of the 'celebrity terrain' and the construction(s) of individual stars. He places the celebrity at the 'interstices of the private and the public realms of the movie industry' (Marshall 2014, 84), thereby alluding to – to remain in the nomenclature of *histoire croisée* – the celebrity as a point of 'intercrossing' him/herself. In fact, in terms of the analysis of the role played by the celebrity in the silent screen era and the possibility of a common Danish-German film culture, applying Werner and Zimmermann's notion of 'intercrossings' on the celebrity persona seems rather sensible. Thus, in the following we would like to suggest a reading of the celebrity as explicitly the point of 'intercrossing' between arts and audiences, cultures and communities.

In Marshall's understanding, the celebrity terrain is a space constructed and inscribed by the media, the critic, the public, the fan, and, once created, the celebrity persona becomes a 'terra nullius', free to be claimed by a culture or audience, 'each of which initiates its own negotiation of what the celebrity terrain signifies' (Lee 2016, 40). But how exactly would we then speak about the celebrity terrain in the theoretical frame of *histoire croisée*'s notion of intercrossing?

First and foremost, before turning to the celebrity terrain itself, it is important to keep in mind that the endeavour to define a common culture between two spaces (the Danish and the German film culture) assumes the understanding of these spaces as otherwise separate communities which come to meet – and entangle themselves – on different grounds. Hence, the 'Danish' transnational celebrity moves fluidly between these different communities and cultural contexts while simultaneously providing the canvas for different inscriptions by different recipients of differing cultural backgrounds (and spanning different times through the medium of his/her art). The notion of 'scale' and the 'transnational' in Werner and Zimmermann's model of *histoire croisée* is not of little importance in this case:

> [T]he transnational cannot simply be considered as a supplementary level of analysis to be added to the local, regional, and national levels according to a logic of a change in focus. On the contrary, it is apprehended as a level that exists in interaction with the others, producing its own logics with feedback effects upon other space-structuring logics. (Werner and Zimmermann 2006, 43)

'Transnationality' would then be defined along the lines of stars as border-crossing cultural agents and shows itself in the 'mobility and flexible citizenship that silent screen stardom could enable' through the media that 'allowed celebrities to move across space and cultures relatively quickly' (Lee 2016, 43). It entails not only the transnational celebrity's capacity to bridge space and cross borders physically and artistically, but also calls for the celebrity to become a space, a 'terrain' in Marshall's words, him/herself. The celebrity mediates between cultures and communities, forming a nexus of entangled possibilities of ascriptions and identifications which, gathered in the entity of the celebrity, necessarily interact with and produce these 'feedback effects'.

In terms of 'scale', the individual celebrity is placed in a highly complex way: on an economic level, individuals like Urban Gad and Asta Nielsen spiralled the progress towards the long feature film, but always in relation to other border-crossing individuals coming from the other side; that is Germany, like Ludwig Gottschalk, who brought the ground-breaking film *Afgrunden* (*The Abyss*, 1910) to German audiences, and in relation to corporations that had already established cross-border networks. On a cultural level, individuals like Olaf Fønss transported ideas and knowledge on the silent screen, that is in books like *Tysk Skuespilkunst* ('German Art of Acting', a collection of portraits of individual actors, 1931), again in interaction with other individuals (the actors figuring in the book), and in relation to the knowledge he himself collected throughout his acting career in Denmark and Germany alike. On a social level they spoke to German and Danish public audiences through the press as cause and object of conversation, and on a complex and more intimate level they touched the individual fan, contributing to shaping their understanding of lifestyle and social mobility (Marshall 2014), but also in terms of emotional investment (Duffet 2013).

The examination of fan magazines in the German language area has shown that we cannot separate the reception of Danish stars in Germany entirely from national discourses. From the late 1910s onwards, the press, and the new emerging format of the fan magazine, spread information about celebrities' backgrounds, sometimes sharing personal and intimate information on the stars. The media coverage of individual actors in journals and fan magazines alike speaks unambiguously for the distinct popularity of actors from Denmark in Germany, but, more importantly, also for a general public awareness of the fact that they were *Danish*. However, interestingly, the different strategies of how to construct a supposed 'Danishness' of Danish silent screen stars in Germany in the 1910s and 1920s did not impede their incorporation into a decidedly German national discourse. The celebrity understood as a space, a terrain of potential for social, cultural and individual inscription at the same time, thus becomes the node of differing discursive inscriptions, by necessity laden with social, cultural and individual ideology. It is precisely through this flexibility, the openness for varying constructions of one and the same individual celebrity persona, and the possibility of being fitted into multiple discourses at a time, that the star as a crossing point of different conceptions on a larger scale undermines discursive ascriptions.

In his study *Celebrity and Power. Fame in Contemporary Culture*, Marshall identifies different entities that profit immediately from defining the celebrity in their own terms, one of which is the cultural production side. To the cultural producers the celebrity 'acts as a form of insurance [. . .], a kind of guaranteed return on investment for the production company' (Marshall 2014, 13, see also Dyer 1998, 10–11) – a role the Danish stars undisputedly performed very well in the German language area. Asta Nielsen and Olaf Fønss are among those stars that seldom failed their purpose as box-office draws. They were marketed tactically – an assumption allowed by the phrasing of an advert in *Der Kinematograph* cited by Peter Lähn (1994, 18) – and coherently for the audiences they were to enthuse. The Loiperdinger and Jung anthology *Importing Asta Nielsen. The International Film Star in the Making 1910–1914* (2013) shows this in a remarkably convincing way in the case of Asta Nielsen.

Olaf Fønss' fame arguably began with *Atlantis* (1913) and reached its peak during the production years of the *Homunculus* series (1916–1917), which made him extremely popular in the German language area (Nørrestedt 1994, 119–20; Quaresima 1996). Browsing through contemporary magazine entries on Olaf Fønss, enthusiastic descriptions of his acting and also his whole persona including his family life, feed the assumption of an emerging celebrity culture which introduced the star as a commodity in the 1910s.

Scandinavian actors were easy to market and arguably became more accessible to German audiences when subjected to a narrative of common Danish-German/Germanic heritage. It appears to have been of some importance to the German media to uphold the blending of 'Danishness' and 'Germanness': The narrative of a Germanic heritage that Danish stars were subjected to figured mostly in fan magazines and might have served to

Figure 3.1 Olaf Fønss on the cover of *Die Filmwoche* in 1923 shortly before the inflation reached its peak: The price of the issue was 3 billion marks! Danish Film Institute, Olaf Fønss collection, Scrapbook 1920–1924.

fuel general consumer culture far more than it featured in individual communication between fan and star, as will later be seen. An early German example of this process of using a film star to put commodities on the market is the Asta-Nielsen-perfume (see illustrations in Haller 2009, 329). In evaluating the possibility of a common Danish-German film culture in the 1910s, the construction of the individual celebrity as an economic investment and his/her emerging introduction as a commodity on the cultural market should not remain unappreciated. After all, the economic success of Danish stars in the German language area depended partly on how marketing 'aligned them as a group with their audience' (Marshall 2014, 92).

The influence Danish films had on the German silent film production side, culturally and economically, can feasibly be attributed to some key individuals – albeit it should always be acknowledged that these individuals were part of a bigger picture – who mediated powerfully between Denmark and Germany as social/cultural/economical/political communities, thereby interlacing, entangling, Danish film and German film. Danish silent film celebrities are to be defined precisely as such key individuals. Interestingly, from the survey of fan magazines, it appears that the contemporary construction of these celebrities' 'Danishness' could differ enormously. Julie Allen in *Icons of Danish Modernity. Georg Brandes & Asta Nielsen* (2012) identifies two main discourses on 'Danishness' circulating in the 1910s: that of a publicly cultivated, rather conservative stereotype within Denmark (an endo-stereotype), on the one hand, and a more modern Danish stereotype across Europe (an exo-stereotype) and other continents influenced by figures like Nielsen and Georg Brandes who conveyed 'cultural modernity' on the other (Allen 2012, 19). Interestingly, while Olaf Fønss posed an image that functioned to adapt to both the Danish endo- and the Danish exo-stereotype, Asta Nielsen was not properly re-installed to conform to the endo-stereotype until after her death, instead catered to a progressive, extravagant exo-stereotype during her lifetime.

Taking a closer look at how the 'Danishness' of Fønss and Nielsen was negotiated in German media, it is important to underline that their personal lives and careers were extremely tightly knit to Germany. Olaf Fønss came into fully realising his popularity in Germany in 1914 following a visit to his brother's residence in Munich, where he was enthusiastically celebrated when he appeared at several premières throughout Germany (Fønss 1930b, 117–25). His cooperation with the Deutsche Bioscop and the realisation of the film series *Homunculus* marked his entrance as a powerful and popular cultural agent into the German language area (Nørrestedt 1994, 120). The cooperation with the Deutsche Bioscop, and arguably his popularity amongst fans in Germany, were crucial to his international success. Simultaneously, he occupied prestigious positions on the economic side of the Danish silent film industry (Nørrestedt 1994, 120–1). During his career as a film star, Fønss' residence alternated between Denmark and Germany. It might not be entirely wrong to assume that his professional and financial success strongly depended on both countries and cultures. Fønss, who assiduously collected his fan mail and filled four weighty scrapbooks with newspaper and magazine articles published about himself between 1912 and 1932, today stored at the Danish Film Institute, was very aware of his popularity with German and Danish audiences alike, and took care to appeal to business partners and fans of both German and Danish background. Fønss' celebrity in Germany and the German language area is visible from 1914 onwards in magazines and fan letters of the time. It is conspicuous that the percentage of fan letters written in German to Fønss is extremely high, at more than 80 per cent, while Wieth's German language fan post accounts for 57 per cent and Nielsen's for 38 per cent (however, one should take into consideration that these two later collections are highly selective and therefore not really comparable).

The enthusiastic media coverage of his persona and the content of the fan mail he received cater to the image of a hero of many. In a German newspaper article entitled 'Olaf Fönss' service to German Cinema' the author asserts: 'A mind like Goethe's rests on Viking shoulders' (Fredrik 1920), creating an image of the celebrity Fønss highly laden with national ascription, and composed by melting two images into one another; one inherently German, the other inherently Danish, but both inherently Germanic. In an intriguing examination of 'transnational celebrity identities', Katja Lee identifies different strategies that Canadian transnational stars Maud Allan, Mary Pickford and Emma Albani developed in order to 'accommodate the demands and cultures of multiple spaces' (Lee 2016, 39). The ambiguous national construction of the celebrity Olaf Fønss as a Viking and a Teuton might also have served as a strategy to facilitate identification with the actor for Danish and German audiences, while simultaneously consolidating the German claim on the Danish star. It seems almost as though the German press would create a public image of Fønss that managed to successfully incorporate both 'Danishness' and 'Germanness' into one Germanic representation and harmoniously bridging two national discourses. It is interesting to observe how the German press worked to promote a Germanic image of the actor, referencing not only to Denmark and his Danish heritage but to Scandinavia and typical Northern tropes: Fønss is thus described as 'the blonde, earthy figure of legendary Vikings full of grit and strength' with 'clear steel eyes' (Borchardt 1919a, 13). References to Scandinavia and typical allusions to the 'northlands' (Wagener 1923, 24), the Scandinavian fjords ('P.O.' 1920), and the Vikings are gladly invoked by magazine authors, oftentimes explicitly describing Fønss as a Teuton (see for instance Fredrik 1920).

Asta Nielsen, of course, did not fit the picture:

> She came from the north, from the cool land of blonde beauties – who could believe that in this slender figure with jet-black hair and burning big eyes there was a passion such as is peculiar only to southern women! She came from the north and brought with her all the ardor of the south. (Hermann 1913/14)

Unlike Olaf Fønss, Asta Nielsen did not seem to lend herself to match the 'Germanic' stereotype. Julie Allen has provided ample evidence of this (2011, 2012, 2013). Nielsen's shape was that of a 'gazelle', her temperament was that of a Spaniard (Aubinger 1913), her body that of a French woman: Her 'slender figure' was thought to correspond 'closely to the athletic, somewhat androgynous body type that was already becoming fashionable in France' (Allen 2013, 49). Nielsen's exotic look was inscribed with different conceptions of nationality. Among her roles were a French Noblewoman (*Die Verräterin*, 1911, *The Traitress*, also: *A Woman of the People*), a Spanish girl (*Der Tod in Sevilla*, 1913, *Spanish Blood*), a Greenlandic indigenous character (*Das Eskimobaby*, 1918, 'The Eskimo-Baby') and a young English lady (*Der fremde Vogel*, 1911, *A Strange Bird*, also *The Course of True Love*). It is reported that she wore a wig of light blonde hair for the production of *Die Kinder des Generals* (1912, *Falsely Accused*) on the occasion of acting the role of a German girl (Figure 3.2): 'long blond braids that made her look more like the stereotypical Nordic ideal of beauty' (Allen 2013, 45). This need to put on a blonde wig is very telling in terms of her 'failure to embody the Danish norm' (Allen 2013, 49). The Danish author Sophus Claussen saw her in *Afgrunden* in Paris and complained in the Danish newspaper *Politiken* that Nielsen 'falsifies' the image of Denmark abroad, as she exhibited a 'passionateness [. . .] which we [. . .] do not have' and that she is 'much too black' (Claussen 1911). Nielsen was not perceived as the typical

Figure 3.2 Asta Nielsen wearing a blond wig in *Die Kinder des Generals* (1912). Danish Film Institute.

Dane. According to Allen, this held true for her reception in Denmark and in Germany alike. In fact, Nielsen was regularly characterised by a 'perceived inherent foreignness' (Allen 2011, 82). Yet, her 'Germanisation' took place through the physical act of relocation and with her move to Berlin she became 'a Berlin compatriot' (Loiperdinger 2013, 107), which complicated her reception in Denmark.

The discrepancy between different national ascriptions and her own self-perception posed a dilemma for Asta Nielsen. Her discomfort with having to define her identity in a national discourse is arguably one of the most illuminating examples when trying to read the celebrity as a formative point for differing personal implications of national affiliation: 'I felt international because my art was', she said in retrospect in an interview after her career had ended ('Filmkameraet var som hele verdens øje' 1948). But faced with the expectation to express a self-representation in the conventional nationalised discourses during her career, she resorted to a strategy of ostensibly serving multiple discourses of national affiliation at the same time, which were thereby undermined in their exclusivity: while she wrote about Denmark as her fatherland ('Vaterland') in 1928 (Nielsen 1928), she also referred to Germany as her fatherland ('Fædreland') in a 1930 interview with her close friend Fønss (Fønss 1930a, 122) – perhaps feeling encouraged by this interviewer, whom she might have assumed shared her misgivings about clear-cut national identities as a result of their similarly transnational Danish-German film careers. These misgivings became even more discernible when she called Germany her 'second' fatherland in other contexts (Nielsen 1998, 93). No doubt, a discourse of exclusive nationality was not sufficient to frame her identity.

The contradictory manner in which Nielsen resorts to national affiliations indicates a state of betwixt-and-between, which was not resolved until after her death. With regard to Nielsen's contemporary Olaf Fønss, a similar picture presents itself. The general public, and especially those who defined themselves as Fønss-fans, were knowledgeable about his nationality, especially after the great success of the *Homunculus* films, and he, too, became the terrain for negotiations of nationality. The geographical proximity of Denmark and Germany, the already existing co-operations and trade-offs between the Danish and German film industries, will undoubtedly have played their part in positing Danish stars at the centre of discourses surrounding 'Danishness' and 'Germanness'.

When trying to place the celebrity within a common Danish-German film culture, individual stars like Fønss and Nielsen stood as, and acted as, the intersection between different communities (cultural producers, audiences, fans). The 'celebrity terrain' became the ground on which different needs (economical/cultural/ideological/identificatory) met, intercrossed and influenced each other. Through their art, their mobility and their semiotic openness, these Danish celebrities invited varying inscriptions, not least of national kinds which at the high tide of wartime in the mid-1910s were hardly escapable, but which were at the same time undermined and subverted by the power of the celebrity terrain to be continually overwritten.

Fan Mail and its Own Nationality

Preserved fan mail to Danish film stars is outstanding source material to shed light on not just the question of a Danish-German common film culture in the silent era, but also on a multitude of other topics, like the emergence of film fandom and fannish practices in the 1910s and 1920s, the audience's reception of specific films, the history of gender constructions, not least with regard to what is considered to be the typical fan, or epistolary rhetorics. Generally, the contemporary press coverage was dominated by descriptions of fan mail as a product of 'letter writing lunacy' (Carter 1920) among screen-struck, mostly female film fans. Many stars painted a picture of fan mail's content (and its senders) in articles and memoirs that is, to say the least, quite one-sided. With the exception of Clara Wieth, who wrote in retrospect about those 'exciting letters and *billets-doux* with tributes to one's blondness and nordic sentiments' (Pontoppidan 1965, 210), the other stars from Denmark seem to have considered their fan mail and fans in general a nuisance at best, and suggested that fans were often psychologically imbalanced. Both Fønss and Nielsen admitted in their memoirs that they used employees to answer the masses of mail and that these employees even faked their signatures (Nielsen 2022, 168–9; Fønss 1932, 116).

However, the fan mail passed down in the archives allows us to contrast these pathologising media accounts and personal reminiscences of annoyance with authentic letters.

True, in this bulk of letters and postcards there are not only numerous confessions of love, even marriage proposals. There are also a few instances of epistolary stalking. A certain Sofie Ruppert from Bohemia, for instance, wrote more than fifty ecstatic letters to Olaf Fønss between 1914 and 1930 – and at least four less rapturous ones to Clara Wieth – without, as far as we know, ever receiving a written reply. Olaf Fønss was even confronted with a suicide threat. But the expression mode of the letters varies between rapturous and demure, between naïve and highly self-reflexive, if not ironic, and even the content cannot be lumped together. In many letters, the Danish star is addressed as a diary-like confidant,

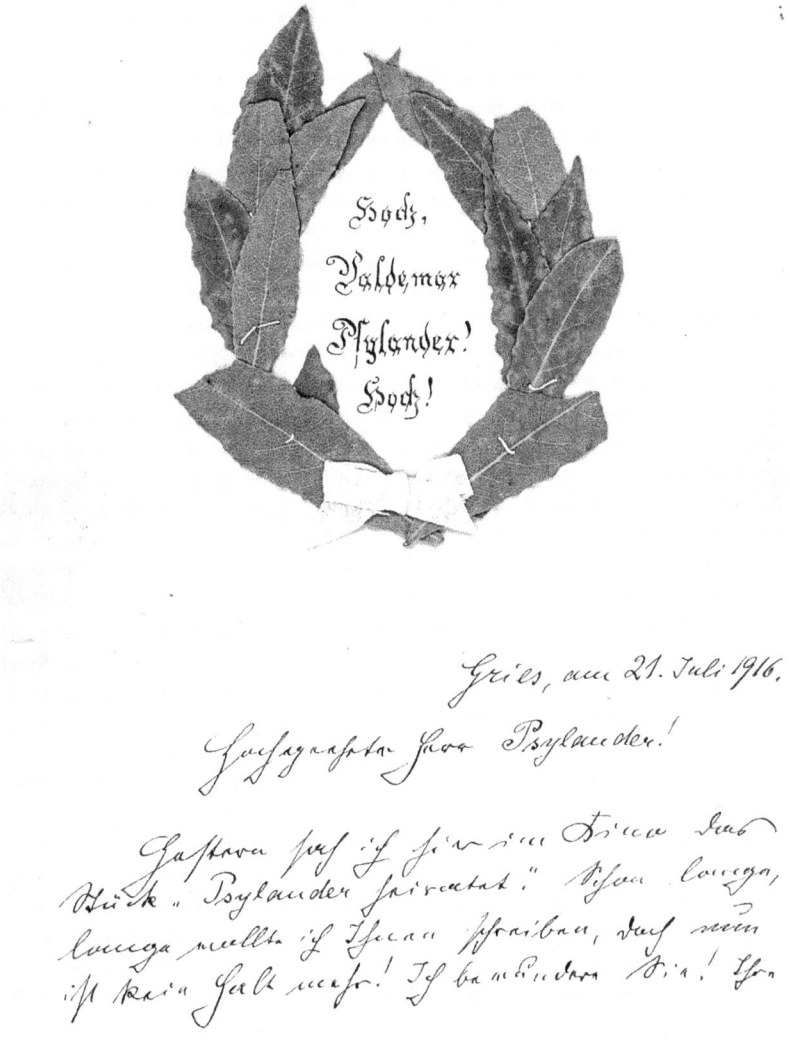

Figure 3.3 The only still existing fan letter to Valdemar Psilander, written by Maria von Wallenstern in 1916, is typical for the utmost care and even display of splendour many of the fan letters show. Danish Film Institute.

with whom one wishes to 'chat' intimately, resulting sometimes in quite moving letters, which offer insights both into the depressing prospects of the fans in their lives and their attempts just to get noticed in their individual uniqueness as well as into the contemporary possibilities for dealing with love emotions, especially for the so-called 'Backfische' – young girls. As elaborated upon in the previous section, in these letters the star functions as a projection screen, a *terra nullius* that can be claimed and inscribed by the fan.

However, considering the multitude of topics addressed in these letters, which we explore in an ongoing research project, it is astonishing that notions of 'Danishness' or 'Northernness' seem not to have played an important role. True, there are exceptions: Lotte Sommer from Rostock, for example, was hoping for Olaf Fønss' forgiveness in 1918 because 'Danes are probably a bit gentler in general' (Sommer 1918) – 1864 is obviously long forgotten. Others mention Fønss' geographic 'Northernness' and substantialise it by referring to stereotypes about the North. Women from the realm of the Habsburg monarchy (and later from Austria) were particularly given to this discourse. In 1920, a woman from Vienna with an indecipherable name sent a fan letter to Fønss, describing the reasons for her admiration: 'Since childhood, when other girls dreamed of the south, of their journeys there, my longing was always directed towards the north' (Anonyma 1920). Zlata Kanzlarić from Zagreb confessed in 1917 her fondness for Northerners ('Nordländer'), explaining that '[p]erhaps the reason is that you are the opposite of us impulsive Slavs' (Kanzlarić 1917). Mathild Adamec from Prague assumed in the same year that her fascination with Fønss might be due to 'the way of the deep-thinking Norwegian [. . .]. I admire very much the Norwegians, because they are people who are mentally especially capable' (Adamec 1917), and in Vienna Marianne Wildom acknowledged in 1919 her 'great fondness for Norway. It must be a beautiful country and a noble people' (Wildom 1919). The mistaking of Fønss for a Norwegian underlines how much Norway at this time epitomised Northernness in the German language area; that is, how the conception of differing Nordic nation states often succumbed to a single stereotypical image of Scandinavia, but also the extent to which a Danish actor like Fønss was inscribed in this omnipresent discourse about 'Northernness'.

But in most of the letters, the only flagging of Clara Wieth's or Olaf Fønss' 'Danishness' or 'Northernness' as a form for alienness consists of an occasional speculation about whether the Danish actor or actress would be able to read the letter written in German. Some express their regret for being unable to write in Danish in order to facilitate communication with the star from Denmark. A few of the fans actually write in (some kind of) Danish, blend Danish (or inter-Scandinavian) phrases into the German text or announce that they are going to learn Danish. However, a very large majority of the extant letters and postcards from the German language area do not make language a subject of discussion at all.

Figure 3.4 The ardent fan Sophie Ruppert sent more than fifty letters to Olaf Fønss between 1914 and 1930. This is one of at least eight portraits she included with her letters. The writing reads 'in perpetual memory'. Danish Film Institute.

This is arguably unsurprising, given that German at that time was the *lingua franca* in many parts of Europe and especially in Northern Europe (the company archive of the Nordisk at the Danish Film Institute attests to this). Still, not even other potential cultural differences are mentioned in the letters, such as the Kurrent handwriting (Figure 3.4), which posed an indisputable obstacle to a smooth German-Danish letter communication. It was unknown outside of Germany and is quite a task to decipher without practice. Significantly, the Kurrent handwriting is mentioned only once in Fønss' bulk of fan mail, when a certain Eveline Förster-Müller from Berlin comments on her using the Latin cursive instead of the Kurrent in 1922. Although she regrets that her Latin letters are poorly legible due to her lack of practice, she will not use Kurrent because 'the German letters are more unfamiliar to you, I guess' (Förster-Müller 1922).

Are we allowed to interpret this failure to mention linguistic and/or cultural differences in fan mail as a tacit assumed sign of cultural commonality, an indication of a common Danish-German (film) culture in the eyes of the German fans? Suspiciously, in letters from outside

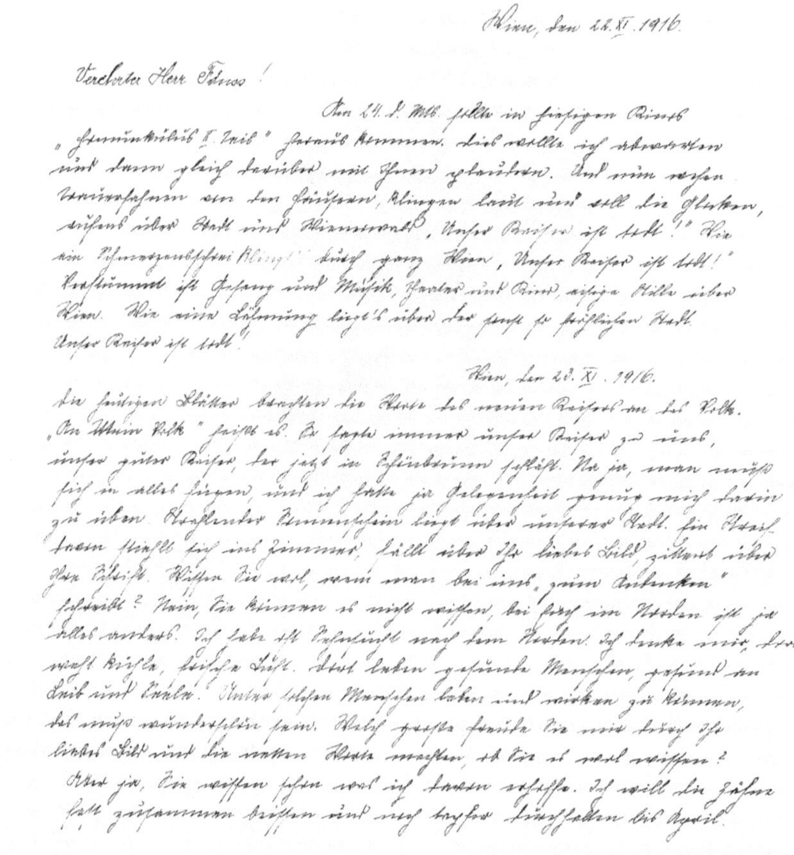
Wien, den 22.XI.1916.

Verehrter Herr Fønss!

Wien, den 23.XI.1916.

Figure 3.5 Lotte Johanssen's fan letter to Olaf Fønss from 1916 is written in a very readable Kurrent, yet it takes familiarity with Kurrent to decipher the letter. Danish Film Institute.

the German language area we encounter the same lack of emphasis on linguistic and/or cultural differences. Wieth's collection contains letters from fourteen languages, Fønss' from eleven, and Nielsen's from twelve – even including non-*lingua francas* like Czech, Romanian, Russian, Estonian or Hungarian. Looking at such letters makes you wonder: how could the fans expect the star to understand their letters without employing an expensive translation agency (which the star probably would not bother to do)? Obviously, the fans could not, and still it did not seem to stop them from writing. However, such letters clearly do not point to, say, a common Hungarian-Danish culture, but rather at a commonality of a different kind – or rather a comm*u*nality, testifying to a strong bond in a community.

In order to understand this communality, we have to abandon the reference to the notion of national cultures, even be it their bridging, annulment or abrogation. We need to change our lenses coloured by a discourse on nationality with a focus on the specifics of fandom culture. It is a commonplace in fandom studies that emotionally involved fans aim at bridging the gap between their mundane, trivial existence and the 'star', metaphorically placed far away on the firmament. They do this by putting up pictures of the star in their intimate domestic spaces, for instance, or by trying to keep informed about the star's doings, and not least by trying to establish an epistolary communication with intimate overtones. All these traits are present in the fan mail to Danish stars from the German language area, as mentioned above. Postulating familiarity with and proximity to the star – gradually sliding towards identifying with the star – is characteristic of fandom and explains why cultural differences are minimised and why a generalised trait of communality is the norm, not the exception in all fan letters, independent of their provenance. Otherwise these letters would not be fan letters in the first place.

The fans' apparent lack of interest in questions of national origin and culture, while at the same time being part of what one might call 'a common fan culture', reveals that there are other 'imagined communities' at play than just national ones – and perhaps even more important ones at the level of the individual. Anderson's concept invites a transfer to the realm of fandom, a description of fandom as an alternative nation: the 'nation' of fans is without doubt 'imagined because the members of even the smallest nation will never know most of their fellow-members, meet them, or even hear of them, yet in the minds of each lives the image of their communion' (Anderson 1983, 15). This imagined communality rests on a perpetual media synchronisation of the expectation horizon of its members, as it is done by the films and the media coverage about the star, but also by practices such as letter writing and scrapbooking. Accordingly, scholars of fandom studies have emphasised fannish activities such as 'a creation of an interpretive community, [. . .] an extension into the rest of living, and an alternative social grouping' (Staiger 2005, 114).

Some fans may not have wanted to be a part of this 'fandom nation', as it potentially disrupts the illusion of a unique personal relation to the star; but even in cases where the personal relation is at play, the fandom nation was indirectly acknowledged when letter writers started out by claiming a superior fan status in comparison with all the other fans. The aforementioned woman from Vienna with the indecipherable name claimed that she 'alone grasped the spiritual aspect of your art, and that made me so happy and shaken that I believed you were playing for me alone!' (Anonyma 1920). Normally, however, fans underlined their belonging to the fandom nation. This could happen on a local level by describing themselves as part of a dedicated group of fans in their hometown, as when the saucy question 'We wonder if our Olaf kisses as sweetly in real life – as it looks in the movie?' was asked by self-declared 'little girls from the Prater', a beer garden and amusement park in Berlin ('Ungenannt' 1917). Following the breakthrough of fan magazines after the end of World War I in the German language area, references to a global level of a medially synchronised fan communality became very common, sometimes with an ironic self-reflexive twist. Hilde Riese started her letter in 1923 with the lines:

> I hope you will not throw this letter into the fire without reading it. Smile rather 'sublimely', as it befits celebrities, about the crushes of young girls in all countries; I take it for granted that also there in Copenhagen the Backfische (I am such a one of 17 years) have crushes on you. As for me, this is very much the case. (Riese 1923)

Especially in the nationalistic war-ridden 1910s, fans were well aware that their 'fandom nation' transcended national identities and could conflict with the 'other' nation claiming hegemony. In the German language area, fans fortunately did not have to do without the films with the stars from Denmark during the war, although some fan letters comment on deplorable interruptions in the film supply. In the British market, however, the situation was different. When German films were banned in 1916, a certain L. Boyce wrote rather unpatriotically to Asta Nielsen on hearing this announcement that such a ban

> [. . .] would break my heart, if I thought I should never see you again. [. . .] I could not possibly live without you [. . .]. I should have been quite contented for the rest of my days, if I only could have seen your films, but now they are going to take them from me, to ruin my happiness, interest in work, and everything. (Boyce 1916)

The Question of 'Danishness' and Forms of Danish-German Commonality

Boyce's letter is only one of many examples of the personal 'emotional investment' (Duffet 2013, 138) audiences all over the world made in

Danish stars. Their fan communities spanned the globe; their art spoke to a variety of cultural audiences and lent itself to be imbued with different cultural, moral and ideological meanings (Ogawa 2013). To the fans, they remained mostly outside the national discourse, which the media, however, could not do without. On the individual scale – the relation between fan and star – conceptions of nationality seem to lose their weight. Although the commonality with the Danish star is – implicitly or explicitly – proclaimed in the fan letters, it mostly did not rest on specific notions of 'Danishness', but rather on a (fictitious) intimacy made possible by the primary media (the films) and information from the framing secondary media (the press coverage).

The examination of fan magazines in the German language area has shown, however, that we cannot separate the reception of Danish stars in the German language area entirely from national discourses. The Danish (or at least Northern) origin of the stars was well known in the German press, often even emphasised, and conceptions of 'Danishness' clearly played a role when writing about them (instead of to them). The semantic openness of the celebrity terrain allowed the press to construct Danish stars in the German language area in a paradoxical way: 'Danishness' invoked oxymoronically both a romanticised, backward-oriented idea of 'Northernness' and at the same time some kind of avant-garde in the literal sense, that is showing a way to a modern world understood in a teleological way. Not surprisingly, these differing constructions of 'Danishness' can even be observed in other contexts than cinema (Allen 2012).

These contradictions could be negotiated in complex ways on the celebrity terrain, as the press coverage of Olaf Fønss and Asta Nielsen shows. In both cases, a representation of a common Danish-German film culture comes into being by the loss of the specificity of Danish and German film culture in the process of semantisation. In Fønss' case, his star persona avoided contradicting national attributions by calling positively upon a common 'Teutonicity' or 'Germanicness', while Nielsen's star persona negatively refused national or Northern attributions. Nielsen suffered from not being able to fully accommodate herself within this discourse of a shared Northern heritage, but was celebrated as the face of modernity, a cosmopolitan woman, as international as her art, forming ties not only between the German and the Danish film culture, but others as well – her influence reached as far as Brazil, Australasia and Japan (Loiperdinger and Jung 2013).

Stars like Asta Nielsen and Olaf Fønss enable us to speak of a common Danish-German film culture, albeit forcing us at the same time to acknowledge the complexity that underlies such an assumption. As diverse as 'cinema' as an institution and set of practices is, so is the answer to the question of how 'Danish' the stars from Denmark were for the German audience and what this 'Danishness' implied. Previous research publications like the edited volume *Schwarzer Traum und weiße Sklavin* (Behn 1994) have provided ample examples of instances in which the Danish cinema and German cinema interacted. In the reference frame of *histoire croisée*, these precise points of intercrossing are to be seen as meeting grounds where the Danish and the German film cultures come together to be renegotiated as entangled ones. These entanglements were also shaped by individual artists like Olaf Fønss and Asta Nielsen. The material surveyed highlights not only the relevance they had for the Danish and the German film culture respectively, but also how they – and other stars from Denmark in the German language area – brought the two together.

References

Adamec, Mathild to Olaf Fønss, 9 October 1917. Danish Film Institute, Olaf Fønss collection, 451.

Allen, Julie K. 2011. 'Denmark's Ugly Ducklings. Georg Brandes and Asta Nielsen's Metacultural Contributions to Constructions of Danish National Identity.' *Scandinavian Studies* 83, no. 1, 63–90.

———. 2012. *Icons of Danish Modernity. Georg Brandes & Asta Nielsen*. New Directions in Scandinavian Studies. Seattle: University of Washington Press.

———. 2013. 'Ambivalent Admiration. Asta Nielsen's Conflicted Reception in Denmark, 1911–1914.' In *Importing Asta Nielsen: The International Film Star in the Making 1910–1914*, edited by Martin Loiperdinger and Uli Jung, 39–51. KINtop Studies in Early Cinema, vol. 2. New Barnet: John Libbey Publishing.

Anderson, Benedict. 1983. *Imagined Communities. Reflections on the Origin and Spread of Nationalism*. London: Verso.

Anonyma to Olaf Fønss, 20 January 1920. Danish Film Institute, Olaf Fønss collection, 1025.

Aubinger, Josef. 1913. 'Asta Nielsen – Urban Gad.' *Zeit im Bild*, 1192–3.

Bálazs, Béla. 2001. *Der sichtbare Mensch oder die Kultur des Films*. Suhrkamp-Taschenbuch Wissenschaft, vol. 1536. Frankfurt am Main: Suhrkamp.

Behn, Manfred, ed. 1994. *Schwarzer Traum und Weisse Sklavin: Deutsch-dänische Filmbeziehungen 1910–1930*. München: edition text+kritik.

Biltereyst, Daniel, Richard Maltby and Philippe Meers. 2019. 'Introduction. The Scope of New Cinema History.' In *The Routledge Companion to New Cinema History*, edited by Daniel Biltereyst, Richard Maltby and Philippe Meers, 1–12. Abingdon, Oxon: Routledge.

Borchardt, Dr. 1919a. 'Olaf Fönss'. *Elegante Welt* 8, no. 12, 12–13.

———. 1919b. 'Gunnar Tolnæs in Berlin.' *Elegante Welt* 8, no. 24, 13–14.

Boyce, L. to Asta Nielsen, 20 February 1916. University Library Lund, Asta Nielsen collection.
Carter, Charles. 1920. 'Letter Writing Lunacy.' *Picture Play-Magazine*, Nov. 1920, 43–4.
Claussen, Sophus. 1911. 'Films –.' *Politiken*, 5 May 1911.
Danish Film Institute. 2021. '"Verdens Valdemar".' Last modified 9 December 2022. https://www.stumfilm.dk/stumfilm/temaer/verdens-valdemar
DanLitStummFilm. n.d. 'Droop, Marie Luise [geb. Fritsch]'. Accessed 21 May 2022. http://danlitstummfilm.uni-koeln.de/portraits/portrait.php?id=Droop,%20Marie%20Luise%20[geb.%20Fritsch]
Droop, Marie Luise. 1918a. *Die Lieblingsfrau des Maharadschas I und II. Filmroman*. Eisbärbücher, vol. 1. Leipzig: Haupt & Hammon.
———. 1918b. 'Gunnar Tolnaes, der Liebling der Damenwelt.' *Illustrierte Filmwoche* 6, no. 2, 16.
Duffet, Mark. 2013. *Understanding Fandom. An Introduction to the Study of Media Fan Culture*. New York and London: Bloomsbury Academic.
Dyer, Richard. 1998. *Stars*. New Edition with a Supplementary Chapter and Bibliography by Paul McDonald. London: British Film Institute.
Fee, Annie. 2015. *Gender, Class and Cinephilia: Parisian Cinema Cultures, 1918–1925*. Ph.D. diss., University of Washington.
'Filmkameraet var som hele verdens øje. Samtale med stumfilmens store kunstnerinde, Asta Nielsen, der bedre kan lide den enkeltes venskab end populariteten fra de mange'. 1948. Undated clipping from non-identifiable newspaper, but obviously from 1948. Asta Nielsen collection, Danish Film Institute, Copenhagen.
Förster-Müller, Eveline to Olaf Fønss, 2 July 1922. Danish Film Institute, Olaf Fønss collection, 1247.
Fredrik, L. K. 1920. 'Olaf Fönß im Dienst des deutschen Films.' Dated 28 August 1920. Clipping from non-identifiable newspaper. Olaf Fønss' scrapbook 1919–1921, Danish Film Institute, Copenhagen.
Fuller, Kathryn H. 1996. *At the Picture Show. Small-town Audiences and the Creation of Movie Fan Culture*. Washington & London, Smithsonia Institution Press.
Fønss, Olaf. 1913. 'Omkring Atlantis.' *Filmen*, 15 October 1913, 5–11.
———. 1930a. *Danske Skuespillerinder. Erindringer og Interviews*. Copenhagen: Nutid.
———. 1930b. *Films-Erindringer gennem 20 Aar*. Copenhagen: Nutid.
———. 1932. *Krig, Sult og Film. Filmserindringer gennem 20 Aar*. 2nd vol. Copenhagen: Alf. Nielsen.
'Gert.' 1920. 'Gunnaritis.' *Wiener Eisbär. Unterhaltungsblatt für Kinofreunde* 3, no. 15, 1 March 1920, 6.
Gestrich, Constanze. 2008. *Die Macht der dunklen Kammern. Die Faszination des Fremden im frühen dänischen Kino*. Berliner Beiträge zur Skandinavistik, vol. 15. Berlin: Nordeuropa-Institut.
'Gunnar Tolnäs.' 1917. *Elegante Welt* 7, no. 14 (4 February 1917), 7–9.

'Gunnar Tolnæs in Berlin.' 1919. *Illustrierte Film-Woche* 7, no. 6, 38–9.

Haller, Andrea, 2009. '"Nur meine Asta! und damit basta!" Ein Blick in die Frauen- und Fanzeitschriften der 1910er Jahre.' In *Unmögliche Liebe. Asta Nielsen, ihr Kino*, edited by Heide Schlüpmann, Eric de Kuyper, Karola Gramann, Sabine Nessel and Michael Wedel, 325–36. Vienna: Verlag Filmarchiv Austria.

———. 2010. 'Film, Fashion and Female Movie Fandom in Imperial Germany.' In *Not so Silent. Women in Cinema before Sound*, edited by Sofia Bull and Astrid Söderbergh Widding. Acta Universitatis Stockholmienis. Stockholm Studies in Film History, vol. 1, 325–38. Stockholm: Stockholm University.

Hermann, Walter. 1913/14. 'Asta Nielsen'. *Illustrierte Kino-Woche* 1, no. 16, 187.

'H.G.' 1914. 'Carlo Wieth.' *Illustrierte Kino-Woche* 2, no. 19 (7 May 1914), 222.

'H.S.' 1914. 'Ebba Thomsen (Zu unserem Titelbild.).' *Illustrierte Kino-Woche* 2, no. 20, 236.

Jacobsen, Wolfgang and Heike Klapdor. 1997. 'Merhameh – Karl Mays schöne Spionin. Ein Dialog über die Autorin Marie Luise Droop.' In *Triviale Tropen. Exotische Reise und Abenteuerfilme aus Deutschland 1919–1939*, edited by Jörg Schöning. Ein CineGraph Buch, 124–41. München: edition text + kritik.

Jacobsohn, Egon. 1915. 'Unsere Flimmersterne.' *Elegante Welt* 4, no. 26 (22 December 1915), 7–9.

Johannsen, Lotte to Olaf Fønss, 22 November 1916. Danish Film Institute, Olaf Fønss collection, 285.

Jung, Uli and Martin Loiperdinger. 2013. 'Introduction.' In *Importing Asta Nielsen: The International Film Star in the Making 1910–1914*, edited by Martin Loiperdinger and Uli Jung. KINtop Studies in Early Cinema, vol. 2, 1–11. New Barnet: John Libbey Publishing.

Kanzlarić, Zlata to Olaf Fønss, 8 May 1917. Danish Film Institute, Olaf Fønss collection, 511.

'Kino und Elegante Welt.' 1918. *Elegante Welt* 7, no. 10, 16–17.

Kvam, Kela. 1997. *Betty Nansen. Masken og mennesket*. Copenhagen: Gyldendal.

Lähn, Peter. 1994. 'Afgrunden und die deutsche Filmindustrie. Zur Entstehung des Monopolfilms.' In *Schwarzer Traum und weiße Sklavin. Deutsch-dänische Filmbeziehungen 1910–1930*, edited by Manfred Behn. Ein CineGraph Buch, 15–29. München: edition text + kritik.

Lee, Katja. 2016. '"What an elastic nationality she possesses!" Transnational Celebrity Identities in the Late Nineteenth and Early Twentieth Centuries'. In *Celebrity Cultures in Canada*, edited by Katja Lee and Lorraine York, 37–55. Waterloo (Ontario): Wilfrid Laurier University Press.

Lewandowski, Herbert. 1921. 'Olaf Fönss.' *Film-Tribüne* 3, no. 5, 7.

Loiperdinger, Martin. 2013. '"Die Duse der Kino-Kunst". Asta Nielsen's Berlin Made Brand.' In *Importing Asta Nielsen: The International Film Star in the Making 1910–1914*, edited by Martin Loiperdinger and Uli Jung. KINtop Studies in Early Cinema, vol. 2, 93–112. New Barnet: John Libbey Publishing.

Loiperdinger, Martin and Uli Jung, eds. 2013. *Importing Asta Nielsen: The International Film Star in the Making 1910–1914*. KINtop Studies in Early Cinema, vol. 2. New Barnet: John Libbey Publishing.

Marshall, P. David. 2014. *Celebrity and Power. Fame in Contemporary Culture*. Minneapolis and London: University of Minnesota Press.
Nielsen, Asta. 1928. 'Mein Weg im Film.' *B.Z. am Mittag*, 24 September 1928.
———. 1998. *Breve 1911–71*, edited and selected by Ib Monty. Copenhagen: Gyldendal.
———. 2022. *The Silent Muse: The Memoirs of Asta Nielsen*, edited and translated by Julie K. Allen. Rochester: Camden House.
Nørrested, Carl. *See also* Nørrestedt, Carl.
Nørrestedt [sic], Carl. 1994. 'KOPENHAGEN – BERLIN – KOPENHAGEN. Olaf Fønss (1882–1949).' In *Schwarzer Traum und weiße Sklavin. Deutsch-dänische Filmbeziehungen 1910–1930*, edited by Manfred Behn. Ein CineGraph Buch, 116–24. München: edition text + kritik.
Ogawa, Sawako. 2013. 'Asta Nielsen and *Shimpa* Films in Japan.' In *Importing Asta Nielsen. The International Film Star in the Making 1910–1914*, edited by Martin Loiperdinger and Uli Jung. KINtop Studies in Early Cinema, vol. 2 321–326. New Barnet: John Libbey Publishing.
Orgeron, Marsha. 2009. '"You Are Invited to Participate": Interactive Fandom in the Age of the Movie Magazine.' *Journal of Film and Video* 61, no. 3, 3–23.
'P.O.'. 1920. 'Olaf Fönss.' *Die Filmwelt*, no. 31/32, 2.
Pickford, Mary. 1955. *Sunshine and Shadow. An Autobiography*. New York: Doubleday.
Pontoppidan, Clara. 1965. *Eet liv – mange liv. Første halvdel: til 1925*. Copenhagen: Hasselbalch.
Quaresima, Leonardo. 1996. 'HOMUNCULUS: A Project for a Modern Cinema.' In *A Second Life. German Cinema's First Decades*, edited by Thomas Elsaesser, 160–7, 309–12. Amsterdam: Amsterdam University Press.
'Das Resultat unserer Rundfrage.' 1914. *Illustrierte Kino-Woche* 2, no. 1, 7.
Riese, Hilde to Olaf Fønss, 21 June 1923. Danish Film Institute, Olaf Fønss collection, 1379.
Ryan, Barbara and Charles Johanningsmeier. 2013. 'Guest Editor's Introduction: Fans and the Objects of Their Devotion.' *Reception. Text, Readers, Audiences, History* 5, no. 1, 3–8.
Schenstrøm, Carl. 1943. *Fyrtaarnet fortæller*. Copenhagen: H. Hagerup.
Schröder, Stephan Michael. 2005. 'Fra Babel til Nørrebro, fra Berlin til Frederiksberg: Filmens internationalisering og nationalisering.' In *Kultur på kryds og tværs*, edited by Henning Bech and Anne Scott Sørensen, 114–32. Aarhus: Klim.
———. 2020. 'On the "Danishness" of Danish Films in Germany until 1918.' *Kosmorama* #276 (www.kosmorama.org).
Sommer, Lotte to Olaf Fønss, 25 March 1918. Danish Film Institute, Olaf Fønss collection, 744.
Staiger, Janet. 2005. *Media Reception Studies*. New York: New York University Press.
'S.W.'. 1924. 'Olaf Fönss – wieder in Berlin.' *Die Filmwoche* no. 8, 144.
'Ungenannt' to Olaf Fønss, 3 March 1917. Danish Film Institute, Olaf Fønss collection, 454.

'Die Völker und der Film.' 1925. *Berliner Illustrirte Zeitung* 34, no. 2 (11 January 1925), 61.
Wagener, Siegfried. 1923. 'Der Künstler Olaf Fönss.' *Die Film-Woche*, no. 2. in October, 24–5.
Werner, Michael and Bénédicte Zimmermann. 2006. 'Beyond Comparison: Histoire Croisée and the Challenge of Reflexivity.' *History and Theory* 45, no. 1, 30–50.
Wildom, Marianne to Olaf Fønss, 29 May 1919. Danish Film Institute, Olaf Fønss collection, 957.
Zernack, Julia. 1997. 'Nordenschwärmerei und Germanenbegeisterung im Kaiserreich.' In *Wahlverwandtschaft. Skandinavien und Deutschland. 1800–1914*, edited by Bernd Henningsen, Janine Klein, Helmut Müssener and Solfrid Söderlind, 71–87. Berlin: Jovis.

CHAPTER 4

How 'German' was German Film in Denmark during the Silent Era?

Lars-Martin Sørensen

This chapter analyses how Danish media perceived and presented German film culture throughout the two decades of international silent cinema from 1910 to the advent of sound in the late 1920s. To some extent, it takes the opposite perspective of the previous chapter: the newspaper and trade press articles scrutinised here do not offer access to individual attitudes and opinions. They do, however, allow for insights into the broader framework within which public opinion on the contact points between Danish, German and perhaps a common Danish-German film culture was formed.

Public notions of 'German film' in Denmark during this period were intertwined with broader notions of 'Germany'; Danish-German film culture played out against the backdrop of international political and economic relations between the two nation states. Therefore, the influence on public discourse exerted by the major political shifts of the era must be included in the analysis.

The introductory chapter has already presented a sketch of Danish-German cultural and political relations during the silent era and the influential events of the half century leading up to the advent of moving images. However, the perception of all things German in the primary sources studied in this chapter – Danish dailies and the film trade press – was obviously not shaped only by the legacy of major historical events like the Second Schleswig War, World War I and the Danish incorporation of North Schleswig in 1920. While events like these are certainly important, the practicalities and routines of day-to-day relations with neighbouring countries also play their part in the construction of public discourse. So in order to illuminate the changing position of German films in Denmark, one needs to establish a suitable point of departure. A good place to start this exercise is, as pointed out by Schröder and Zerlang (2011), the year 1908, because in 1908 nothing particular happened in the relationship between Denmark and Germany. The Second Schleswig War was almost half a century in the past, with World War I not yet looming in the horizon. Film trade between the two countries had only just started. As a baseline from which to gauge the climate between the two neighbours and its immediate background, 1908 appears an advantageous starting point, even if this study as a whole operates within a slightly different period. In 1908

> the development towards a less tense neighbour relations had advanced significantly. The German ambassador to Copenhagen could record that even if the [Danish] sentiment could not be described as decidedly pro-German, it was by no means directly anti-German either. Such a verdict would have been unthinkable even a few years before. (Frandsen 2011, 24, citing a letter dated 3 September 1908 from the ambassador to the Reich Chancellor)

So, broadly speaking, Danish bitterness over lost wars and the humiliations suffered by the Danish-oriented minority in Schleswig was apparently wearing off by 1908, at least according to the German ambassador cited above by Steen Bo Frandsen, a Danish scholar of Border Region Studies. While this judgement may ring true with relations in diplomatic circles, the sentiments aired in popular culture and subsequently in writings on film in Danish dailies are of a more complex and conflicting nature.

In 1909, for instance, a newcomer to Danish film production, the company Fotorama, which was based in Denmark's second largest city, Aarhus, produced *Den lille Hornblæser* ('The Little Trumpeter'). Based on a patriotic poem about the First Schleswig War (1848–1851), the film fanned Danish nationalist sentiments and became a box office success, selling more than 150,000 tickets nationwide (Jensen 1969, 32). The profitability of patriotic war films did not go unnoticed in Copenhagen, where another newcomer to film production, the company Kinografen, premiered with its nationalist war film *En Rekrut fra 64* (*A Recruit from 64*) on 1 August 1910. Only twelve days later, Aarhus-based Fotorama struck back with *En Helt fra 64* ('A Hero from 64') – both films pointing to the fatal year 1864 in their titles; the year Denmark was reduced to a small state after the defeat in the Second Schleswig War. Both the '64 films are strongly nationalistic, the closing scene of *En Rekrut fra 64* even spelling out in the final intertitle the protagonist's thirst for revenge on the German killers of the farm girl who saved him from Prussian captivity: 'The farmer takes him to the girl's grave and he thinks: If only I could take revenge', it reads. The film refrains from demonising the Prussian enemy, but it does align the audience firmly with the Danish protagonist, so even if it does not come across as directly anti-German, it certainly glorifies bravery on the Danish side and – as mentioned – to some extent justifies the Danish

Figure 4.1 'The Little Trumpeter' high on the fortifications fighting the Prussian invaders. Danish Film Institute.

protagonist's thirst for revenge. Only a fragment of *En Helt fra 64* survives. Judging from the seventeen minutes preserved and digitised, focus was on the suffering of the Danes, and only one scene of the Prussians exists, in which demonisation is not a feature.

En Rekrut fra 64 and *En Helt fra 64* were both screened in Germany, where the Danish nationalist perspective apparently did not stir up notable dissatisfaction among German audiences or media. *A Hero from 64* was marketed as 'a national war drama' by the German distributors. There is no indication that that the officious German censors removed the ending scene or even the final intertitle of *En Rekrut fra 64*. Stephan Michael Schröder, who has studied the German reception of the two films, concludes that

> the Second Schleswig War of 1864 seems not to have played any important role in the reception of the Danish films. This was because remembrance of the war in Germany and Denmark around 1910 was characterized by a fundamental asymmetry. While the war had generally had an identity-shaping function in Denmark (not at least because of the suppressed Danish-speaking population in Prussian

Schleswig-Holstein), it was quickly forgotten in Germany, superseded by later wars against Austria and France. (Schröder 2020)

The fundamental asymmetry pointed out by Schröder pertains not only to war remembrance, but to numerous other aspects of Danish-German relations and film culture. As I shall show below, very broad and stereotyping notions of 'Germanness' bordering on the anti-German were part of the Danish discourse on German films while contemporary German perceptions of 'Danishness' were anything but hostile, romanticising rather than critical (Schröder 2020). Additionally, there is the tendency of the early Danish film trade to see the German market as all-important, while German film remained, largely speaking, non-existent, or at least went unmentioned by the Danish press throughout the first decade of the twentieth century.

For entrepreneurial film bosses like Ole Olsen, the founder of Nordisk Films Kompagni, looking south to Germany was the obvious choice. Olsen had established the first foreign subsidiary to the company the same year as the company proper, in 1906. It was located in Berlin's Friedrichstrasse. The year 1907 brought Olsen a runaway success, a film on the shooting of two lions, coincidentally imported from a German zoo. The film, *Løvejagten* (*Lion Hunting*), sold an unprecedented 259 copies, became one of the company's greatest box-office hits and spearheaded the international breakthrough of Nordisk Films Kompagni (Thorsen 2017, 24). The following year, in 1908, Nordisk took part in 'The First International Cinematograph Industry-Exhibition' in Hamburg (Schröder 2011, 124 ff.) and won a gold medal and a prize of honour. The medals of the diploma decorated the letterhead of Nordisk's stationary during the following years – winning in Germany became part of Nordisk's brand. Moreover, Olsen devoted an entire chapter – including a photo of a silver cup – of his somewhat anecdotal autobiography to the victorious participation in the Hamburg event (Olsen 1940, 85–90). Olsen allows the fact that the entire competition was a scam and a scandal to go conveniently unmentioned (Schröder 2011, 125). In short, from the outset Germany was by far the most important market for the emerging Danish film industry and an attractive arena for the practitioners of the trade. Viggo Larsen, the director behind *Løvejagten*, who also played one of the leading characters in the film, migrated as one of the first of many Danish film professionals to Germany in late 1909 to pursue an almost lifelong career in the film trade (Engberg 1994, 8). As detailed by Adriaensens in this volume, the cinematographer who shot *Løvejagten*, Axel Graatkjær, also had a long career in Germany.

Figure 4.2 Three Danes and a German shooting *Engelein* (1914). From the left: Axel Graatkjær, Asta Nielsen, Urban Gad and Karl Freund. Danish Film Institute.

The Sources

As mentioned above, Danish film professionals' appetite for the German film market and the resulting entanglements apparently did not cause an interest in German films and film culture in Danish media in the early years of moving images. A truncated search for articles on or even mention of the phrase 'German film' in the more than 35,000,000 digitised pages of Danish language dailies accessible through the portal 'Mediestream' results in no hits for 1908.

Coming across newspaper or film trade press articles on 'German film' before the 1910s is highly unlikely since articles on film as such were rare. Cinema was considered a vulgar temptation, primarily aimed at and enjoyed by the lower orders. Therefore, it was not a suitable topic for journalists specialising in 'the arts' and film professionals, especially actors trying to make a career on stage, insisted on anonymity as far as their film roles were concerned. Therefore, it is hard to find information on the individuals behind the early productions. This, of course, changed dramatically by 1910 and the breakthrough of international film stars like

Asta Nielsen and Valdemar Psilander. The first trade press publication, *Nordisk Biograf-Tidende*, did not emerge until 1909. A significant share of the around twenty trade press pamphlets and magazines published during the 1910s and 1920s are, generally speaking, focused rather narrowly on Danish films, companies, cinema and censorship regulations and film stars. Now and then stories concerning international film culture do pop up, but very often these stories are about trade relations, not articles with qualitative subject matter on films from other countries. This tendency was very strong in the first decade of silent cinema. Films were, generally speaking, not yet discussed in public in terms of nationality, even if early film programmes occasionally listed shorts with titles that made their national origin immediately apparent, as in the case of the first film screening in Copenhagen in 1896, which included titles like *From an English Race Track* and *Surf at Dover* (see Tybjerg 2022).

Ten years after 1908, in 1918, the number of hits for the same search on 'German film' is nine and in 1928, the search results in 235 hits. For comparison, a search for 'American film' results in 209 hits for 1918, 'French film' hits 10 articles, 'Swedish film' 14, 'English' only 3 and 'British' none. The newspaper collection of the Danish Royal Library to which the Mediestream-portal offers access is, of course, incomplete. Therefore, we cannot take for granted that the search engine provides a 1:1 picture of the exhibition of 'German film' in the Danish press. The number of dailies fluctuated over the years, new papers emerged, others ceased to exist and some papers had subsidiaries in different parts of the country that would print part of the articles published by the main paper, thus resulting in more hits for identical articles. In addition, the number of preserved dailies in the collection presumably also fluctuates from one year to the next.

The general tendencies of the search results are, however, in line with the general film historical developments. It is uncontroversial to state that German cinema's international breakthrough started in 1919–1920. From 1919 to 1920, the number of hits almost triple, from five to thirteen. The increase in the numbers of Danish newspaper articles 'hit' by a search for 'German film' in the base grows steadily throughout the 1920s. What is more, not only does the quantity of articles increase, but the length and quality of the articles also rises. Having undertaken the search and read the little more than 1600 accessible articles dating from 1910 to 1930, I feel I can safely say that international film criticism and detailed reporting on international film culture and trade in Danish papers matured from 1920 onwards. Up through the 1910s, the majority of newspaper articles are rather short notices stating that a certain film was opening at a certain cinema, although there are exceptions to this general rule. Both the advent of the international star system and the outbreak of World War I prompted articles on foreign stars and trade relations. Even the short notices often shed at least some light on how German film was perceived and presented to the public. Therefore, the dailies are the primary sources of this chapter.

The trade press, of course, targeted a narrower segment of film professionals and film *aficionados*. Their importance to this study is secondary. Generally speaking, trade press articles were longer than newspaper articles and therefore often offered more detailed insights into the image of German films as it was constructed for those with a professional interest in cinema. Up through the period, trade press publications grew from mere pamphlets published primarily as promotion materials by production companies and cinemas into proper magazines for members of trade organisations, most importantly the Copenhagen cinema owners' association.

Drawing primarily on these sources, the analysis comes in three parts: First, the pre-war years, from 1910 to 1913, where, briefly put, most references to German film dealt with Danes in Germany. From 1913 onwards, German films were increasingly discussed in their own right, most often with a distinct focus on famous German actors, or with a respectful nod to German high culture. During the pre-war period, negative and stereotypical views of 'Germanness' were quite frequently aired.

Second, during the war years 1914–1918, trade relations became an important topic; in particular, the fate of Nordisk's interests in Germany. Denmark's official neutrality in the war influenced public discourse on Germany and German culture profoundly.

The third part of the analysis deals with the post-war years, 1918–1930. Just prior to German cinema's definitive international breakthrough in 1920, admiration for German capabilities in filmmaking abounded, especially with respect to detective films and historical films. Part of the German success rubbed off on Danish-born filmmakers pursuing a German career with their 'Danish films from abroad' (see *Randers Amtsavis* 20 December 1923, 12). This development, however, coincided with the Danish incorporation of North Schleswig in 1920. Initially, this caused some turbulence with the film culture of the German-oriented minority in the border region; later a growing anxiety towards Germany in film censorship and public discourse is evident (Sørensen 2020). Unsurprisingly, the geographical place where the two countries meet was an arena of both coexistence and conflict and the relocation of the border boosted the public articulation of national sentiment.

The Pre-war Years

The breakthrough for Danish film – and for Asta Nielsen and director Urban Gad – in the German market left a clear imprint on the German trade press in late 1910. To take just one example, the German periodical *Der Kinematograph* published no less than three full-page adverts and an in-depth article on the merits of the film *Afgrunden* (*The Abyss*) in December 1910 – only a few months after the film premiered in Denmark. 'A sensational drama', 'sold out every night' the adverts proclaimed. The in-depth article made great efforts to analyse both the emotional needs that motivated film audiences to attend the film and how the film met these needs in a clever and artful manner: 'Here, you sense the calm and confident mastery that characterizes every great work of art', a critic using the pen name Niko writes in *Der Kinematograph* ('Abgründe', December 1910).

Research on German films in Danish dailies and periodicals does not produce the same clear-cut example of one film spearheading a decisive breakthrough. German film becomes a noticeable topic in Danish pre-war publications only gradually; in 1912 a handful of articles are on the hit list of the beforementioned truncated search for 'German film' in Danish dailies, roughly counting the number doubles throughout 1913. In 1911, only an advert for a German film pops up.

The articles in 1912, however, are all concerned with Danes in Germany – clearly, at this point; 'German film' is only of interest to Danish papers if prominent Danes are involved. Unsurprisingly, the Danes involved are Asta Nielsen and Urban Gad, who moved to Germany after the runaway hit *Afgrunden*. The Danish commentators' somewhat self-centered perspective degenerates into derogatory remarks on 'Germanness' in several of the pre-war newspaper articles. For instance, in a review of *Die Verräterin* (*The Traitress*, 1911), which opens with the exclamation 'A genuinely German film!', the Copenhagen daily, *Riget*, writes: 'There is no doubt that the film will have its effect in Germany. The author, however, cannot expect us to take it seriously in our country. It is simply too clearly *made in Germany*' (*Riget*, 25 March 1912, 2, italics and English in original). In the same vein, a film featuring comedian Max Linder is up for review one year later in the countrywide daily *Social-Demokraten* (23 August 1913, 5). The film is dismissed as 'German comedy of the most heavy handed kind' and national differences are again evoked: 'To Danish tastes, the main character is not as irresistible as is presumably the case in his home country.' The reviewer was evidently unaware that Linder was a Frenchman, and the film (the brief description fits *Le Duel de Max*, 1913) is mistaken for a German one. Errors of this sort were commonplace and testify to the at times rather lenient approach to facts practiced by contemporary journalists writing on film culture.

The only admission in the otherwise harsh verdict on the above-mentioned film, *The Traitress*, is the fact that Asta Nielsen plays well. Another Copenhagen daily, *Berlingske Aften* (26 June 1912, 3), aims almost the same line of critique at another Nielsen vehicle, *Die Macht des Goldes* (*The Might of Gold*, 1912). The film is described as 'extremely bad in its composition' and 'Asta Nielsen is not given the opportunity to show her talent in it. The remaining actors are German.' Here, the implication is that the German film is bad; Asta Nielsen is talented but to no avail and the German cast not worth mentioning by name. It also goes unmentioned here and in the review of *Die Verräterin* that Urban Gad, who married Asta Nielsen that same year, directed both films.

The expressed view that the capacity of one talented actor to make even poor films worthwhile watching gradually also becomes a recurrent trait in the growing number of articles on Nielsen's German counterpart, Henny Porten. She, too, is often singled out as the positive touch to otherwise dull movies from Germany. For instance in *Berlingske* (11 November 1913, 4): 'It is all immensely Germanic, very sad and not just slightly boring', which, the article proceeds to say, is counteracted by Porten's 'somewhat interesting' performance.

In 1913, the first unreservedly positive reviews of German films appear. For instance in *Berlingske* (1 November 1913, 3), where the film *Schatten des Lebens* ('Shadow of Life', 1912) starring Henny Porten receives praise as a 'beautiful German film' and Porten is referred to as 'well known'. Indeed, beginning in September 1913, Porten's films were released as being part of 'The 1st Henny Porten Series', positioning her as a star comparable to Asta Nielsen (if not quite as well paid).

Summing up, the main impression conveyed to newspaper readers was that German films were of poor quality. Several articles rested their case at labelling the films as 'German', 'immensely Germanic' or 'too clearly *made in Germany*', which equalled 'bad', not to be taken seriously by us even if they, the Germans, do. This was the case even with films that had a considerable creative input from Danish-born film professionals. As we shall see in the following, the clear-cut notion of films partly made by Danes working for a German production company as plain and simply 'German' gradually gives way to more composite classifications of national origin – but not until the general reputation of 'German film' as such increases during the post-war years.

The newspaper articles of the early 1910s on film are, generally speaking, short notices of around 100 words, whereas the trade press published longer articles, some of which qualify as features or background articles. Unlike the newspaper articles, however, only very few trade press articles deal with individual films from Germany. On the agenda is Germany, her market, stars and film culture rather than specific films. And here, the image of German film culture is more ambiguous and contradictory than the impression you get from reading the dailies.

The most important trade press publication of the 1910s undoubtedly is the members' magazine of the Copenhagen Region Cinema Owners Association titled *Filmen* ('The Film'), published twice a month from 1912 through 1919.

National identity, as Benedict Anderson reminds us (1983, 6–7), is always imagined in relation to other nations. The national self-image promoted by *Filmen* obviously changes over time and interacts with the image of Germany and German film culture. Through the pre-war years, when Danish films successfully conquered foreign markets and Danish born actors, most importantly Asta Nielsen and Valdemar Psilander, became international stars, the image of a small nation punching way above its weight was frequently aired. One example is an anecdotal essay published in March 1914 (*Filmen* vol. 2, no. 10, 163–4) written with understated humour by the pseudonym 'Fantomas'.

The article conjures up the image of a cheerful international party of men having a good time at a café in the Latin Quarter of Paris. First introduced by the Danish narrator are the 'swarthy gentlemen from the Balkans and Russia. Soon a couple of young Frenchmen joined' and as the story unfolds, more and more nationalities come together round the café table. Each nation is offered a brief verdict on its defining characteristics and place in the international context: Russia is the somewhat lethargic bear, the Spaniards are sort of okay, whereas the Germans are well known but not well liked and their army needs a good bashing on occasion. Trouble arises when it is the Danish narrator's turn to explain that he comes from Denmark. Nobody understands; no one can place Denmark on the map even though 'Scandinavia' as a concept is known – the capital of Scandinavia being 'Tivoli', the story goes. The narrator makes a new attempt by namedropping famous Danish authors like Georg Brandes and Hans Christian Andersen, still to no avail. On the verge of desperation, the author mentions Asta Nielsen and Valdemar Psilander – and then, finally, the rest of the party showers praise on the minuscule country that has fostered international film stars of such magnitude. The author no longer feels squeezed in between the big powers.

While the story told obviously never took place, the imagined situation is pivotal to the self-understanding of Danish film culture of the pre-war years: a small national state but a great film nation. The smallness, of course, has to do with the lost war and the German annexation of North Schleswig. Imagining Denmark as small vis-à-vis big Germany was a recurring feature of writings on the contact points between the two countries. In the very first issue of *Filmen* (vol. 1, no. 1, 18) published in October 1912 for instance, a brief notice stated: 'During the first quarter of this year, Germany imported 18 million Marks worth of film, primarily from France and England' – or, in other words: the German film trade is *big*. The notice was printed in a recurrent section of short snippets of news entitled 'Stumper og Strimler', which roughly translates to 'Clips and Flicks'. Yet even though Germany was considered big, most frequently only short snippets of news on all things German were published in Denmark, while longer articles on German subject matter only appeared infrequently. The importance of the German film trade to Danish film professionals is clearly visible in the 'Clips and Flicks' section, for instance in mid-January 1913, where the section consists of all in all six brief notices over one and a half pages, four of which deal with German matters. Three advertisements flank the notices; two of the ads come from German companies, Drägerwerk in Lübeck, a producer of bulbs for film projectors, and a Berlin film laboratory (vol. 1, no. 7, 110–11). One of the notices served as a harbinger of times to come: the German Minister of War had issued a new decree from the *Kaiser* that forbade military personnel from taking part in film shoots. Only officers in command could permit the filming of troops doing military drills, and only if the film would not expose military secrets. Sharpened military conditions in Germany are already on the radar of the Danish trade press by January 1913.

Besides being big and often relegated to the 'Clips and Flicks' columns of *Filmen*, the most striking feature in the coverage of German subject matter is that 'Germany' appears to be almost synonymous with 'Berlin'. So-called 'Berlin Letters' was a recurring format of both Danish dailies and *Filmen*. One such letter, signed 'A.R.' and describing the stronghold of the German film trade, Berlin's Friedrichstrasse and the café Trocadero, was published in November 1913. The author first marvels at the number of Berlin film factories, the countless workers staffing those factories and the admiration shown to Berlin's new demigods, the film directors, whose task it is to pick and choose from the 'human material' so readily offered up for sale at the Trocadero café in Friedrichstrasse. Then the mood changes as the focus shifts to the impoverished proletariat of child actors created by crass film capitalism:

> The supply here is so immensely higher than the demand and that pushes the prices down. Moving images may have done much good, and undoubtedly, the future belongs to cinema. However, it has created its own strange and unsettling proletariat, which is nowhere more clearly visible than at this café. ('Berlinerbrev' 1913, 28)

The children at the café, the author continues, are no longer 'merry, lively and natural children, but premature grownups, who can laugh and cry on command', all day long you can see them 'slumped in chairs smoking cigarettes' – the image conjured up is one of misery and destitution.

The article tells the story of the victims of massive industrial production volume; indirectly implying that this particular problem is German and that 'we' do not have this in Denmark. The subtle comparative perspective comes about with the use of little words like 'here' in the sentence quoted above: 'The supply here . . .' It is but one example of an 'unwaved flagging of banal nationalism', to use the terminology of British sociologist Michal Billig. He cautions that even if the discursive everyday construction of nationalism is banal in the sense that it is inconspicuous, it is not necessarily benign (Billig 1995, 6, 10). By suggesting that work conditions in the German film trade are inhumane as compared to those in Denmark, and that big is certainly not beautiful, the text does not directly fan an anti-German flame. Rather, it serves as a note of caution to the intended readership of Danish film professionals, urges them to keep their industry small and beautiful, and fades out with a glimpse of optimism: the German film actors' union – *Genossenschaft deutsches Kinoschauspieler* – will be opening an office in Friedrichstrasse in order to mitigate the circumstances for the children at the Trocadero café and heighten awareness of the phenomenon of film acting by children as such.

In March 1914, child acting was a prominent feature in Benjamin Christensen's *Det hemmelighedsfulde X* (*Sealed Orders*), where the fourteen-year-old German boy Otto Reinwald played the son of the leading character, Lieutenant van Hauen. In October 1915, Otto, his three sisters and their mother are in focus in an article in *Filmen* ('Filmens Ansigter' 1915). The Reinwald family had taken up residence at Nordisk Films Kompagni, where Otto was again part of a Danish film production and hence among the German actors who pursued a career in Denmark. Between 1914 and 1917, Otto Reinwald played in six Danish features, the beginning of a life-long film career as an actor and a producer. The article celebrates Otto Reinwald and his family as eminent actors, including the little sister Hanni Reinwald, whose potential in film acting is praised. In the same issue of *Filmen*, German actor Erna Morena is introduced to Danish readers as a new star in German cinema and compared to Henny Porten ('Ny Stjerne').

Figure 4.3 German child actor Otto Reinwald in director Benjamin Christensen's striking framing. *Sealed Orders* (1914). Danish Film Institute

In 1913, Porten had snubbed Nordisk Films Kompagni: after signing a contract with Nordisk, she changed her mind and stayed with Messter in Berlin. Breaking the contract resulted in Porten paying a 34.000 Mark fine to Nordisk. *Filmen* brought a neutrally worded article on the Porten affair in July 1913 ('Rygte' 1913). The praise showered on both the Reinwald family and Erna Moreno in fall 1915 is just one of many signs that the appraisal of German film in Denmark gradually began to change during the war years. It was still, however, primarily German-born film professionals with direct relations to Danish companies who made the big headlines and were the topic of longer articles, and articles on German film culture often served to highlight the Danish position by comparison, either explicitly or implicitly.

The War Years

Denmark declared its neutrality when World War I broke out. Hostilities had only been underway a couple of days when on 2 August 1914, the Danish Ministry of Foreign Affairs summoned the editors of the leading newspapers to a meeting – representatives from the Ministry of Defence and the Ministry of Trade also took part. Officials stressed the importance of maintaining 'balance' and walking the tightrope of neutrality in wartime. Direct censorship would not be introduced, but it was impressed on the gentlemen of the press that they were expected to observe strict neutrality and to exercise the 'utmost cautiousness' in mentioning the warring nations (Mchangama & Stjernfelt 2016, 621). In the wake of the initial meeting, a list of twenty topics best avoided or only mentioned in the press with 'the utmost cautiousness' was circulated among the editors, who were also warned in no uncertain terms that if harmful messages or statements were published, censorship and punishment would be the result. All in the name of national security, of course (622).

Against this backdrop, it is unsurprising that the articles published by Danish dailies during the war years are almost suspiciously lukewarm in their negotiation of German film and film culture. The same goes for the trade press, and the numerous Danish war films produced just before and during World War I are strikingly neutral. Recognisable uniforms and flags were avoided and while films like *Ned med Vaabnene!* (*Lay Down Your Arms!*, 1914), *Mit Fædreland, min Kærlighed!* (*Through the Enemy's Lines*, 1915) and *Pro Patria* (1915) differ in the respect that some are pacifist films and some are war dramas, they all bemoan the evil of war and advocate peaceful coexistence. Outright pacifism is on the agenda in the sci-fi *Himmelskibet* (*A Trip to Mars*, 1918), which was co-written by the general director of Nordisk Films Kompagni, Ole Olsen, who had ample reason to promote a course of neutrality since it meant selling the company's films to the great warring nations on both sides of the trenches. In fact, the company's production guidelines stipulated a course of cautiousness against offending or alienating foreign censorship, powers and audiences (Thorsen 2016).

In 1914, the designation 'a German film' as opposed to, for instance, 'a film by director X' or 'a Henny Porten film' still dominates the short newspaper notices on film premieres. The majority are neutral in their wording and in their verdict. Only a couple of articles – both of them published before the outbreak of war – stick out as mildly negative: the Copenhagen daily, *København*, writes on the opening of the German film *Die Tangokönigin* ('The Tango Princess', 1913) that 'calling this film a good film would conflict with the truth, so we are not going to call it a good film' (8 February 1914, 9). Another critical article, published in *Social-Demokraten* (17 June 1914, 4), draws a well-known dividing line:

> The film *might* have achieved its intended eerie effect, if the leading role had been executed with imagination, but the German actor, in whose hands the role is placed, is not capable – at least not to Danish viewers – of producing the necessary shivers down the spine, but merely pulls [unintended] smiles.

The position is glaringly clear that while the Germans may well be satisfied with this kind of acting, we, the Danes, are accustomed to better standards. The film in question, however, is *Der Student von Prag* (*The Student of Prague*, 1913), partly the brainchild of Danish-born director Stellan Rye and widely acclaimed as an artistic milestone in German cinema. The male lead was played by Paul Wegener, who soon rose to international stardom – in the eyes of Danish critics, too. Again, a film with a considerable creative contribution by a Danish-born director is rejected as German and 'not to our tastes' in a review written by a journalist who does not mention – probably does not know – the Danish angle on this story. The same goes for a much more positive review in the same paper, *Social-Demokraten* (4 October 1914, 4), of a film titled *Frelst* or *Frelst fra den vaade Grav* ('Saved from a watery Grave'), in which Wanda Treumann performs 'with artfulness'. Unfortunately, I have been unable to establish the proper German title of the film and there is inadequate information in the short notice for further research. In the early 1910s however, Wanda Treumann and the abovementioned Viggo Larsen formed a couple both professionally and in private. When Wanda Treumann appeared on the big screen, her husband Viggo Larsen either directed, was part of the cast or both. Just as Stellan Rye's contribution to *The Student of Prague* goes unnoticed in this paper, so does Viggo Larsen and Wanda Treumann's partnership in the mention of yet another 'German film'. As stated earlier, the quality of film journalism in the early 1910s frequently leaves quite a bit to be desired, and the verdicts were often handed down in less than 100 words.

The newspaper *Social-Demokraten* – the organ of the Social Democratic party – was one of the pioneers among dailies when it came to writing longer film reviews. In October 1914, the paper printed a review almost 400 words in length of a film premiere at the Palads theater in Copenhagen (30 October 1914, 4). It concerns the successful premiere of the German biopic *Richard Wagner* (*The Life and Works of Richard Wagner*, 1913), which was accompanied by a live orchestra and a male choir and made the audience 'interrupt the show with ovations a couple of times'. Praise for the film and the orchestra is unreserved, although the paper sees fit to state that 'the great composer can hardly be said to be embraced with hero-worship by the broad audience in this country as opposed to his status in Germany'. Here, again, contrast between Danish and German positions is part of the narrative, even if the review is positive. Another striking feature is the article's respectful nod to German high culture. Similar tendencies can be traced in the production of the Danish big-budget production *Atlantis*, made by Nordisk the year before, in 1913. The film was based on a 1912 novel by renowned German author Gerhard Hauptmann. There is little doubt that Nordisk chose Hauptmann's novel for two primary reasons. First, the plot resonated with the sinking of the *RMS Titanic* in 1912, and second, Nobel Prize winner Gerhard Hauptmann's reputation bestowed the film with an air of high culture perhaps intended to counter a potential critique for sensationalism and doubtful taste in the choice of topic only one year after the tragic and monumental catastrophe. Hauptmann, his art and his personal history were sufficiently famous to make headlines in a two-page cover story of the Aarhus trade press magazine *Biografteaterbladet* in January 1913 (issue 1).

The war years put trade relations high on the agenda of both dailies and the trade press. As mentioned above, Denmark as a nation state pursued a policy of neutrality, supported by the pacifist films made. However, steering a completely neutral course in the end proved impossible for Nordisk Films Kompagni, and the business adventure of Danish film in Germany spearheaded by Nordisk would soon come to an end.

The first inkling of the dire straits ahead may have become evident with Danish film professionals in in July 1915, when Germany suddenly prohibited all film exports. The reaction to this draconian measure in Danish media was bewilderment. One paper conspiratorially asked whether the Germans were planning to use film stock to produce explosives (*Fyens Stiftstidende*, 26 July 1915, 4). *Filmen* asked their contacts in Berlin why German authorities were inflicting such heavy losses on their own film industry. Reportedly, enemy agents had copied secret missives on film to smuggle out of Germany ('Tyskland' 1915, 168). Perhaps the ban is only

Figure 4.4 Marketing film as fine art. Poster featuring the name and image of Nobel Prize winner Gerhard Hauptmann. Danish Film Institute.

a temporary measure until authorities have found a way to control film export, the anonymous writer speculates. The developments in Germany are described as 'unsettling' to Danish film; they may cause problems for production companies that use German labs for copying. This trade, another article in the same issue of *Filmen* notes, has already caused raised eyebrows with British and Russian authorities due to their ongoing boycott of Germany ('Kopierings-Vanskeligheder' 1915, 168).

On November 15, the crisis escalated considerably. The British consulate in Copenhagen refused to certify Danish films for export to the United Kingdom, because German films had allegedly been smuggled to Great Britain in the guise of Danish ones (*Østsjællands Folkeblad*, 25 November 1915, 3). While the British market was less important to Danish film exports than the central European one, the implicit accusation of collaborating with the Germans was a serious matter. Not least for leading company Nordisk and Ole Olsen, who was placing his bets and sizeable investments on a lucrative future selling films from neutral Denmark to the warring nations and 'only' facing serious competition from Hollywood (Thorsen 2020, 205). In February 1915, the company had doubled its share value and was investing heavily in the German market. Nordisk's expansion in Germany, however, soon aroused suspicion and open critique from the German film trade. On 15 April 1916, the esteemed trade magazine *Lichtbild-Bühne* warned against 'the Northern peril' caused by the '*Schreckgespenst*' ('terror-spectre') of Nordisk Films Kompagni and the company's expansionistic threat to German film (201). The affair did not receive much attention in the Danish press until October, when *Lichtbild-Bühne* accused Nordisk of selling French film stock in Germany and thus violating the German trade embargo against enemy goods (*Nationaltidende*, 10 October 1916, 1). In a brief article on the title page of the paper, manager Frost from Nordisk vehemently denies that any such transaction has taken place and lashes out at *Lichtbild-Bühne*, which has allegedly 'systematically persecuted Nordisk Films Kompagni'. Ten days later, another paper carried the same story, albeit without the quote about *Lichtbild-Bühne* (*Randers Dagblad og Folketidende*, 20 October 1916, 4). Both articles were brief and, despite the controversies being reported, kept to neutral terms – none of the papers commented on the unfolding events.

The same neutral wording and somewhat surprising brevity recurs when the Danish press breaks the news that Nordisk has sold all its assets in Germany one year later. The Berlin correspondent of one paper reports that a 'great conglomerate that completely regroups the entire German film trade has been formed' and that the new company has bought all

Nordisk's assets (*Horsens Folkeblad*, 18 December 1917, 8). The article is, again, brief, neutral in its wording and abstains from putting the affair into any kind of broader perspective, even if the forced sale of Nordisk's assets in Germany in 1917 – in hindsight – arguably amounts to the most dramatic event ever experienced by any Danish film company. Whether the tone and scale of reporting is due to ignorance of the scope and seriousness of the events, or the paper is just respecting the official line of observing the beforementioned 'utmost cautiousness' in reporting on German conditions, is an open question. In *Filmen*, the trade press seems somewhat mystified at what has taken place in Germany. The magazine brings a short notice quoting the 'laconic message' published on the affair, and refers to having unsuccessfully asked Nordisk for a comment ('Nordisk' 1917, 58). Apparently, the company was anything but communicative on the forced sale of its German assets. Another trade press magazine neatly summed up the conditions in 1919:

> the situation worsened day by day until the last year of the war when it became absolutely impossible. The English did not want films printed on German stock and the Germans did not want films shot on British stock. If you were so unfortunate that one of your extras was named Braun or Schneider, your film was at risk of being scrapped by the allied countries, or you had to provide birth certificates for all of your staff etc. In the end, it was categorical import bans across the board. ('Dansk Filmsindustri' 1919, 33)

This rather blunt statement was published after the big guns had fallen silent, however. During the war years, the impression that restraint practiced in the name of neutrality reigned supreme is difficult to dismiss.

The Post-war Years

Concurrent to the intensified focus on trade relations and the conspicuous restraint in the negotiation of all things German, the overall reputation of German film in the Danish press improved during the war years. Henny Porten's films, for instance, went from being labelled 'German films with Henny Porten' to 'Henny Porten films'; the star image gradually became more important than the national labelling. The leading conservative Copenhagen daily, *Berlingske Tidende*, introduced a recurring column devoted to film premieres under the headline '*Den stumme Scene*' ('The Silent Stage'). Here, films from Germany would be introduced and appraised like films from any other nation – derogatory remarks on their 'Germanness' dwindled and had all but disappeared by mid-1918. To take just one example, the column mentions two German productions on 31 July 1918 (4) among five short notices on film premieres in Copenhagen. One is described as 'a German film' whereas the other is introduced as a 'three-act film by Conrad Wiene starring Wanda Treumann' with no mention of national origin. The three remaining notices concern 'an Olaf Fønss film', using the fame of the Danish star as a brand for the film, 'an Italian work by Ambrosius Danzig' and finally 'the great American film drama "Joan of Arc"' (DeMille's *Joan the Woman*, 1916). The discussion of films from different nations is even; if there is a famous star, the star name is the brand, if not, nationality will do.

Another perceptible development is that the Danish press repeatedly highlights certain German genre specialties. Detective films gradually become a 'German genre', one in which 'the audience follows the unfolding plot with excitement' (*Berlingske Tidende*, 22 November 1918, 4). The historical drama, however, is the genre in which the Danish esteem for German film rises most clearly. The monumental three-part epic film *Veritas Vincit* ('Truth Triumphs') by director Joe May had been a 'spectacular success' in Germany (Rogowski 2003, 15), and it attracted considerable attention when it opened in Danish cinemas in 1919. Joe May and his wife Mia would soon become household names in Denmark. The film was promoted in adverts as 'an excellent piece of cultural history' (*Østsjællands Folkeblad*, 7 November 1919, 3) and praised for its deep pondering on humankind's most important problems, 'a characteristic of modern German literature', another paper writes (*Aalborg Amtstidende*, 12 October 1919, 5). So even if May's epic historical film in some respects leaned towards the sensationalistic and colourful, it was promoted and conceived of as a sober historical film, even elevated for its likeness to 'high cultural' forms of expression like German literature.

The breakthrough for German historical drama – and for German cinema as such – came in 1920, spearheaded by Ernst Lubitsch's *Madame Dubarry* (1919). The film catapulted Pola Negri to instant stardom in Danish papers and made Emil Jannings an even bigger star than he already was. New films starring Pola Negri immediately became 'Pola Negri films' in newspaper headlines (*Social-Demokraten*, 28 May 1920, 6). Another indication of *Madame Dubarry*'s importance to Danish discourses on German film can be found in the sheer quantity of hits found by a Mediestream portal search for 'Madame Dubarry' in 1920 versus a search for 'Veritas Vincit' in 1919. The latter results in 119 hits, *Madame Dubarry* 432. Lubitsch's breakthrough film on the mistress of Louis XV of France opened at Danish theatres in November 1919. By New Year's the film had been mentioned in Danish newspaper articles 126 times, more times than *Veritas Vincit* had throughout the entire year of 1919.

By January 1920, quotes from raving newspaper reports on the film were used in advertisements:

> What style and culture! What a macabre imagination in the last torturing scenes! This truly is a work of poetry, a gloomy song of death and doom, on strong passions that steal away humans, drive them to flee on the wings of swans towards the highest peaks, then slings them into the abyss . . . (*Berlingske Tidende*, 15 January 1920, 6)

For German film in Denmark, the success of *Madame Dubarry* in 1920 equalled the importance for Danish film in Germany of *The Abyss* in 1910. In April 1920, Lubitsch struck Danish box-offices again with another historical blockbuster, *Anna Boleyn*. Again, Emil Jannings starred as the noble ruler, this time as Henry VIII. Henny Porten, who by then had been a star in Denmark for years, played his unfortunate wife, who cannot produce a male heir.

By June 1921, German film was presented as world leading in the Danish press (*Jyllandsposten*, 11 June 1921, 5). In a long article, penned for the paper under the pseudonym 'Sorosis' from New York, an ongoing cultural battle between the US and Europe, first and foremost German film, is laid out. American writers have reportedly succumbed to their own greed by making quick bucks on 'Nick Carter novels' and have been beaten at home by British authors like Wells, Galsworthy and Bennett. American films have become 'so stereotypical that no intelligent human being can be bothered to waste time watching them'. At the same time, well-crafted German successes like *Madame Dubarry* and *Anna Boleyn*, produced for a fraction of the price of their American counterparts, are 'flooding the American market'. In this article, and several others like it, German film is depicted as leading a European offensive of artistic films against American film's crass commercialism and outright stupidity. The American side meets the German onslaught by demanding protectionist measures and making accusations against the two most famous German films for propagandising against America's closest allies – France and Great Britain – as a prelude to 'the next military standoff': does *Madame Dubarry* not deal with the French Revolution – one of the most serious uprisings in human history? And does *Anna Boleyn* not discredit the British throne? The bias of the Danish writer is clear: American protests and products are met with contempt; German films represent European artistic values. Moreover, somewhat surprisingly perhaps considering that the year of publication is 1921, the writer is counting on a 'next military stand-off' between Germany, France, Britain and America.

This was one of two primary ways the Danish press negotiated the sudden prominence of German cinema. Some, like the writer of *Jyllandsposten*'s letter from New York, took the success of German-made films in the American market as proof that crass commercialism and affluent decadence characterised Hollywood fare, made for and by unintelligent people. Seen in this light, artistic and sophisticated film – and in this case: literature, too – from Europe only took its fair share of public attention and the market over there. In this respect, German film spearheaded by the producing company UFA came to play a significant role in the post-war years as creators of 'high cultural artefacts' that not only constituted sober alternatives to American 'Nick Carter-culture', but also gave Hollywood fierce competition on the domestic market. Left untold by Danish dailies in this context is often that the German film industry rose to international prominence sheltered behind a protectionist import ban that lasted from 1916–1921 (Grainge, Jancovich and Monteith 2007, 123–4). Simultaneously, Hollywood's dominance in the European market was steadily growing, not least in Denmark, where the domestic flagship, Nordisk Films Kompagni, had been forced to sell off its assets in Germany during the war and suffered economically from the collapse of the Russian market due to the civil war and subsequent revolution.

The other way the Danish press handled the German successes involved stripping films of their 'Germanness'. Jens Locher, a prolific writer, editor and film publicist, from 1921 ran a weekly full-page section called *Films-Avisen* ('The Film Paper') in the newspapers of the Ferslew group, including *Nationaltidende* and *Dagbladet*. On 30 October 1921, the section included a long article, 'Den tyske Film', signed JL (presumably Locher himself), that described recent developments in the German cinema. Locher opens by stating that even if there were rare exceptions, German films from the pre-war period were generally speaking 'sensationalistic films or tasteless comedies'. After the war, however, the extremely low exchange rates for German marks and one director had turned the tide by directing historical dramas – Lubitsch with his *Madame Dubarry* and *Anna Boleyn*. Locher continues:

> The first thing, one needs to say concerning these films is that they do not seem 'German' in the annoying sense of the word. For the first time, a German director has complied with international standards and the result is worldwide victory.

The success of and admiration for Joe May's films received similar treatment in *Social-Demokraten* (1 April 1922, 3) in a brief article on the premiere of May's exotic *Das indische Grabmal, erster Teil – Die Sendung des Yoghi* (*Mysteries of India, Part I: Truth*, 1921) starring Danish born Olaf Fønss:

> 'Mysteries of India, Part I: Truth' is actually completely cleansed of the errors and tastelessness that until recently gave German film the black stamp: 'Made in Germany' – even in the eyes of immature viewers. [. . .] a director like Joe May is more of an American than a German; he has a firm grip on monumental effects.

The introduction to the article hails the 'immeasurable successes' of German film internationally – as do numerous other contemporaneous articles. However, Danish reviewers' and reporters' admissions of German capabilities and progress very often come with reservations concerning the 'Germanness' of the films, reservations hinged on the implicit premise that if it is good, the film in question cannot be truly German. Or – as we shall see below – the reason why it is a good film is explained by the fact that a Dane was centrally involved in its making.

Highlighting Danish participation and essentially appropriating the films was an important aspect of this Danish way of negotiating the German successes by deemphasising their 'Germanness'. Feature articles on Danish film professionals pursuing careers in Germany had become commonplace by the early 20s. In addition, articles had grown from mere notices to full-page cover stories or several page film sections (see for instance *B.T.*, 17 May 1920, 9–10). By 1923, the UFA film *Tatjana*, about the Russian revolution, starring Olga Tschechowa, was promoted by adverts in Danish dailies with a header above the title in bold proclaiming that this is 'A Danish film from abroad'. Below the very brief blurb on the film, a second hook line announces that: 'It is a German film influenced by **Danish** film culture' (bold in original). *Tatjana* was directed by the Dane Robert Dinesen and co-written by Harriet Bloch, the first woman to become a professional scriptwriter in Denmark and author of around 150 films, 100 of which were produced by Nordisk. So, in this manner, a film made in Germany was draped in Danish colours to Danish readers – or, in different terms, 'de-Germanised' in an advert intended to appeal to the presumed tastes of Danish palates.

This frequently aired attitude also has a reciprocal aspect: whenever Danish-born superstar Asta Nielsen's German-produced films fail to please Danish reviewers, the explanation offered is that she has been 'Germanised'. An article published on Nielsen's recent films in *Dagbladet* (3 October 1922, 4), for instance, states that 'in the past, the best films from Germany were *Asta Nielsen films*, which very quickly lost their initial touch of Denmark and were completely engulfed by "das grosse

Figure 4.5 A 'Germanised' Dane and an international celebrity from Germany. Asta Nielsen and Henny Porten cheek to cheek in *I.N.R.I.* (1923). Danish Film Institute.

Vaterland"'(italics in original). Seen in this light, the article continues, it is probably good news for Danish audiences that domestic censorship has banned the screening of Nielsen's *Fräulein Julie* ('Miss Julie', 1922). As the paper puts it: 'We were not allowed to see "Miss Julie", and those who saw it anyway say that that was only fair. "Hamlet", however, we did see and then wished for censorship to have refused us that pleasure'. Despite this bashing, the anonymous writer hopes for Asta Nielsen's return to Denmark, 'in order for this remarkable talent not to be entirely swallowed up by a "Germanism" that will do her no good'.

In the arena of pop cultural journalism, the existence of a common film culture in the cosmopolitan sense of the concept, where nationality becomes secondary or even irrelevant to the participants, is hard to trace. International celebrity status to some extent grows to overshadow national origin; the best example of this is incarnated by Henny Porten, the first German-born actor whose films become labelled by her name rather than national origin. But generally speaking, the Danish press upholds rather than dissolves national boundaries. To Danish newspaper readers, strict divisions between them and us were maintained in the public discourse on Danish-German film relations by what appears to be ingrained suspicion among Danish writers against the notion that anything 'good' could also be 'German'.

As pointed out in the preceding, there are instances where German films are dealt with in an unbiased, matter-of-fact manner by the Danish press, especially during the first post-war years. In the wake of the war, however, the question of 'Germanness' vis-à-vis 'Danishness' soon became an urgent concern, not least to the Danish-oriented population living under German rule in part of North Schleswig. As mentioned in the introduction, a plebiscite was held in the disputed region in 1920, resulting in a border relocation. Understanding Danish antagonism against all things German as the immediate outcome of the boost to Danish national sentiment in winning back lost territory is of course captivating, and probably part of the background for why German successes that could not be ignored were explained away by the press as 'un-German'. It is, however, a short term explanation, or perhaps more precisely; a short term speculation, since direct causation is absent in the articles dealing with German film's success in Denmark and internationally in the early 20s.

During the war years, however, German authorities responsible for disseminating film propaganda to Scandinavia met what appears to be the same ingrained scepticism. Starting in 1916, the German Army targeted a number of neutral and allied countries with film propaganda, first military films; later feature films became part of the propaganda operation (Goergen 1994, 30). Two years later, in 1918, more than 200 staff were busy distributing German film propaganda to Denmark, Sweden and Norway (31). Even though considerable effort and means were invested, the Danish part of the operation failed spectacularly for a number of reasons. Influencing public opinion in favour of Germany, which was the expressed aim, proved particularly difficult in Denmark, whereas the Swedish reception of German propaganda was more positive (31, 35). The Copenhagen branch of the operation even warned Berlin that 'strongly partisan films' should not be distributed: 'In particular, the film *Das Säugetier* was absolutely unsuitable' for Danish audiences (quoted in Goergen 1994, 33). *Das Säugetier* ('The Mammal', 1917) is an animated anti-British short, featuring an obese giant John Bull sitting on the British Isles casting greedy looks at the riches of the rest of the world. He gradually metamorphoses into a giant octopus embracing the globe, until German submarines and zeppelins attack and put an end to Bull's global, colonial stranglehold.

The warning against distributing crass militaristic propaganda like *Das Säugetier* to Denmark not only shows that the films employed were differentiated according to the presumed preferences of national audiences. It also suggests that the German film professionals and officials assumed that Danish audiences would be unreceptive to anti-British propaganda.

When the propaganda operation was scrapped in 1918, one of the conclusions drawn was that 'big, attractive German features were best suited to gather crowds, who could be leisurely entertained' and thereby somehow influenced in favour of Germany (39). The success of Joe May, Lubitsch and others, however, did not become Germany's gain in Denmark, partly because the international entanglements of cinema could explain the 'Germanness' of their films away, partly because moviegoing does not erase memories of war and the humiliation of defeat. Finally, and perhaps most of all, because 'Germanness' as such is an amorphous and flexible concept, well suited to conveniently match just about any situation where Danish feelings of inferiority call for balancing measures vis-à-vis the powerful southern neighbour.

References

'Abgründe.' 1910. *Der Kinematograph*, no. 207, December 1910, n.p.
Anderson, Benedict. 1983. *Imagined Communities: Reflections on the Origin and Spread of Nationalism*. London: Verso.
'Berlinerbrev.' 1913. *Filmen* 2, no. 2: 27–8.
Billig, Michael. 1995. *Banal Nationalism*. London: Sage.
'Dansk Filmsindustri.' 1919. *Kino-Revuen* vol. 1, no. 3, 33.
Engberg, Marguerite. 1994. 'Zwischen Kopenhagen und Berlin. Ein Überblick.' In *Schwarzer Traum und Weisse Sklavin. Deutsch-dänische Filmbeziehungen 1910–1930*, edited by Manfred Behn, 7–14. Munich: edition text + kritik.
'Filmens Ansigter. Sødskene Reinwald.' 1915. *Filmen* 4, no. 1: 6.
Frandsen, Steen Bo. 2011, 'På vej imod en ny normalitet. Et signalement af det dansk-tyske naboskab i 1908.' In *1908, et snapshot af de kulturelle relationer mellem Tyskland og Danmark*, edited by Stephan Michael Schröder and Martin Zerlang, 20–35. Hellerup: Spring.
Goergen, Jeanpaul. 1994. 'Neue Filme haben wir nicht erhalten. Die deutsche Filmpropaganda 1917/1918 in Dänemark.' In *Schwarzer Traum und Weisse Sklavin. Deutsch-dänische Filmbeziehungen 1910–1930*, edited by Manfred Behn, 30–40. Munich: edition text + kritik.
Grainge, Paul, Jancovich, Mark and Monteith, Sharon. 2007. 'Competing with Hollywood: National Film Industries outside Hollywood.' In *Film Histories*, edited by Paul Grainge, Mark Jancovich and Sharon Monteith, 120–46. Edinburgh: Edinburgh University Press.
Jensen, Bernhardt. 1969. *Da Aarhus var Hollywood. Et kapitel af stumfilmens historie*. Aarhus: Universitetsforlaget i Aarhus.
'Kopierings-Vanskeligheder.' 1915. *Filmen* 3, no. 20 (1 August), 168.

Mchanganma, Jacob and Stjernfelt, Frederik. 2016. *Men – Ytringsfrihedens historie i Danmark*. Copenhagen: Gyldendal.
'Nordisk Films Co.s tyske Interesser.' 1917. *Filmen* 6, no. 5: 58.
'Ny Stjerne, En.' 1915. *Filmen* 4, no. 1: 2–6.
Olsen, Ole. 1940. *Filmens Eventyr og mit eget*. Copenhagen: Jespersen & Pio.
'Rygte og et Dementi, Et.' 1913. *Filmen* 1, no. 18: 242.
Rogowski, Christian. 2003. 'From Ernst Lubitsch to Joe May: Challenging Kracauer's Demonology with Weimar Popular Film.' In *Light Motives: German Popular Film in Perspective*, edited by Randall Halle and Margaret McCarthy, 1–23. Detroit: Wayne State University Press.
Schröder, Stephan Michael and Zerlang, Martin, eds. 2011. *1908, et snapshot af de kulturelle relationer mellem Tyskland og Danmark*. Hellerup: Spring
———. 2020. 'On the "Danishness" of Danish Films in Germany until 1918.' *Kosmorama* #276.
Sørensen, Lars-Martin. 2020. 'The People of the Borderland – A Forbidden Film, a Powerful Neighbour, and Film Censorship as Foreign Policy.' *Kosmorama* #276.
Thorsen, Isak. 2016. '"Vi maatte passe paa" – Selvcensur og selvregulering i Nordisk Films Kompagnis production'. Kosmorama #262.
———. 2017. *Nordisk Films Compagni 1906–1924, the Rise and Fall of the Polar Bear*. East Barnet, Herts: John Libbey (= KINtop studies in early cinema; vol. 5).
———. 2020. 'Schreckgespenst aus Dänemark.' *Dansk-tyske krige: Kulturliv og kulturkampe*, edited by Torben Jelsbak and Anna L. Sandberg, 201–21. Copenhagen: Copenhagen University Press.
Tybjerg, Casper. 2022. 'The First Danish Film Shows Revisited: A Historiographical Study.' *Kosmorama* #281.
'Tyskland forbyder Udførsel af Films.' 1915. *Filmen* 3, no. 20 (1 August): 166–8.

CHAPTER 5

Sherlock Holmes in Transit

Palle Schantz Lauridsen

On 25 September 1908, a Sherlock Holmes film opened in Danish movie theatres. It was the first of twelve one-reelers produced by Nordisk Films Kompagni. A week later, the company's Berlin branch promised cinema owners 'sold out theatres' if they bought that same film. It was after all a story 'of unprecedented excitement from beginning to end' (*Der Komet*, 3 October 1908) as the company boasted.

Twenty-one years later, Sir Arthur Conan Doyle, the author of the original Sherlock Holmes stories, went to see a film in Copenhagen. He was on a spiritualist lecture tour and took time off to watch the last German silent Holmes film, *Der Hund von Baskerville* (*The Hound of the Baskervilles*). He told journalists that he was satisfied with the film (*Politiken*, 27 October 1929).

The twenty-year period between the first Danish Sherlock Holmes film, which was also distributed in Germany, and the last German Holmes film, which was also distributed in Denmark, is highly interesting when trying to understand the entanglements of the film cultures of the two countries. The Holmes stories came from England but soon circulated 'beyond their country of origin' (Damrosch 2003: 4), turning them into world literature. Adding in the number of adaptations in other media, one might even refer to the totality of Holmes 'texts' as *world culture*.

In this chapter, I investigate the Danish and German Holmes films that came out in the silent era as exemplary of the entanglement of the Danish-German film cultures and, more broadly speaking, the entanglement of the Danish-German *media* cultures. The first of these Holmes films were Danish and they (co-)kickstarted a craze for the detective film (Hesse 2003, 55 pp.), while subsequent films cemented the success of the genre. The films reconfigured a literary prototype, which is why it is important to understand the transmedia relations between the films, the literary sources and other media at the beginning of the twentieth century.

Copenhagen, 1907

In April 1907, a popular theatre in Frederiksberg – a municipality encircled by Copenhagen – presented the stage play *Baskervilles Hund* (*The Hound of the Baskervilles*). Several critics noted that while the play was evidently an adaptation of Conan Doyle's novel, it was in fact of German origin. The critics all liked the novel, but none of them liked what they saw on stage. The fact that the play was German presented no problem to the critics at the outset.

The Frederiksberg show was the first of numerous exchanges between Danish and German adaptations of the Sherlock Holmes stories. Up until the Danish opening of the 1929 *Hund von Baskerville* film, the detective crossed the border between Denmark and Germany in several contemporary media. In addition to the theatrical play, borders were literally crossed in a series of printed penny dreadfuls and in several Danish and German films. Danish and German actors and directors took the detective in hand in their neighbouring countries and many of the resulting films were shown in both countries. The need to understand these exchanges from the point of view of entangled history is self-evident.

These Danish-German exchanges of an originally British print media phenomenon are in focus here. From one point of view theatrical plays, penny dreadfuls and silent films were distinct mediatic configurations of the Holmes stories; but from an audience or user perspective they were all equally important as configurations of the character and the stories in the overall media environment, 'the entire body of available media at any given time' (Hasebrink and Hepp 2017, 364). As audiences at any given time and place may choose from a variety of possibilities within the existing media landscape they are, as Danish media scholar Kim Schrøder has demonstrated, 'inherently cross-media' (Schrøder 2011, 6) and the concept of transmedia experiences on the side of audiences (Meyer & Pietrzak-Franger 2022, 4) is fruitful when describing their meetings with cultural artefacts such as Holmes. Consequently, it is necessary to try to understand all the Holmes configurations in the Danish-German media environment during the silent era while aiming, as I do here, to examine the entanglements of Danish and German Holmes films.

Only a few of the films discussed in this chapter are extant and thus it is impossible to do, say, comparative stylistic or narrative analysis of the Danish and subsequent German Holmes films by director and actor Viggo Larsen. The source material of the chapter is therefore basically made up of written material from newspapers, film magazines and digital and analogue archives.

Above all, the chapter refers to three film actors and/or directors who – like their films to some extent – crossed the geographical borders between Denmark and Germany while working with, among other things, Sherlock Holmes: the Dane Viggo Larsen and the Germans Alwin Neuss and Ferdinand Bonn. Viggo Larsen directed and played the central character in several Danish Holmes films. Immediately after moving to Berlin, he made additional Holmes films there. Alwin Neuss played Holmes in a Danish film before playing the character in Germany. Ferdinand Bonn, for his part, wrote the play mentioned above, and a few years later played in a few films shot in Copenhagen by Nordisk Films Kompagni, before returning to Germany where he shot almost a dozen Holmes films.

Adaptive Transit

The first story about Sherlock Holmes, the consulting detective from Baker Street 221B, was published in England in 1887. Forty years later, the sixtieth and last one was published – the last written by Arthur Conan Doyle, that is. From a very early stage, Holmes was used in stories written or performed by others – in pastiches, imitating Doyle's style, and in numerous other adaptations rarely recognised by Conan Doyle.

Franco Moretti has noted that London was one of the two European centres – Paris was the other – for the dispersion of literary works in the 1800s, and that countries other than Britain and France were always at the periphery of this dispersion (Moretti 1998, 37, 173–4). Conan Doyle's stories indeed spread from London and translations were generated in other countries like Denmark and Germany. Having 'settled' in these 'peripheral' countries, the stories sometimes were transformed and at other times exchanged between them without any 'detour' to the centre.

In some cases, translators domesticated Doyle's stories. In Denmark, translators chose (partly) Danish names, such as Baker Gade or even 'Bagergade', 'gade' being Danish for 'street', instead of Baker Street, or changed an English name such as Mary Jane into its Danish equivalent, Marie Johanne. This was the case when – in 1898 – minor local Danish newspapers serialised *A Scandal in Bohemia* as *Kvindelist* ('Women's Wiles') (Lauridsen 2022, vol. 9, no. 8). With the purpose of increasing the intelligibility of the stories and making them less unfamiliar, some passages were omitted, others added, and especially the opening paragraphs were rewritten, in German as well as in Danish translations. This practice is obvious in the first Danish magazine translation of the first Holmes novel, *A Study in Scarlet* (Doyle 1898b), and in the first German newspaper serialisation of the second novel, *The Sign of Four* (Doyle 1894). Other things being equal, the change in cultural environment must have resulted in different understandings of the stories depending on their locus of reception. Crude as they may seem, these translations constitute only the minimal form of literary exchange and must be characterised as one of the simplest forms of adapting a cultural product into a new cultural environment.

Relating to the translation of the Holmes stories, Germany in some cases functioned as a country of transit. The first Russian publications, for example, were translated from German (Piliev 2005). In all the cases in which Holmes crossed the border between Denmark and Germany, however, the exchange took place on a secondary but no less important level, which one might label adaptive transit: the texts were first adapted into, say, another language such as German, and from there into another such as Russian. The 'texts' exchanged were national adaptations which – in each of the two countries – to some degree took Conan Doyle's stories and characters as their point of departure. Regardless of whether they can be understood as cases of adaptive transit or adaptations of imports from the English centre, many of those adaptations should be considered local rather than national. Few media reached all parts of the two countries and the fact that, say, a theatrical play opened in Copenhagen or Berlin was no guarantee that it was performed elsewhere in Denmark or Germany.

Some national (or local) adaptations stayed local. An example is the series of Holmes cartoons published in 1910–1911 by Danish humourist Storm P. in the newspaper *Ekstra Bladet* (Lauridsen 2018). It remained – and for more than 100 years was forgotten – in Denmark, just as the German Holmes films produced by the KoWo company between 1917 and 1919 seem to have stayed in Germany (Ross 2003, 22). They did not, at any rate, travel to Denmark. It made no difference that Holmes was played by Ferdinand Bonn, who – as we shall see – was known by Danish cinema audiences.

Even though the Holmes universe had its centre in England, a significant adaptive transit took place between Denmark and Germany during the period between 1907 and 1929. It took place on stage, in printed media and not least in cinema, where Danish as well as German production companies early on took to Holmes and exchanged films and personnel across the border in the entangled German-Danish film culture.

Sherlock Holmes in Denmark

In Denmark, Holmes first made his appearance in newspaper serials, the first of which – a translation of Conan Doyle's second Holmes novel,

The Sign of Four – was published in the summer of 1891. During the following fifteen years, practically all of the Holmes stories were circulated in a variety of translations in an increasing number of local Danish newspapers and magazines (Lauridsen 2022, vol. 9, no. 8). One and a half years after the first Danish serialisation, Conan Doyle's first Holmes novel, *A Study in Scarlet*, became the first of the Holmes stories to be published in Danish in the less ephemeral media of the book. The rest of the stories published by Conan Doyle up until 1902, including *The Hound of the Baskervilles*, made it to the Danish book market. Of crucial importance to the popularisation of Holmes in Denmark was the play *Sherlock Holmes*, opening in Copenhagen on 26 December 1901. The play was a Danish version of William Gillette's American play from 1899, which bore the same title. Neither Gillette nor Conan Doyle received any royalties, which was in accordance with the fact that Denmark had not signed the Berne Convention for 'The Protection of Literary and Artistic Works'. The play became a huge box-office success in Copenhagen. During the following months, travelling troupes performed the play – or similar plays – across the country. Simultaneously, *The Hound of the Baskervilles* was published in Danish, first – almost simultaneously with its first publication in the British *The Strand Magazine* – as a weekly magazine serial (1901–1902), and later as a book in two impressions (1902) and as a newspaper serial in at least sixteen newspapers (1902–1903). So, a little more than ten years after the first publication of a Holmes newspaper serial in Denmark, 1902 marked the turning point of Holmes' career in Denmark. In the following decade, he remained very popular across a variety of media. When, starting in 1908, Nordisk Films Kompagni launched the first of twelve Holmes films, they knew for sure that Holmes, nationally and internationally, was a well-known and popular character. As an indication of the international entanglement of the undertaking, one might add that the idea of a Danish company producing adaptations of stories of an English origin came from Nordisk's Norwegian representative in New York (Kopibog VII, 792, July 22, 1908). Holmes' international popularity was also the reason why a German publisher from 1907–1911 published numerous 'original' (that is, not authored by Conan Doyle) penny dreadfuls 'starring' Sherlock Holmes. These instalments were translated from German into a variety of languages (Nordberg 2005). Danish was one of them.

Sherlock Holmes in Germany

Sherlock Holmes also arrived in Germany in the 1890s and became a steady success after the turn of the century (Glücklich 2018). In March 1892, the

Figure 5.1 The first issue in one of the Danish series based on the German penny dreadfuls shared its colourful front page drawing and its story with issue 20 in the German series.

publishing house Lutz from Stuttgart bought the rights for translating the first two Holmes novels for the German speaking region, covering not only the vast territory of the German Empire, approximately one and a half times larger than the Federal Republic of Germany of today, but also nations and regions with smaller or larger German-speaking populations in such countries as modern-day Austria, Hungary, Switzerland, Czechoslovakia and Poland.

Lutz published its first Holmes novel – *Späte Rache* (*A Study in Scarlet*) – in 1894 as volume 10 in a series called *Kriminal- und Detektiv Romane*. The following years Lutz published other Holmes stories in the same series; starting in 1902 they launched a special Sherlock Holmes series. Both series were reprinted several times. There seems to have been only a few German serials compared to the Danish market. This pronounced difference may be because Lutz probably bought the rights for the short stories published after the first two novels for the German-speaking region; it may also in part be explained by noting that the newspaper database of the *Deutsche Digitale Bibliothek* is not as comprehensive as its Danish equivalent. It is striking that most hits concerning newspaper serialisations of Holmes stories in the German digital archive derive from the cities of Karlsruhe and Düsseldorf as newspapers from these cities are digitised. Similarly, screenings of Holmes films found in the archive centre on those same two cities.

The Berlin-based publishers Verlagshaus für Volksliteratur und Kunst published a series of episodic Holmes stories from 1907 through 1911. In German, these sorts of publications are referred to as 'Großchenheften'. Modelled after American dime novels, they were written by anonymous German writers, and they presented a Holmes quite different from the one Conan Doyle had penned. German Holmes solved crimes across the globe, whereas his English predecessor basically stayed in London and in places he could reach by train from London railway stations (Moretti 1998, 135–8). Holmes' companion in the German adventures was not a man of his own age (Dr Watson) but Harry Taxon, a boy. The omission of Dr Watson meant that the stories were no longer, as they had been in Conan Doyle's originals, the accounts of Watson's adventures with or memoirs of Holmes. Instead, the German stories had third person heterodiegetic narration. The German stories were far more violent and bloody than Conan Doyle's and in the new stories Holmes was often in dire straits, locked up or on the verge of drowning, *et cetera*, none of which happened in Conan Doyle's stories. The penny dreadfuls were action-packed stories aimed at young audiences, and as such were a sign that this part of the population was becoming commercially interesting for the emerging media industries.

In total, 230 issues of the series were published in Germany. Only nineteen were translated into Danish (Nordberg 2005: 19), but most of the penny dreadfuls published in Denmark were about other heroes. Nick Carter, a modern, urban and American detective, became particularly popular – and infamous. He lent his name to the moral debate about the alleged harmful effects caused by these publications: The Nick Carter Debate. Their German origin did not pass unnoticed: in 1908, Mr Wilhelm Tryde, a Copenhagen bookseller, was interviewed by a Copenhagen newspaper, *Berlingske Politiske og Avertissements Tidende*. Tryde, the chairman of the Booksellers' Association, had no kind words for the penny dreadfuls. He did not like their form of distribution, being sold in 'cigar shops' (25 November 1908, Evening Edition) and not through regular bookshops. He also did not like their German origin, which, strangely enough, he condescendingly characterised by switching into English:

> The pamphlets reveal their German origin because of their murdering of the Danish language and the many Germanisms [. . .]. Every Danish book seller disapproves of this foreign literature, which – even in paper and print quality – reveals that it is 'made in Germany' [English in the original], because of its sensational and unwholesome contents.

Tryde's remark is one of the very few in the material of this chapter that explicitly comments on the fact a particular cultural artefact originates from Germany while simultaneously equating its country of origin with poor quality.

Sherlock Holmes on Stage

In Denmark as well as in Germany, Holmes was an established literary figure before the stories about him were adapted into other media. The first non-literary adaptations took place in the popular theatre. In both countries, plays with some relation to a play written by American actor and writer William Gillette, in collaboration with Sir Arthur Conan Doyle, were staged. As mentioned above, a Copenhagen Theatre, Folketeatret [The People's Theatre], was very successful in adapting the play in 1901. In Germany the play was translated a bit later, in 1905

> to be immediately followed by a string of similar plays, some loosely based on the famous Gillette play. The success of these plays in the 1906 season almost inevitably led to the world's first stage adaptation of *The Hound of the Baskervilles* [. . .] (Ross 2003, 6)

Only a few weeks after that first stage adaptation of *The Hound . . .* two additional plays by the title of *Der Hund von Baskerville* opened in Germany. Both were to have great impact on the 'destiny' of the hound in Germany. Michael Ross argues that the significance of the plays

> can hardly be exaggerated for the further development of German *Hound* versions. It can be said that all later adaptations, at least up to 1955, were based as much on either or both of these plays as on the canon. (Ross 2003, 8)

One of them, Ferdinand Bonn's *Der Hund von Baskerville*, soon came to Denmark. As we saw earlier, this was the first time a Danish audience would have encountered a German Holmes adaption. The other *Hund von Baskerville* stage play, written by Richard Oswald and Philip Julius, formed the basis of two screen adaptations by Oswald, which were also shown in Denmark. The first, from 1914, was directed by Rudolf Meinert; the second, the 1929 version that Conan Doyle saw in Copenhagen, by Oswald himself.

The Danish adaptation of Bonn's play opened on 1 April 1907, at the amusement theatre Frederiksberg Teater. Its manager, Emil Wulff, had decided to end the season with the play, which had premiered at Bonn's own Berliner Theater in Charlottenstraße just two and a half months earlier.

The play, *Baskervilles Hund. Sherlock Holmes sidste Hændelse. Folkekomedie i 4 Akter* ('The Hound of the Baskervilles. Sherlock Holmes' Last Incident. Melodrama in 4 Acts'), was performed up to and including 28 April.

As was the case with the play which made Holmes popular on stages across Denmark in 1901–1902, Bonn's play was a substantial adaptation of Conan Doyle (Lauridsen 2020b). Though Germany, as opposed to Denmark at the time, had signed and implemented the Berne Convention for 'The Protection of Literary and Artistic Works', Conan Doyle could not prevent Bonn from using the title, characters or plot elements from his 1902 novel. Making additions, omissions and variations of his own, Bonn could even claim to have written an original piece, an 'eigenthümliche Schöpfung' (Gesetz 1901, §13) as it is called in the German 1901 copyright legislation, and the play was accepted as such by a Berlin court of law (Lauridsen 2020b, 42). Bonn also generically modulated Conan Doyle's Gothic tale towards romance, just as he added some – quite strange – philosophical discussions between Holmes and the villain.

The play was a success with Berlin audiences. Theatre manager Wulff watched it in Berlin, bought the rights and soon staged in back in Denmark. Bonn's play crossed the border between Germany and Denmark, and Danish audiences' first rendezvous with a stage production of *The Hound of the Baskervilles* thus was a striking example of adaptive transit.

The show at Frederiksberg Teater was met with rotten reviews and subjected to public contempt in a satirical ballad (*Aftenbladet*, 7 April 1907). Many critics realised that Wulff had brought the play back from Berlin and – though they phrased it differently – agreed with the critic from *Berlingske Tidende* who thought that the novel was 'murdered, first in a German dramatisation and later in a Danish translation' (2 April 1907). While the play was of crucial importance in Germany for the future of *The Hound of the Baskervilles* as a commercial property, in Denmark it was no success. It only ran at the Frederiksberg Teater, was roughly handled by the press and even held up to ridicule. Nevertheless, it somehow made Bonn known among Danish critics and the movie business, and on a small scale kicked off the Danish-German Holmes entanglement.

Ferdinand Bonn and Nordisk Films Kompagni

Danes not only got to know Ferdinand Bonn as the author of the stage version of *The Hound of the Baskervilles*. A few years after the staging of the play, Bonn in 1912–1913 appeared in four films produced by Nordisk Films Kompagni – and later Danes could see him in one of the ten Holmes films he made in Germany. His position in the Danish-German film culture in the 1910s is a good example of the entanglements between Danish and German popular culture in the period. I shall therefore present it in some detail, even though his German Holmes films never became as important in Denmark as they were in Germany.

Bonn signed a contract with Nordisk on 15 March 1912, and the newspaper *Social-Demokraten* noted that the film company had 'employed the well-known German actor Ferdinand Bonn as a film writer as well as a director and player' (12 March 1912). The contract, however, which can be found in the Nordisk Films Kompagni Collection at the Danish Film Institute, says nothing about direction, and only states that Bonn must deliver 'manuscripts for 6 larger films in which he personally will play the main character'. It ended up with just four films, all shot during the summer of 1912. In a letter to Bonn, dated 23 April 1913, Harald Frost of Nordisk Films Kompagni writes: 'Concerning the remaining two roles, we take the liberty to inform you that we have not given up on them, and ask you to inform us when you will arrive in Copenhagen to perform them' (Kopibog II, 25). In two subsequent letters, one from May (II, 25), another from June (II, 26), Frost explicitly again asks Bonn to give notice of his day of arrival. After that, no further attempts seem to have been made, and Bonn never showed up to shoot the last two films mentioned in his contract. Directed by August Blom, all four films were marked by the production policy established by Nordisk in the spring of 1911. Thus, they were long films, more than one reel, and were presented as art films. They also had to follow Nordisk's rules for scriptwriters: 'The action must take place in the present day and play out among the upper classes' (quoted in Thorsen 2017, 106).

Bonn had never worked with cinema before. When, after his summer in Copenhagen, he returned to Berlin, he told *Lichtbild-Bühne* that filming was 'a very interesting and consequently also a very pleasant occupation' (23 November 1912, 38). Since cinema was silent, he was not restricted to the manuscript's lines and was able to improvise. He was particularly happy to escape the critics whom he had never liked – and who never liked him. In his autobiography, *Mein Künstlerleben* ('My Life as an Artist', 1920), eight years and several films later, he recalls:

> When film appeared, I said to myself that admittedly it was not pretty, and not great art either, but one does not have to learn a lot of nonsense by heart, and it is divine even that the images move quietly across the screen while you are sitting safely at home and have to fear neither the audience nor especially the press. (Bonn 1920, 225–6)

Back in 1912, Bonn, however, had criticised Nordisk's rules for scriptwriters. They specified: 'Crimes like murder, theft, counterfeiting and the like must absolutely not be shown but only suggested' (quoted in Thorsen 2017, 106). Bonn – when writing about it in the autobiography – found that limitations of that sort made it impossible for him to write scripts for Nordisk. He had written four manuscripts, but Nordisk's main office in Copenhagen turned them down, considering them 'unusable' (Kopibog XX, 189, 8 May 1912). The Berlin branch was asked to try to persuade Bonn to write new manuscripts and pressed for them (Kopibog XX, 326, 20 May 1912), but it seems most likely that he never wrote any. If, Bonn argued, punishable actions could not be shown, it was impossible to stage Oedipus or Shakespeare, in which case all theatres might as well close for good (*Lichtbild-Bühne* 47, 23 November 1912, 38). Maybe that was his way of explaining why Nordisk turned down his manuscripts. And maybe Bonn's somewhat patronising attitude towards filming was the reason why Danish author of several film historical booklets, Arnold Hending, some forty years after the events, concluded that Bonn did 'seem a bit embarrassing' at the studio due to his 'self-assertive behaviour' (Hending 1951, 17). He had, Hending continued, after all 'passed 50 and had peaked, when he received the request from Nordisk'.

According to the contract, the films were to be shot during June, July and August 1912, and Bonn arrived in Copenhagen at the end of June. In Denmark, the films premiered in the period between September 1912 and July 1913.

When Danish cinemas advertised the four films, some mentioned Bonn's name, others did not; the very few and very short reviews of the films typically mentioned other names since actors more well-known to audiences played important roles. Bonn's name was up against the Norwegian Ragna Wettergreen and local stars Robert Dinesen, Else Frölich, Clara Wieth and Valdemar Psilander.

One of the films, *Historien om en Moder* ('The Story of a Mother', 1912), was reviewed in a few Danish newspapers. *Social-Demokraten* referred to Bonn's acting as 'lively' (27 September 1912), whereas *Nationaltidende* called him 'the controversial German actor' and added that the role as the father of the child 'does not truly give him the opportunity to appear in all his glory' (28 September 1912). *Fredericia Dagblad* presented him as 'the leading man of the Imperial Berlin Opera' (3 October 1912). The following day, an advertisement for Kosmorama, a movie theatre likewise in Fredericia, referred to Bonn as 'the leading force of the German National Theatre' (*Fredericia Social-Demokrat*, 4 October 1912). He was not an opera singer and though in 1902–1903 he had been employed at Könichlisches Schauspielhaus in Berlin's Gendarmenmarkt (Müller 2004, 125), he had only been the leading man at his own theatre. Nevertheless, he could, of course, be called the 'outstanding German actor' (*Demokraten*, 25 November 1912), and his reputation was hardly diminished when it was reported that he was paid the extravagant amount of 25,000 Danish kroner for his part in the film (*Fredericia Dagblad*, 3 October 1912). The sum of 25,000 Danish kroner must have been far off the mark. According to the contract, Bonn was to receive 3000 German marks for the first film and 2300 marks for the subsequent ones. Had he fulfilled the contract and produced six manuscripts and played the leading man in all of them, his earnings would have totalled 14,500 marks, the then equivalent of 13.000 kroner. In the end, however, none of his scripts seem to have been accepted, and he only appeared in four films.

Bonn was one of the cards played by Nordisk when the company placed its bets on long 'artistic' films from 1911 onwards. His name, however, does not seem to have been much in use on the Danish market, and as noted correctly by Bonn there was no reason to be afraid of the critics, since his four Danish films received practically no reviews. It should, however, be remembered that Nordisk was an international company with a written policy insisting that movie plots 'must be suited to an international audience' (quoted in Thorsen 2017, 106); a company with a large volume of business in Germany, where Bonn was an established name. Therefore, it is no surprise that a German trade magazine published a full-page advertisement for *Die Tragödie einer Mutter* with Bonn's name in the headline as 'the great German actor' (*Lichtbild-Bühne* 37, 12 September 1912, 9).

The Danish market was obviously of little importance to Nordisk. Based on data in the distribution protocols of Nordisk Films Kompagni (DFI XII:33, p. 28, 44, 56, 64), the four Bonn films sold a total of 391 copies, only eight of which – two of each – were sold in Denmark, corresponding to a home market share of 2 per cent. The remaining 383 copies were sold abroad, with Germany (25 per cent) and Russia (21 per cent) topping the list of recipients. The average number of copies sold by Nordisk in 1912 was 69, and 52 in 1913 (Thorsen 2017, 195). Thus, the Bonn films sold better than average in the period; why this is the case is impossible to know.

According to his autobiography, Bonn did not consider film a part of his 'life as an artist'. Nevertheless, he did not give up on the new media after his involvement with Nordisk. Quite the contrary. He founded his own production company and produced eight films during the years 1913–1916 (German Early Cinema Database), and throughout his career, he appeared in more than sixty films. (Müller 2004, 153). He starred as Sherlock Holmes in ten films, one of which was screened in Denmark in December 1914. The film, *Sherlock Holmes contra Dr. Mors*, was an adaptation of Bonn's first play about Holmes.

Holmes on Film

Between 1908 and 1920 German production companies released almost fifty films (Vaughan 2019) that related to Sherlock Holmes in one way or another – and even more Holmes-themed films (nine of non-German origin) were screened there (Ross 2003). Today, most of these films can only be documented by titles announced in German cinema advertisements – the actual films are lost. Some were probably only loosely based on the writings of Conan Doyle, while others were adaptations of German plays, and some just borrowed the character and probably treated him in what was considered a commercially sound way. What does exist – in some cases – is a number of summaries, but whether they describe the films properly is impossible to know. It is evident that such summaries often tell only part of the story and serve as teasers for audiences. They were basically advertisements and supplementary explanations of (parts of) the films (Sandberg 2001).

In 1910, actor and director Viggo Larsen left Denmark to pursue a career in Berlin. He had played the part of Holmes in Danish films which he also directed – and he continued playing Holmes in several German films. Years later, he told a reporter that:

> 'There goes Sherlock Holmes!' the boys on the streets shouted in Berlin. They had seen me as the detective in a few serial films we had shot in Valby [where Nordisk had its studio], but they did not know my name. (Hr. Bert 1955)

Figure 5.2 Sherlock Holmes (Viggo Larsen) eavesdropping in *Droske 519* (*Cab 519*). Danish Film Institute.

The interview took place more than four decades after the events, but if Larsen's memory served him well, the story signifies the popularity of the Nordisk Sherlock Holmes films in Germany. There is ample evidence to document that Larsen's Sherlock Holmes films were screened in Germany. All the films are listed in the so-called 'title books' where Nordisk meticulously translated titles and intertitles for foreign markets, and German is one of the languages used. In some cases, printed and/or typed programme texts exist, also in German. Also, advertisements in trade magazines and newspapers testify to the screening; but apart from this empirical evidence, it seems impossible to conclude anything specific as to their circulation and reception in Germany.

From the founding of the company in 1906 until he was fired at the end of 1909, Viggo Larsen had directed almost every film produced by Nordisk Films Kompagni. He directed the first six of their Holmes films (1908–1909) and starred in – depending on the sources – five or six. In 1909, he also directed and starred in other detective and crime films: one about the detective Pat Corner, three about Nat Pinkerton, whose fame came from penny dreadfuls, and two about the criminal mastermind, Dr Nikola. From 1910, Larsen was part of the Berlin-based German film industry, and in his first films in Germany, he turned to Sherlock Holmes.

Larsen's Danish Holmes films include a two-part series in which Holmes is up against Raffles, the gentleman thief who originally appeared in several stories by Sir Arthur Conan Doyle's brother-in-law, E. W. Hornung. Among Larsen's six German Holmes films, the first five constituted a series in which Holmes meets the gentleman thief, the Frenchman Arsène Lupin, who had been created as a literary character by Maurice Leblanc a few years before. In one of his first stories (1906), Leblanc has Lupin outsmart Sherlock Holmes. In later editions and additional stories, he changed the name of the detective into Herlock Sholmès. Some of Larsen's Holmes/Lupin films were screened in Denmark.

Roughly speaking, there were three German Holmes series on the Danish market in the 1910s: Larsen's Holmes/Lupin films from 1910–1911 and two series of films that screened during the years 1914–1916. Four of all these films were increasingly distant relatives of *The Hound of the Baskervilles* and of Oswald's and Philip's 1906 play, while the last two, *Sherlock Holmes contra Professor Moriarty* (1911) and *Sherlock Holmes contra Dr. Mors* (1914), took Ferdinand Bonn's first Holmes play from 1906 for their inspiration.

At least three of Larsen's Holmes/Lupin films were shown in Denmark: *Der alte Sekretär* ('The Old Secretary') in August 1910; in October 1910 *Der blaue Diamant* ('The Blue Diamond'). In some newspapers, the latter was advertised as a 'Berlin Art Film' (*Demokraten*, 10 October 1910). The next two films in the German series, *Die falschen Rembrandts* ('The Fake Rembrandts') and *Die Flucht* ('The Escape'), probably did not reach Denmark, but the final episode, *Arsène Lupins Tod* ('The Death of Arsène Lupin'), opened in Copenhagen on 10 March 1911. In August 1911 yet another of Larsen's German Holmes films – *Sherlock Holmes contra Professor Moryarty* [*sic*] – made it to Denmark.

As if Holmes *versus* Lupin and Holmes *versus* Professor Moriarty did not suffice, yet another 'versus film' opened in Denmark in the middle of December 1914. Here Holmes was up against another adversary in *Sherlock Holmes kontra Dr. Mors*. The film critic of *Berlingske Tidende* found the battle between the two 'rather thrilling', even if he also thought that 'one has seen more subtle and cleverly directed films in this genre' (11 December 1914). *Social-Demokraten* noted that the film showed that 'Conan Doyle can be successfully dramatized for the movies' (12 December 1914), but also critically commented: 'The film is full of dress changes and re-disguises so that at times you have no idea who is who.' Holmes was played by Ferdinand Bonn, but only *Politiken* recognised him, and only found the film entertaining at all because 'Bonn as Sherlock Holmes is something of a character' (11 December 1914), who composed Holmes in a 'mixture of serious superiority and condescending conviviality'.

Alwin Neuss as Sherlock Holmes

Following the wave of 'versus films', Conan Doyle's most popular Holmes story, *The Hound of the Baskervilles*, served as the background to six German films, four of which were also distributed in Denmark.

During the first years of World War I, four German Baskerville films opened in Denmark. They all starred Alwin Neuss, who had also played Holmes in one of the Holmes films by Nordisk, *Den stjaalne Millionobligation* (*The Stolen Legacy*, 1911). Trying to furnish some of their output with a sheen of artistic prestige, Nordisk hired Neuss, who became the first German actor to work for the company. Neuss enjoyed a certain degree of fame in Germany with some fifteen years of stage experience, mostly as a 'free-lance actor' (Hending 1951, 8). He and Nordisk must have signed a contract, but it probably does not exist, at least not in the files at the Danish Film Institute. As to why he was hired, the closest we get is Hending's suggestion that Neuss had 'friends of influence' who had mentioned him favourably (8), maybe, one could add, to the company's representatives in Berlin. He starred in a total of eight films at Nordisk in 1910–1911, most of them – such as the Holmes film – along the traditional

Figure 5.3 Alwin Neuss as Sherlock Holmes in *Den stjaalne Millionobligation* (*The Stolen Legacy*). Danish Film Institute.

lines of the company's productions as well as *Hamlet*, shot with lots of extras in original renaissance costumes partly 'on location', that is at the castle in Elsinore (7–10).

Back in Germany, Neuss starred in four films related to the Baskerville story: *Der Hund von Baskerville* (1914), *Das einsame Haus* ('The Solitary House', 1914), *Das unheimliche Zimmer* ('The Uncanny Room', 1916), and *Wie erstand der Hund von Baskerville / Die Sage vom Hund von Baskerville* ('How did the Hound of the Baskervilles Emerge' / 'The Saga of the Hound of the Baskervilles', 1916).

The first of Neuss' German Holmes films was quite widely distributed in Denmark and well received by newspapers. The critic in *Folkets Avis*, along with his colleagues at *Social-Demokraten* and *Roskilde Tidende*, found the new film thrilling. Advertisements mentioned Conan Doyle or Sherlock Holmes and several boasted that it had been 'screened simultaneously in seven of Berlin's largest movie theatres and everywhere to full houses' (for instance *Politiken*, 2 November 1914). In the context of this chapter, it is noteworthy that the Berlin success was singled out.

'The contents of the narrative are probably well-known to most people', the *Folkets Avis* wrote (5 November 1914), but the film differed from Conan Doyle's novel on several points. The main plot was the same and dealt with an unknown heir, Stapleton, who – assisted by a live version of the mysterious hound from a family legend – tried to position himself as the next heir to the family estate. The setting was contemporary – not the 1880s as in Conan Doyle's novel. There were cars and an ingenious system of communication by which Holmes summons Dr Watson, who is well advanced in years: Holmes pushes a few buttons and elsewhere in the building his message, 'Komme zu mir, Watson' ('Come to me, Watson'), emerges on a large screen. The scene marks the only appearance of Watson, who plays a central role in the novel: he narrates it and is the central character, while Holmes is absent in half of the scenes.

Alwin Neuss' Holmes is a modern urban man wearing a suit and soft hat. He is composed, almost cool and self-confident, as in the incident where he finds out that Stapleton has mounted a bomb with a fuse in a chandelier at Baskerville Hall, he quietly waits and asks for a cigarette as the fuse slowly burns down. It is not until the very last second that he offhandedly shoots off the fuse with his revolver and uses the still burning part of the fuse to light his cigarette. Oswald used that very same idea in his and Julius Philip's 1906 play (Ross 2003, 7). Neither the surroundings nor Baskerville Hall itself display the foggy, gothic atmosphere from the novel. *Social-Demokraten*, whose critic believed the film to be English, found that the 'famous hound probably looks a bit more good-natured than one would have imagined' (8 November 1914).

The remaining films of the series did not attract much attention. *Das einsame Haus* ('The Lonely House'), called *Undervandshuset* ('The Submerged House') in Danish, was advertised as a separate continuation of *The Hound of the Baskervilles,* and called an 'exceptional sensation detective drama' (*København*, 1 February 1915), and Holmes as well as Conan Doyle were mentioned in several advertisements. They also informed audiences that the success of the first film was the reason why it was decided 'despite the enormous expenses to shoot yet another of the world famous Scherlock [*sic*!] Holmes novels by the author Conan Doyle, known around the entire globe'. One may wonder how the film can be a separate continuation as well as an adaptation of yet another Holmes novel, as Conan Doyle wrote no sequel to '*The Hound*'. The solution to this paradox is that the film has nothing to do with Conan Doyle's story but is a continuation of the first film in the series. The story, as it is paraphrased by Ross (2003, 11), brings back the villain, Stapleton, who once again tries to lay his hands on Baskerville Hall. He builds a house that can be submerged into a lake. Here he holds Henry Baskerville and Mary Lyons captive until Holmes tracks their whereabouts. When everything seems lost for Stapleton, he tries to flood the house, so that he himself, the young lovers and Holmes will drown, but 'in the last moment Holmes discovers the mechanism', as noted by the German trade magazine *Der Kinematograph* (quoted from Ross 2003, 18). The Danish daily *Politiken* mentions that 'Holmes raises the strange house and its two prisoners to the surface again' (2 February 1915) and ironically comments on the film as part of a serial:

> This is all undeniably very exciting, but even more exciting it will be to see whether Mr. Stapleton, who blows himself up at the end, can be patched together again and found useful for continuous appearance.

He could – and he did appear in the next instalment, *Das Unheimliche Zimmer* ('The Uncanny Room'), which opened in Copenhagen on 28 February 1916 as *Sherlock Holmes Sejr* ('The Victory of Sherlock Holmes'). The film has Stapleton escaping from prison with one goal only: to take revenge on Holmes. He does so by 'refined means' (*Der Film*, 10 May 1919, quoted from Ross 2003: 19) by 'appalling inventions such as an entire room which is lowered to crush Sherlock Holmes' (*Politiken*, 4 March 1916). According to *København*, Holmes succeeds in 'forcing his adversary into a moor where he is swallowed by the quagmire' (4 March 1916). Stapleton ends his days in a similar manner in Conan Doyle's novel, with the quite significant difference that Holmes does not *force* him into the mire; rather Stapleton flees there on his own initiative.

Figure 5.4 Advertisements for *Baskervilles Hund* (*Politiken*, 2 November 1914). The dog looks quite good-natured as opposed to Conan Doyle's description in the novel: 'Never in the delirious dream of a disordered brain could anything more savage, more appalling, more hellish be conceived than that dark form and savage face which broke upon us out of the wall of fog'. (Doyle 2017: 651)

This time Stapleton was done for. However, one additional film in the Baskerville series was produced. In Germany it was banned by the censors until after the war (Ross 2003, 20), but it opened in Denmark on 31 July 1916. As opposed to the two previous films, a hound was part of the cast in *Sagnet om Baskervilles Hund*. A Copenhagen theatre printed the following in the advertisements for the film:

> No crime novel has ever agitated the public mind to the same extent as the story 'The Hound of the Baskervilles', now known throughout the entire world. Therefore, it is highly natural that a bold screen version of the legend connected to 'The Hound of the Baskervilles', will be of the greatest interest everywhere – especially when the representation, like here, is full of vivid fantasy and strong mystery. (*Politiken*, 16 July 1916)

Apparently, the film was loosely based on the legend of the hound told by Conan Doyle as the background for the story. In the film, it takes place in the sixteenth century, where a lecherous knight sets his mind on a virtuous countess. Having been rejected by her, he employs radical methods:

> enveloped in an animal's skin he throws the area into anxiety and horror and kidnaps her. The returning count approaches the primordial ancestor of all detectives, Holmes, who lives as a hermit. He (even back then) quite easily exposes the kidnapper and hands him over to blood justice. (*Der Film*, 19 July 1919, quoted by Ross 2003, 19)

København printed a short review of the film noting that it was 'full of mystery and horror' (1 August 1916) and 'the uncanny dog itself' showed itself in 'a new and unknown apparition'. The newspaper jokingly continued:

> It is recommended for those who suffer from the heat of the summer to look at this film. The many horrifying incidences send cold shivers down your spine in a refreshing way without any unhealthy effects on the nervous system.

When the two films, which had been banned by censorship during the war, opened in Germany in 1919, they appear to have been so popular that yet two more films were added to the Baskerville series: *Das Sanatorium Macdonald* ('The Macdonald Sanatorium') and *Das Haus ohne Fenster* ('The House with no Windows'). Neither of the two were screened in Denmark.

The Final Silent Holmes Film

In 1929, Richard Oswald returned to *Der Hund von Baskerville*. As mentioned earlier, he had written a play based on the book in collaboration with Julius Philip in 1906; the play that was adapted for the 1914 film directed by Rudolf Meinert. In 1929, Oswald directed the film himself. The new *Hound* turned out to become the last silent one; when it opened in Copenhagen on 21 October 1929, a few of the theatres of the Danish capital had been running talkies for two months.

The film sat well with the Danish critics: 'It goes without saying that an exciting film has come out of an exciting book', *Social-Demokraten* had proclaimed on the 1914 version when it opened (11 November 1914). The critic at *Aalborg Amts-Tidende* formulated it similarly, but with a different opinion, when in 1929 he wrote about the new *Hound*: 'A good book unfortunately does not necessarily make a movie quite as good – it is rather the opposite – and *The Hound of the Baskervilles* certainly does appear quite tame on screen' (27 November 1929). Most critics, however, wrote in favour of the film and described it as thrilling, though one found that the few glimpses of the dog failed to produce big thrills (*Politiken*, 22 October 1929). Nobody mentioned the film's German origin.

From an entangled history perspective, the international cast of the film is interesting. Holmes was played by an American actor, Watson by a Russian and the other actors were of Italian, Austrian, English and German origin – and the cinematographer, Frederik Fuglsang, was Danish. After some time at Nordisk in Copenhagen, he left for Berlin in 1916 and worked there until his death in 1944.

A Common Holmes Culture?

In conclusion, the entangling of the Danish-German Holmes culture unfolded on several, intertwined levels. The great variety of media involved made it *mediatic*. It also took place on a *personal* level with film professionals working in both countries, on a *corporate* level and, perhaps especially, on the level of *reception*.

Based on the material in this chapter it is likely that neither Danish nor German audiences or critics in the silent era cared much whether the Holmes films screened across the Danish-German border were made in Denmark or in Germany. The films were part of the general media environment in both countries and interacted with Holmes configurations from other media: translations of Conan Doyle's stories in newspapers, magazines and books, stage productions and penny dreadfuls. As was the case with these other media, the films crossed borders often with practically nobody noticing where they came from – and in some cases even mistaking a German film for an English one. Danish media only mentioned the German origin of a film, or referred to any kind of 'Germanness', in very few cases, and in those cases the purpose was to position the film as something special. For instance, in the 1914 advertisements for *Der Hund von Baskerville*, which mentioned that it had been 'screened simultaneously in seven of Berlin's largest movie theatres and everywhere to full houses', or when another film was advertised as a 'Berlin art film'. It was also mentioned only a few times that Ferdinand Bonn was a well-known actor in Germany. Only the already mentioned Danish bookseller Tryde utilised the phrase 'Made in Germany' pejoratively when in 1908 he complained about the contents, the translation and the quality of the paper of the penny dreadfuls in general.

The actors and directors who worked in both countries seem to have considered them one labour market. On a personal level, working in a new country meant travelling, (temporary) exile, signing of new contracts and maybe new career opportunities. Viggo Larsen directed Holmes films in Denmark before pursuing a career in Germany, kicking it off with Holmes films, in which he replaced one gentleman thief, the Englishman Raffles, with another, the Frenchman Arsène Lupin. Alwin Neuss starred in one

Figure 5.5 When *Sherlock Holmes Sejr* reached the Danish provinces, the advertisements on many occasions featured a drawing of Alwin Neuss' Sherlock (*Randers Amtsavis*, 17 March 1916).

Danish Holmes film, later to become a major Holmes actor in the German film industry in the 1910s. Ferdinand Bonn started wrestling with Holmes in his own plays performed at his own theatre in Berlin, had one of them staged in Denmark, first met the film industry in Denmark and continued in the business when back in Germany he – among other things – did a series of Holmes films.

The number of films and film professionals travelling between the two countries, in a media environment that does not seem to have cared much about the national origin of the individual film, actor or director, underlines that the adaptive transit between the two countries was enacted on a relatively large scale. It is also an indication that – at least at the level of audience reception – it makes perfectly good sense to think of the Holmes films as part of a common German–Danish film culture.

References

Bonn, Ferdinand. 1920. *Mein Künstlerleben. Was ich mit dem Kaiser erlebte und andere Erinnerungen*. Diessen vor München, Verlag Jos. T. Huber.

Damrosch, David. 2003. *What is World Literature?* Princeton: Princeton University Press.

Das Millionentestament (programhæfte). Accessed 27 April 2022. https://video.dfi.dk/filmdatabasen/36454/Stjaalne%20millionobligation,%20Den_36454_Filmprogram.pdf?_ga=2.189815915.171739012.1650801213-1541036113.1650801213.

Deutsche Digitale Bibliothek a. Accessed 27 April 2022. https://www.deutsche-digitale-bibliothek.de/content/newspaper/fragen-antworten?lang=de.

Deutsche Digitale Bibliothek b. Accessed 27 April 2022. https://www.deutsche-digitale-bibliothek.de/newspaper.

Deutscher Film. 2020. Accessed March 2020. https://de.wikipedia.org/wiki/Deutscher_Film#1895–1918:_Pionierzeit_–_Vom_Kintopp_zur_Filmindustrie.

Doyle, Arthur Conan. 1894. 'Das Zeichen der Vier'. *Badische Presse*, March 11 1894.

———. 1898a. 'Kvindelist.' *Holbæk Amts Avis*.

———. 1898b. 'Hævn eller En Opdagers Triumfer.' *A.H. Jordans Revue* 1898, vol. 7–21.

———. 2017. *The Complete Sherlock Holmes*. Accessed 3 June 2022. https://sherlock-holm.es/stories/pdf/a4/1-sided/cano.pdf.

Early Cinema. Accessed 27 April 2022. http://earlycinema.dch.phil-fak.uni-koeln.de/films/index/Filter.FilterByCompany:1/Filter.Company.0:678/Filter.FilterByCompanyType:1/Filter.CompanyType.0:1/keep_frame2:1.

Engberg, Marguerite. 1977. *Registrant over danske film 1896–1914*, I–III. København: Institut for Filmvidenskab.

Gesetz betreffend das Urheberrecht an Werken der Literatur und der Tonkunst (1901). Accessed June 2022. https://de.wikisource.org/wiki/Gesetz_betreffend_das_Urheberrecht_ an_Werken_der_Literatur_und_ der_Tonkunst.

Glücklich, Nicole. 2018. *Die Abenteuer zweier britischer Gentlemen in Deutschland. Auf den Spuren von Sir Arthur Conan Doyle und Sherlock Holmes.* Ludwigshafen am Rhein: DSGH Verlag.

Hasebrink, Uwe and Andreas Hepp. 2017. 'How to Research Cross-media Practices. Investigating Media Repertoires and Media Ensembles.' *Convergence: The International Journal of Research into New Media Technologies.* Vol 23/4.

Hending, Arnold. 1951. *Fremmede fugle i dansk film.* København: Athene.

Hesse, Sebastian. 1994. 'Geile Greisin und Nordischer Galan. Der Detektivfilm der Nordisk.' In *Schwarzer Traum und weiße Sklavin. Deutsch-dänishe Filbeziehungen 1910–1930*, edited by Manfred Behn. München: edition text + kritik.

———. 2003. *Kameraauge und Spürnase. Der Detektiv im frühen deutschen Kino.* Basel: Stroemfeld/Roter Stern. KINtop Schriften 5.

Hobbs, Don. 2021. *The Galactic Sherlock Holmes.* Private edition.

Hr. Bert (1955). 'Dansk film kan fejre sit 50 aars jubilæum.' *Politiken*, April 22 1955.

Lauridsen, Palle Schantz. 2018. *Storm og Sherlock.* København: Fahrenheit.

———. 2020a. 'Talk: Sherlock Holmes og The Hound of the Baskervilles.' DFI, København. Accessed 24 April 2022. https://www.youtube.com/watch?v=1twogxRN8LI.

———. 2020b. 'Kampen om Sherlock Holmes. Forfatterret, moral og teater.' *Peripeti* 32. Accessed 27 April 2022. https://tidsskrift.dk/peripeti/article/view/123728.

———. 2022. *Sherlock Holmes i danske mediekulturer.* E-book. København, Samfundslitteratur.

Meyer, Christina and Monika Pietrzak-Franger. 2022. 'Nineteenth-century Transmedia Practices. An Introduction.' In *Transmedia Practices in the Long Nineteenth Century*, edited by Christina Meyer and Monika Pietrzak-Franger. New York & London: Routledge.

Moretti, Franco. 1998. *Atlas of the European Novel, 1800–1900.* New York & London: Verso.

Müller, Brigitte. 2004. *Ferdinand Bonn. Frauenheld, Lebemann und Weltverbesserer.* Marburg: Tectum Verlag.

Nordberg, Nils. 2005. *The Misadventures of Sherlock Holmes, World Detective.* Nykøbing Sjælland: Sherlock Holmes Museet.

Piliev, George. 2005. 'A Study in Russian.' Accessed 21 April 2022. http://www.acdoyle.ru/about/sherlock%20holmes%20in%20russia.html.

Ritzheimer, Kara L. 2016. *'Trash', Censorship, and National Identity in Early Twentieth-Century Germany.* Cambridge: Cambridge University Press.

Ross, Michael. 2003. 'Footprints of a Gigantic *Hund*.' *Baker Street Journal* 53.

Sandberg, Mark B. 2001. 'Pocket Movies: Souvenir Cinema Programmes and the Danish Silent Cinema.' *Film History*, vol. 13.

Schrøder, Kim. 2011. 'Audiences are Inherently Cross-media: Audience Studies and the Cross-media Challenge.' *Communication Management Quarterly* 18, no. 6.

Thorsen, Isak. 2017. *Nordisk Films Kompagni 1906–1924: The Rise and Fall of the Polar Bear*. East Barnet: John Libbey.

———. 2020. '"De kan gaa paa Lokumet og . . . Kunst" – eller hvorfor A.W. Sandberg tog til Tyskland.' *Kosmorama* #276. Accessed 5 November 2020. https://www.kosmorama.org/artikler/hvorfor-sandberg-tog-til-tyskland.

Vaughan, Nicko. 2019. *Cut to: Baker Street. The On-Screen Adventures of Holmes and Watson*. London: MXPublishing.

CHAPTER 6

Female Stars of German Cinema in an Entangled Danish Film Culture: Asta Nielsen, Pola Negri and Brigitte Helm

Helle Kannik Haastrup

This chapter analyses how female German film stars were an integral part of 1920s Danish film culture, using transmedia theory as a framework to demonstrate specific examples of how the entangled nature of Danish film culture manifested itself across different types of media. Taking my cue from Daniel Biltereyst and Phillip Meers, entanglement 'at the heart of cinema' is in this context specifically concerned with female German stars and their cross-media representations in a Danish film cultural context (Biltereyst and Meers, 2020, 6). The entanglement of film culture lies both in the analysis of the transmedia circuits in this period and in the transnational status of the star images of Asta Nielsen, Pola Negri and Brigitte Helm. These stars were almost by default regarded as modern 'new women' both on- and off-screen (Frymus 2020, Petro 1989, Weinstein 2012). On-screen because of the roles they played, which were often characterised by strong agency, even if they frequently ended up either married, imprisoned or executed. Both Pola Negri and Asta Nielsen are examples of stars who were often '*auteurs* of their own films, *the raison d'être* and guiding spirit' sometimes in fruitful collaboration with directors, too (Haskell 1987, 88 italics in original). Off-screen because they pursued successful careers and were prominent and fashionable figures in the cultural public sphere: Asta Nielsen had been a huge star since the early 1910s and was still regarded as a great actress; Pola Negri had her breakthrough around 1920 and continued her career in Hollywood; Brigitte Helm famously broke through in 1927 with *Metropolis*. Pola Negri and Brigitte Helm were known for their vampish femme fatale roles on-screen; still they were both regarded as fashionable 'flappers' off-screen. In contrast, Asta Nielsen was regarded as neither a vamp nor a flapper; her repertoire included cross-dressing roles as well as embodying complex characters based on the works of Strindberg and Dostoyevsky.

Early cinema culture was highly transnational and in Denmark, the major stars dominating the mainstream media were not Danish, with only a few notable exceptions, such as popular comic duo Pat and Patachon. The popular stars came from a range of different countries (Denmark, Hungary, Italy, Germany, Sweden, Poland, United Kingdom and the US) and starred primarily in American and German films. It was also in this period that the full promotional force of the Hollywood transmedia stardom was taking form in a Danish film cultural context, resulting in the perception of film culture as inherently transnational. This all changed or was redefined with the coming of sound in the late 1920s.

Film Historical Context for 1920s Danish Film Culture and Research Questions

Extant studies on Danish film history characterise the 1920s as a decade of decline based on the lack of international success of Danish cinema compared to the early 1910s (Engberg 1999, Tybjerg 2013). At this point in time Asta Nielsen's career in Germany was shifting gear (Allen 2013, Engberg 1999, Jerslev 1995, Loiperdinger and Jung 2013) and many of her German films did not open in Danish cinemas due to censorship. The highlights of this period include the art films of Carl Th. Dreyer, in particular *La Passion de Jeanne d'Arc* (*The Passion of Joan of Arc*, 1928) and the international success of the Pat and Patachon comedies. Audience successes also included a few Danish melodramas such as those directed by A. W. Sandberg: *Vor fælles Ven* (*Our Mutual Friend*, 1921), *Fra Piazza del Popolo* (*From Piazza del Popolo*, 1925) and *Klovnen* (*The Clown*, 1926) (Tybjerg 2013).

However, from the perspective of entangled history, the 1920s are particularly interesting because they are characterised by significant Hollywood dominance in Danish film culture as well as German cinema gaining ground (Tybjerg 2001, 76). In the early 1920s, approximately 85 per cent of the films shown in Danish cinemas were from the US (Andersen 1924, 40). However, by the late 1920s it was only between 54–68 per cent (Thompson 1989, 128–9), and the closest contender was German film.

The 1920s was also a significant period for modern film culture becoming a *bona fide* mass culture (Kracauer 2004 (1947), Huyssen 1989). In terms of audio-visual entertainment, silent cinema had a pervasive and central cultural and social presence. As the Danish film culture was booming, it was simultaneously entangled with American and German films and transnational stars with significant cultural impact (Tybjerg 2013, 76).

The aim of this analysis is twofold: firstly, to analyse how German films with female stars were represented in a transmedia circuit including critical reception and film cultural engagement in the 1920s. Secondly, focus is on how this new film culture represented the female stars of German cinema through an analysis of three different celebrity portraits of, respectively, Asta Nielsen, Pola Negri and Brigitte Helm in Danish daily newspapers and magazines.

State of the Art

Film culture is evidently a transmedia phenomenon and does not consist only of the movies in the cinemas but must be sought in a wide variety of media texts and discourses. This study is therefore informed by the New Cinema History approach to film culture historiography, where cinema is understood as 'a site of social and cultural exchange' (Maltby 2011, 6). When analysing the entangled nature of film culture, the focus is 'to search for correspondences between a film and the discourses that surrounded it at the time' (Maltby 2011, 6).

In order to map out these transmedia relations and discourses, a useful approach is to adapt the tripartite scheme for the analysis of the circulation of media texts that John Fiske proposed in the chapter on intertextuality of his classic work *Television Culture* (Fiske, 2010). This includes the primary text; the film representing the star in a media fiction. The secondary text is the critical reception such as reviews and commentary, portraits as well as promotion and advertisements. Finally, the tertiary text springs from the audience's engagement in letters to the editor or competition entries in dailies.

Transnational stardom is 'not just a matter of labor that crosses national borders', but includes film stars negotiating 'the tensions between national identity and cosmopolitan culture' (Meeuf 2016, 196, 197). Furthermore, transnational celebrities often 'belong to multiple national discourses' at the same time (Lee 2016, 41). When studying female German stars in Danish film culture, these issues are presented as they unfold in particular media texts: this is why studies of the portrait are relevant. The celebrity portrait as a key journalistic genre became widespread from the 1920s onward, where the new approach was to interview the celebrity in their home and reveal how they successfully managed 'the art of living' (Ponce de Leon 2002, 40). This definition of the celebrity portrait has since been boiled down to four stock elements: the meeting, the demeanour, the current film (or cultural product) and the 'against the grain' aspect (Marshall 2006, 320). In order to understand the portrait genre as part of transmedia film culture and focus on the transnational status of the star, it makes sense to consider the notion of 'the celebrity matrix' based on Richard Dyer's understanding of the interconnected relation between the key elements that constitute a star image: a protestant work ethic, charisma, the display of conspicuous consumption and the performance of authenticity – based on the paradoxical combination of ordinariness and extraordinariness (Dyer 1979, 39–50).

The role of particular film stars in a transnational film culture is productive to study because stars 'are also embodiments of social categories' (Dyer 1986, 18) and therefore when studying German female stars in a Danish context, it is useful to regard them as 'vessels that facilitate the circulations of concepts of femininity, ethnicity and identity' (Frymus 2020, 9).

Asta Nielsen was the first German superstar albeit Danish of origin, but as argued by Julie Allen and others, in the 1920s and onwards her 'personal and professional ties to Germany became a liability for her acceptance in Denmark' (Allen 2020, 178). According to Allen there was speculation as to where 'Nielsen's loyalties—the land of her birth or the land of her professional success' (179). On screen Asta Nielsen did not conform to one particular type, such as either the vamp or the flapper, instead she explored many different female types and 'testing the limits of the feminine space' (Jerslev 1997, 30). However, Asta Nielsen's roles in the 1920s marked a shift compared to the 1910s: 'Nielsen now opted for more serious and nuanced portrayals of female identity [. . .] yet also showing how modern women's options are still limited by their age and beauty' (Allen 2021, 187). In the 1920s she 'continued to embody modernity and feminism on screen [. . .], but her construction of modern female identity was both more mainstream in Germany and more contested in Denmark' (179). For example, in an article with the headline 'The Unique Asta' ('Den Enestaaende Asta) where it was dryly stated that: 'the German taste is not quite the same as ours, even so it is always with great interest that we look forward to an Asta Nielsen opening' (*Vore Damer* 1925, 7 May). (See Figure 6.1)

It hampered her career that many of her films were not shown in Danish cinema in the 1920s due to state censorship. Asta Nielsen's star image, working in the German film industry, was thus inherently transnational and entangled in a Danish film cultural context.

Our second focus is on Pola Negri, who was from Poland but 'became one of the icons of Weimar cinema portraying independent women of strong sexuality' (Frymus 2020, 44). Her international breakthrough with *Madame Dubarry* was directed by Ernst Lubitsch, and because of the film's success in American cinemas, Negri was invited to Hollywood, where she was frequently cast as an exotic vamp (Negra 2001, 159). Pola Negri had a transnational star image incorporating 'connotations of

Figure 6.1 The Asta Nielsen look in 1925: The Unique Asta 'Den Enestaaende Asta'. 1925. *Vore Damer* 13, no. 19. Royal Danish Library, Copenhagen.

Europe and high culture' and was perceived as 'a female foreign celebrity' (Frymus 2021, 42). Her romantic relationships with major male stars Rudolph Valentino and Charles Chaplin mirrored her sexual agency on screen (Frymus 2020, 11). In *Madame Dubarry*, as well as in her other German films, her protagonists were often characterised by an 'active desire' and even as 'sexual aggressors' (McCormick 2020, 78). However, in the Hollywood dramas, she was still cast as the exotic vamp but without a specific ethnicity (Negra 2001, 162), her femme fatale often lacked agency and the stories were softened with a happy end (Negra 2001). She ultimately had difficulty redefining her star image outside of the vamp role and gradually her ethnic and exotic characters were no longer deemed relevant as a type in Hollywood (Negra 2001, 189).

Brigitte Helm was early on 'labelled as *the vamp* of German cinema' (Weinstein 2012, 168). She debuted with *Metropolis* in the double role of the two Marias; the idealistic girl versus the robot vamp seducing the masses. Helm's star image, too, could be interpreted as incorporating these two opposites: the evil vamp as 'the nightmare vision of the New Woman linking her sexuality to technology, modernity and mass culture', whereas the good Maria is the authentic girl (169). Helm was perceived simultaneously as a German national as well as an international star, 'but she did not match the flapper paradigm of the 1920s, nor the homely and healthy paradigms of the nationalist 1930s' (168–9). Helm was on contract with UFA but in 1929 she engaged in an unsuccessful lawsuit against the company. In Helm's view, she lacked control and influence on her roles and image. In 1935, she discontinued her contract with UFA (169).

In this context, the media depiction of these three female stars can tell us about how they embodied '"useful" questions within the social and cultural contexts of their time' (Holmes 2017, 12), such as different roles of femininity. The 'New Woman' was a broad concept addressing the new options and rights of women after World War I, for instance the right to vote and make their own living. In her study of womanhood and femininity in Denmark after World War I, historian Brigitte Søland sketches an 'optimistic narrative identifying the 1920s as the era when women achieved political, economic, and sexual liberation' (Søland quoted in Allen 2012, 197). Female stars were visible examples of successful professionals in the public sphere. In her analysis of the 'die Neue Frau' in a German context, Patrice Petro connects the New Woman to the star image of Asta Nielsen (Petro 1989, 153): 'The image of the New Woman in *Die Dame*, for example, was frequently linked by contemporary critics to the screen persona of Asta Nielsen.' This was also the case with Brigitte Helm in the late 1920s, Weinstein argues, because Helm 'reflected notions about the New Woman in a multifaceted way' (Weinstein 2012, 169).

The entanglement between German and Danish film culture concerns film, stars and cultural engagement, which is why it also makes sense to look at how specific media texts address and articulate the transnational stardom of the female stars of German cinema.

Methodology

In the following, I first give a brief characterisation of the type of the transmedia circuit involving the different media texts in play in the entangled Danish film culture and examples of how popular German cinema and female stars were represented. The focus is on the critical reception in daily newspapers, with exemplary reviews of *Madame Dubarry* (*Passion*) from 1919, directed by Ernst Lubitsch, *Die freudlose Gasse* (*The Joyless Street*) from 1926, directed by Georg Wilhelm Pabst, and Fritz Lang's *Metropolis* from 1927. In addition, the analysis includes new ways of covering film culture in Danish dailies exemplified by the newspaper *B.T.* and the ladies' magazine *Vore Damer*. The media circuit using Fiske's distinctions frames both the film and the stars and/or the ways in which the audience was invited to participate in cultural engagement through competition and participation (Fiske 2010, 110–27).

The second part is the analysis of the three celebrity portraits. The portraits are from the popular ladies' magazines *Vore Damer*: 'Pola Negri and her Hollywood home' ('Pola Negri' 1925) and 'Asta Nielsen at her home' ('Asta Nielsen' 1925). Since there was not a portrait of Brigitte in *Vore Damer*, I use a portrait published in the daily *Klokken 5* under the headline 'At Home with Brigitte Helm' ('Hos Brigitte Helm' 1929).

Entangled Danish Film Culture in the 1920s – a Transmedia Film Culture

In this period, going to the cinema had become well-established as mainstream entertainment. The cinema was part of a transmedia circuit connecting film (the primary text) with an array of print media texts (the secondary texts) framing or re-framing the cinematic experience (Fiske 2010, 116–24). These included reviews, programmes, magazines, photocards and posters offering the audience the experience of different visual media. The circuit finally consisted of different forms of film cultural engagement, the tertiary texts (Fiske 2010, 125–7).

Going to the cinema also offered a different type of access to cultural experiences compared to the theatre because tickets were cheaper, the dress code was more informal and it had a broader appeal as accessible popular culture (Dinnesen & Kau 1983, 23–4). It was also the age of the film palace; the largest movie theatres in Copenhagen were aptly titled Palads-Teatret, Kino-Palæet and World Cinema. Each of these theatres had more than 1000 seats and screenings were accompanied by a live orchestra (Tybjerg 2001, 222–3). As part of the urban landscape, cinemas also typically had large posters or billboards announcing which movies were playing, as well as wall cabinets with stills from the films on the fronts and entrances of the buildings. Kino-Palæet often screened big German film productions, whereas Palads-Teatret mostly favoured Hollywood fare.

In the newspapers, the new films were reviewed on a weekly basis and had been so since before World War I. However, in the 1920s, the coverage of cinema gained prominence in the dailies and included not only reviews and news about upcoming film premieres, stars and directors, but expanded into separate sections or supplements with focus on film. Likewise, the movie theatres not only offered playbills or programmes for each new movie premiere. Palads-Teatret and Kino-Palæet had their own weekly magazines presenting an expanded version of the program, such as *Palads-Teatrets Films Nyheder* and *Kino-Palæets Magasin*. These pamphlets featured articles about the premieres of the upcoming weeks with plenty of photographs. Regular fan magazines were not published in Denmark, but films and stars were prominently featured in ladies' magazines such as *Vore Damer* with star portraits and interviews, fashion reports from Hollywood as well as Paris, London and Berlin.

The critical reception in the daily newspapers focused on reviewing new films that premiered in the big movie theatres like Kino-Palæet and Palads-Teatret, whereas the openings in the smaller movie theatres were mentioned only briefly and in passing. In addition, cinema adverts were now more visually elaborate, with photos or drawings of the star(s) or with quotes from reviews and recommendations.

Three different films are used as cases in the following to exemplify how German cinema and its popular female stars were represented in Danish film culture. The films under analysis are selected based on the availability of reviews framing the film for the reader as well as their popularity at the box-office; that is the number of weeks they played at movie theatres. As mentioned earlier, the films include Pola Negri playing the historical titular figure *Madame Dubarry* during the French revolution, Asta Nielsen sharing her top-billing with newcomer Greta Garbo in *Die freudlose Gasse*, and a big sci-fi production introducing Brigitte Helm in the double role of *ingénue* and malicious robot in *Metropolis*. The reviews expose three different outcomes in the Danish critical reception of German cinema with major stars: the overwhelming success of the period drama *Madame Dubarry*, the very modest run of the realist film *Die freudlose Gasse* and the initial box-office failure of *Metropolis*.

From Massive Success to Unacceptable Realism and a Slow Success Story

Madame Dubarry opened in November 1919 and ran for two consecutive months at the Kino-Palæet. The majority of reviews published the day after the opening described *Madame Dubarry* as an atypical German production, because it was 'better than was usually expected from German (film) productions', (*Københavneren*, 28 November 1919). The major Copenhagen daily *Politiken* concluded that 'German film art and mise en scene have presented something very remarkable here' (27 November 1919). At this time, a run of two weeks was considered a success for a film. The adverts (the secondary texts) promoted the film as 'the best film of the season' and had Pola Negri headlining. One advert included a quotation from Urban Gad, the Danish film director of most of Asta Nielsen's film and her ex-husband, who was still working in Germany. Gad is quoted saying that 'It seems that the Danish audience while watching *Madame Dubarry* finally has discovered Pola Negri. It was about time, because she has already been the biggest film actress of our time for a couple of years' (*Berlingske*, 16 December 1919).

The second example, the Asta Nielsen film *Die freudlose Gasse*, was a kind of comeback for her on the Danish screens when it opened in 1926. From 1923, when the film *Die Tänzerin Navarro* ('The Dancer Navarro') premiered in Copenhagen, the next eight of Nielsen's films were banned by Danish state film censors. Back in 1923, critics did not dispute Asta Nielsen's fame but framed it as German-based, as when for example *Politiken* wrote: 'the most recent Asta Nielsen film in Germany, where our famous countrywoman is regarded as the absolute prima donna of cinema' (*Politiken*, 10 March 1923). Three years later, when *Die freudlose Gasse* opened in Danish movie theatres, the critique was unusually harsh, partly explained by the film being a German one. It also seems to be a turning point in terms of the critics' evaluation of Asta Nielsen's performance. Previously, her acting had always been praised, even if the film divided the critics, as was the case with her female Hamlet adaptation in 1921 or *Die Suffragette* (*The Militant Suffragette*) back in 1913 (Haastrup 2021;

Haastrup 2022). In *Die freudlose Gasse*, the verdict was that 'her original talent had changed into a stiff and unnatural style of acting and she sleepwalks through all nine acts' (*Politiken*, 10 March 1926). The critic in *Nationaltidende* preferred newcomer Greta Garbo and the male lead Einar Hansen, who were both deemed 'excellent', whereas Asta Nielsen 'still has her soulful eyes but film is relentlessly revealing to a face that has lost its youth' (23 March 1926). The film style and subject matter were also criticised as 'a German fasting menu depicting the depression after the war' (*Politiken*, 23 March 1926). *Politiken* concludes with a war metaphor that despite 'actors who are big names in Germany [. . .] the final result was a defeat' (*Politiken*, 23 March 1926).

The final example is *Metropolis*, made by director Fritz Lang, who had had a great success with his Wagner-inspired *Die Nibelungen* from 1924, which ran for more than a month at Kino-Palæet. However, with *Metropolis* in 1927 expectations soared, because the film had been promoted in Danish newspapers as no less than the 'world's greatest picture' (*Nationaltidende*, 5 March 1927). There were even reports in Danish newspapers from the opening night in Berlin: 'It is the greatest film ever made in Germany' (*Klokken 5* 11 January 1927, 4). In *Social-Demokraten*, you could read *Metropolis* as a serial written by Thea von Harbou during the week of the opening night and *Metropolis* was also published as a book. Despite all the commotion, the Danish reviews of the film were mostly negative, but all had praise for the newcomer Brigitte Helm, for instance *Social-Demokraten*, where a German expression was used to describe the lack of substance in a German film (6 March 1927):

> The few times that the spectator was seized by a true and sincere emotion, it was not because of the story, but by the performance of a 19 year old Brigitte Helm [. . .] It was a film with 'Viel Geschrei und Wenig Wolle' ['Much ado about nothing'].

However, *Social-Demokraten* contributed with an additional explanation of why *Metropolis* was unsuccessful. The paper blamed a negative mention on the newscast on the radio predicting that *Metropolis* would become a big box-office failure (11 March 1927). The impact of the new media was perceived as unfair in the article. Since 1926, The Danish Radio Cooperation (*Statsradiofonien*) had been broadcasting on a regular basis and had become a popular part of the media circuit. *Metropolis* only ran for a disappointing five days (5–10 March 1927) in Kino-Palæet, as mentioned above (*Social-Demokraten*, 10 March 1927). Soon after, it opened simultaneously at two smaller movie theatres with five shows a day, to great success, and continued its run for a couple of months. As late as June 1927, three months later, you could still catch *Metropolis* in a Copenhagen cinema. Brigitte Helm, meanwhile, was considered a rising star and received critical acclaim from the very beginning.

Inviting Film Cultural Engagement – Collecting and Producing in the 1920s

Stars of German cinema such as Asta Nielsen, Brigitte Helm and Pola Negri were an integral part of Danish film culture at this time. It was a commercial film culture heavily inspired by the film industries of both Germany and the US and where the audience was addressed differently than in the 1910s. This included invitations in mainstream media outlets to new cultural practices, primarily spread through visual print media and dealing with films, stars and directors.

Figure 6.2 Pola Negri with her signature turban: 'Vore Damers Filmsleksikon – Pola Negri'. 1925. *Vore Damer* 13, no. 47. Royal Danish Library, Copenhagen.

One example of how the daily tabloid newspaper *B.T.* addressed the film-interested audience was the weekly 'B.T. Films Revue', which invited the audience to participate in different types of film cultural practices. This included a section called 'Do You have an Eye for Cinema' ('Har De skarpe Films Øjne'), where readers could write about observations of script errors or continuity mistakes in the films of the week. This qualifies as an example of Fiske's tertiary texts – because the readers wrote to the editor and their input was published. The best observation was given a reward of 25 kroner and the section was a weekly feature in *B.T.* (see *B.T.*, 10 January 1922).

Questions to the editor from readers of 'B.T.s Films-Post', another weekly feature supplying information on films and stars, asked about, for instance, the age of Asta Nielsen and the address of Carl Th. Dreyer. The exact age of Asta Nielsen was described as a 'black secret', even though the editor felt inclined to disclose that she was in her thirties. Carl Th. Dreyer's address on Frederik d. VI's Allé was also revealed (*B.T.*, 17 February 1922).

Another feature was a competition, a lookalike contest, which provided *B.T.* with photographic portraits of readers trying to look like their favourite star. Asta Nielsen's look was popular, as were Norma Talmadge's and Henny Porten's. Competition articles posed the question: 'Do You Look like a Movie Star?' and presented a photo of the star opposite the photo of the reader (7 May 1921). In this manner, *B.T.* invited readers to participate in cultural engagement as a performance in a public forum.

The weekly ladies' magazine *Vore Damer* invited different kinds of film cultural practices, such as collecting portrait photographs of film stars and creating your own 'Vore Damer's Film Encyclopedia' (*Vore Damers Filmleksikon*) (*Vore Damer*, 15 November, 1925). This way *Vore Damer* connected the interest in film stars with serialisation and spurring interest in buying the next issue of *Vore Damer*. The stars included were mostly American stars like Norma Talmadge and Gloria Swanson, but Pola Negri and Asta Nielsen were also featured, as well as Emil Jannings and Pat and Patachon.

Another example of commercial appeal to film-interested audiences was photo cards such as the Sport Cigarettes collectable photo cards (1923–1926). They were cigarette-box-sized small cards with a photo on one side, and a short biography and selection of film titles as well as the production company on the other. An overview of the stars who appeared on the Sport Cigarette cards supports the perception that American cinema dominated the movie theatres, with Norma Talmadge, Mary Pickford, Rudolph Valentino and Douglas Fairbanks as the most frequent, and a single appearance of Danish comic stars Pat and Patachon and the German/US stars Pola Negri and Emil Jannings ('Sport' n.d.). The card series did not include any photos of Asta Nielsen. This selection of stars is perhaps also an indication that Asta Nielsen's films at this time were less mainstream, and that her recent films had not been shown in Danish cinema during this period either.

The letters to the editor and the lookalike contests in the dailies, the film encyclopedia in the ladies' magazine and the card series support that film culture had become mainstream and that film stars were an entangled mixture of American, German and (a very few) Danish performers.

Film culture was a transmedia film culture and a transnational entanglement of the different film companies' and movie theatres' promotion, the reviews and magazines (all secondary texts) and even the collectable photocards that you could get when buying cigarettes. The invitation from daily newspapers and magazines to their readers to engage and participate in film culture with questions, observations or photographs produced tertiary texts. In terms of the entanglement of the 1920s German and Danish film culture, the German films tended to open in the biggest movie theatres, and were deemed important and reviewed. Sometimes German was synonymous with success and quality, as was the case with *Madame Dubarry*. Other times 'Germanness' was unacceptable, as with the stark realism of *Die freudlose Gasse*, where the ageing star, Asta Nielsen, was almost pushed aside by a new one, Greta Garbo. However, Asta Nielsen's talents were usually praised even when her films were unpopular, Pola Negri had successes in *Madame Dubarry* as mentioned above as well as her Hollywood films, and Brigitte Helm got her breakthrough in *Metropolis*. Even though the critics initially disliked *Metropolis*, despite its promotion as the 'world's greatest picture', their evaluation was vehemently ignored by the Danish audience, who enjoyed it, and as shown above, its success kicked in with a slight delay and *Metropolis* eventually became a 'sleeper hit'.

The Presence of Female German Film Stars in Danish Media – Three Portraits

To get a sense of how the female stars of German cinema were represented in Danish mainstream media, the focus is on a comparative analysis of three portraits using genre theory (Marshall 2006) to understand the building blocks of the celebrity portrait, and Richard Dyer's notion of the star image is understood through the celebrity matrix (Dyer 1979). This makes it possible to characterise how the individual star image was presented with regard to authenticity, work ethic, charisma and conspicuous consumption (Dyer 1979, 39–50). The celebrity portrait of a film star is basically an example of an idol of consumption (Lowenthal 2006, 130) and consists of four typical aspects: meeting in a domestic setting, the star's casual demeanour, the star's current work and the revelation of something that goes 'against the grain' of the star's persona (Marshall 2006, 320). The three female stars Asta Nielsen, Brigitte Helm and Pola Negri are also examples of the 'New Woman' as mentioned above (Petro 1989, 30; Weinstein 2012). However, as the portraits of the stars of German cinema demonstrate, from ladies' magazines to daily newspapers, they also represented different types of female cinematic stereotypes.

The first portrait is 'Asta Nielsen at her Home' in *Vore Damer* (2 July 1925). Asta Nielsen's most successful period was a thing of the past in 1925, and her films of the early 20s also favoured the adaptation of classics and melodramas, rather than comedies. Her films still opened in the major cinemas, but from 1923 onward she did not have the same cultural presence in Denmark as before World War I, partly because – as mentioned – her films had been banned. She was the respected artist who had lost her impact with the Danish audience. Even when her films were not well-received, however, her acting talent was still appreciated. In 1925, *Die freudlose Gasse* had not yet been shown in Danish cinemas, but when it was in 1926, as mentioned above, neither the critics nor the audience liked it, but they still appreciated her acting.

The portrait article from *Vore Damer* is illustrated with a photomontage from Asta Nielsen's apartment on Kurfürstendamm in Berlin (see Figure 6.3), including three large photographs, two of which show Asta Nielsen at the centre and her common-law husband, the Ukrainian actor Gregorij Chmara, who is not mentioned at all in the piece but is shown sitting in the background playing a ukulele (9–10). Asta Nielsen is facing the camera, sitting in a large leather armchair in her library, and there are paintings on the walls, including one of herself. She is dressed in elegant yet comfortable dark clothes with a white shirt. Her head is slightly tilted to one side and her feet rest on a pillow even though she is wearing elegant high heels. The image exudes a relaxed yet chic style. The other photos show the couple in the sitting room drinking tea. Asta Nielsen's face is difficult to see but her signature haircut is visible; here, her husband gets the better light. The decor plays an important role, framing the couple with bookshelves, large paintings and even a tapestry. The last photo shows the elegant dining room. The style of décor is not modern, but more of a Victorian home with heavy carpeting, no blank walls and a few select pieces of modern furniture. However, Asta

Figure 6.3 The high priestess of cinema Asta Nielsen: Asta Nielsen at home 'Asta Nielsen i sit hjem'. 1925. *Vore Damer* 13, no. 27. Royal Danish Library, Copenhagen.

Nielsen's apartment has a bohemian vibe, which boasts substantial wealth and cultural capital

The portrait is narrated by a journalist visiting Asta Nielsen in Berlin, and he or she is getting privileged access to Nielsen's inner sanctum. The introduction states that the public interest in her when she visits Denmark is overwhelming, but 'to the broader audience Asta Nielsen is a stranger' (9). This indicates that she is no longer central to the Danish film culture, but still a celebrity.

The journalist describes the apartment interior with many details not shown in the photos: 'When you step into Asta Nielsen's apartment, you are well aware that this is "real life", this is not stylish decorations from a studio'(9). The authenticity is deemed central and invoked from the beginning of the piece: 'The few that actually know the human being Asta Nielsen' – thus indicating the journalist might be one such person – 'will tell you that she is not interested in scenery dust of any kind' (10). In her private life, there is no such thing as pretence, we come to understand (10).

Asta Nielsen's look is shown in the pictures, whereas the demeanour of the star is described as 'living her private life – she is a woman rather than an actress' (10). We are invited backstage into the sophisticated life of Asta Nielsen: the home is 'characterised by its mistress', 'everything is so alive and true in these rooms' and the works of art are something she has collected 'through the years' (9). Having tea in your living room can be seen as an ordinary and everyday thing, but even though the extraordinariness of Asta Nielsen is dominating, she comes off as authentic because she insists on being herself.

There are no references to Asta Nielsen's current work and one explanation is that several of her films at this point have not been shown in Denmark, as mentioned above. The journalist writes that her collection of art and literature, as displayed in her apartment, has helped Asta Nielsen through 'some tough years' (10), and asks rhetorically in the introduction: 'Who is interested in Asta Nielsen films today?' (9).

In the article, the journalist describes the style of the décor as an example of 'hyggens harmonie' ('the harmony of cosyness') based on the mixture of styles: 'baroque and gothic, french rokoko, English renaissance, Empire and Louis XIV, an altarpiece and a tapestry' (9). She goes on to describe to describe how Nielsen has paintings by Rops and Goya, which translate into both cultural capital and conspicuous consumption, and reports: 'There are thousands of books with literature from many countries, Denmark and Germany as well as England, France and Spain, and God knows where' (9). The last remark gives the impressive listing an ironic twist, indicating that Asta Nielsen's interests are impressive, and almost too much. Still, she is defined as 'the high priestess of cinema' in contrast to the 'sugary stars from Hollywood. She is a true human – the others are dolls' (10).

Taken together the article paints a picture of Asta Nielsen as a serious artist, a true human and a transnational film royalty who is popular when visiting Denmark, but who lives on Kurfürstendamm in Berlin. Her charismatic presence is recognised and communicated in the photograph of her in the library, stressing her status as an authentic woman with personal taste. Her conspicuous consumption also has transnational aspects in terms of the European fine arts covering the walls, and her large collection of literature, including both Danish and German works. She even has a painted portrait of herself and is not above flaunting this in her own home. Her protestant work ethic is hinted at: 'For long hours she prepares for her performance' (10). Her authenticity is connected to her personal taste, displaying an extraordinary amount of cultural capital and at the same time performing 'hyggens harmonie' (in English: 'the harmony of cosyness') when having tea with her husband. Asta Nielsen's status as a New Woman emerges from her visual authority, the focus on her career and her accomplishments, taste and star image, and while her husband is seen, he is not mentioned by name. The attention is not on her body or her former trademark skinny look (Jerslev 1995, Haastrup 2022), but rather on her status as a key figure in the German film industry that represents an alternative to Hollywood. German cinema, and Asta Nielsen, are in this portrait considered culturally closer to Denmark because Nielsen is associated with European high culture through the display of her art and book collection, unlike American cinema, which is understood as a popular and commercial culture.

Fashion, Luxury and 'Hygge' in Hollywood – Pola Negri's Hollywood Home

Pola Negri rose to fame playing heroines with a passionate drive, often as an exotic vamp (Frymus 2017; McCormick 2020). Her most successful German film was *Madame Dubarry*, and her subsequent six German-made films were also very popular in Danish cinemas: *Die Bergkatze* (*The Wild Cat*, 1921), *Das Martyrium* ('Martyrdom', 1919) and *Bella Donna* (1923) all ran for two weeks, whereas *Sumurun* (*One Arabian Night*, 1920), *Sappho* (*Mad Love*, 1922) and *Die Flamme* ('The Flame', 1923) ran for more than one month each. The success continued with Negri's American movies, where she was also cast as an exotic vamp; with 'her Italian surname, Polish ethnicity, and connection to the German film industry, Negri remained ethnically vague in the public imagination' (Negra 2001, 161–2).

Off-screen, she appeared modern and more like a flapper, with her romantic connections with American male stars Rudolph Valentino and Charles Chaplin (Frymus 2020, 11–21), which were reported in Danish newspapers. As an imported international star in Hollywood, with considerable success, Negri would soon be followed by others like Greta Garbo and Marlene Dietrich.

In the *Vore Damer* portrait 'Pola Negri and her Hollywood home' ('Pola Negri', 12 February 1925), Negri is presented as a modern and stylish Hollywood star wearing a new outfit in each of the six photographs (see Figure 6.4). The first image in the photo-montage shows her dressed in an elegant housecoat; she is preparing a bath of cream and milk (15) as an implicit allusion to the Egyptian Queen Cleopatra and ultimate luxury. In the next image, she is pictured with a large bouquet of flowers, while in the third she is playing the piano wearing her signature turban. The fourth image shows her feeding goldfish in a pond, wearing a summer dress with pearls and a fashionable bell hat. In the fifth, she has her tennis outfit on while her maid is presenting with her (fan) mail. Finally, in the sixth she is wearing pants as if she is going horseback riding, but she is seen with her dog, and we learn the curious fact from the text that she is actually chasing rats on her property.

This portrait is presumably based on an American original article, since the Danish journalist only provides us with background and refers to how American journalists interpret the photos from Negri's home in a different way, thereby giving the portrait a Danish framing. In the introduction, it is stated that Pola Negri has now settled down in Hollywood; however the journalist argues that her American film career has not yet reached the level of her German films (15). Her reason for moving to the US must be all the 'nice dollars' (15). This was a common critique of stars leaving for Hollywood, stressing the difference between European film and American film, high and low culture.

The photographs tell the story of the looks and demeanour of the star. They all look very much like publicity stills and show curated aspects of her star image: she is seen in a tennis outfit (sporty), she plays the piano (artistic), appreciates flowers (aesthetic sense) and stylish clothes (fashionable). The only backstage information is the awkward photo from the bathroom. Furthermore, her rat-chasing with the dog is interpreted by the journalist as an aspect of her ordinariness – that is something she has in common 'with thousands of her fellow sisters' (16) – an invitation to the reader to engage in identification.

Pola Negri's current work is not directly mentioned but the journalist has not been impressed with her American films so far, although they are

Figure 6.4 Pola Negri and her European 'hygge': 'Pola Negri og hendes Hollywood Hjem'. 1925. *Vore Damer* 13, no. 7. Royal Danish Library, Copenhagen.

getting better, we are given to understand. The 1925 Lubitsch film *Forbidden Paradise* with Negri opened in Copenhagen in March 1926, and was very successful. The revelation of something that is against the grain of what is generally perceived to be the star's persona is expressed by bringing attention to the contrast between the US and Europe, because Pola Negri has managed to create 'hygge' (cosyness) in her 'predesigned Hollywood home' (15) to the surprise of the American journalists. You could argue that it goes against the grain of both dimensions of her image as a vamp and is not in sync with her flapper image either, because 'hygge', in a Danish context, is often understood as creating a relaxed and homely atmosphere with décor and is also related to activities in the home with family and friends. It seems to be quite the opposite of the stylishness that is the key ambience of the photo-montage.

To sum up, Negri's charisma is communicated in the photos and particularly the shot showing her at the piano, because her pose and outfit match her on-screen smouldering vamp characters. The conspicuous consumption is present in her Hollywood villa with a park and staff, and her fashionable clothes (one dress for each photo). In terms of work ethic, this is implicit and primarily told in the brief biography on her growing up in Poland, wanting to be an actress since she was ten. We are also informed that she has taken her last name from the female Italian author Ada Negri (16). Her authenticity is connected to her previous work in German cinema and her European way of decorating her home. The extraordinariness is connected to the conspicuous consumption including the villa, the clothes, the servants and being successful in Hollywood. This way she still comes off as authentic, but it is based on her entangled European background: she is a Polish actress and became famous for her work in German cinema, and now has a career in Hollywood working with her European colleagues, such as directors Ernst Lubitsch and later Mauritz Stiller. Also, her romantic connections with European male stars add to the transnational star image. The portrait also seems to present a different aspect of a star known for her passionate drive, as both relaxed, creative and serious, but also doing everyday stuff for a privileged Hollywood star. The photo-montage shows a very successful star who is a domestic goddess in her own 'cosy' Hollywood home.

The European Film Star Brigitte Helm: UFA-lawsuit, Ordinariness and Vamp-costumes

The *Klokken 5* article 'At Home with Brigitte Helm' ('Hos Brigitte Helm') does not have the lavish photo-montages seen in Nielsen and Negri's portraits (*Klokken 5*, 21 October 1929). It has only one photograph of Brigitte Helm standing on what appears to be a doctor's scale, wearing a seemingly ordinary day dress. Helm had never acted before when she had her international breakthrough with the role of Maria in *Metropolis* in 1927. She was pigeonholed as a vamp on-screen but was the glamourous flapper off-screen, like Negri. In *Metropolis* she was also introduced to the audience in the abovementioned double role as the two Marias, the sexualised robot and the idealistic *ingenue*, two feminine roles corresponding to the two dimensions of her star image. In her following films, she continued with the vamp roles in *Alraune* (*A Daughter of Destiny*, 1928) and *Abwege* (*The Devious Path*, 1928), which were both quite popular in Danish cinemas. Helm's star image was often described as a transnational one: 'Brigitte Helm is undoubtedly one of the most interesting types of women in European cinema [...]. Her acting is intelligent, and she is definitely modern' (*Nationaltidende*, 26 October 1929, 4).

The headline of the portrait is: 'At Home with Brigitte Helm' and the subheading explains that 'Europe's most peculiar film actress – Brigitte Helm. Who does not want to be either a vamp or skinny' ('Hos Brigitte Helm' 1929, 4). The stage is set for an investigation of a star who does not want to play the kind of roles that she is famous for and who does not accept the demands of her company and its power over her body. Furthermore, the interview addresses her 'Germanness' implicitly as an indicator of both cultural and geographical closeness, since the reporter from *Klokken 5* travels to Berlin, where Helm lives in an elegant flat in the bohemian Schöneberg area. Helm's fame also goes beyond Germany, because she is defined as a European, and this is understood as a marker of quality in contrast to stars from Hollywood.

The journalist introduces the article by informing the reader that Helm 'also in Copenhagen has an extraordinarily large audience', meaning that her fame is not 'only' in Germany. When meeting Helm in her 'elegant home', the actress is described as having a 'trailing gait' when coming towards the reporter (4), perhaps implicitly indicating that she is 'performing', giving the journalist a 'to-be looked-at-ness moment' (Mulvey 1975, 809). The intimacy of the meeting is also stressed with a description of her 'funny eyes [...] that can both laugh and cry at the same time' and 'her melodic voice' ('Hos Brigitte Helm' 1929, 4). This way the reader gets the first-hand impression through the journalist. The photo does not offer access to her eyes, and in that sense the portrait presupposes the reader's knowledge of Brigitte Helm's signature look on-screen as the seductive vamp. In the article she is presented as the ordinary girl standing on a scale far from the glamourous publicity stills and her sultry screen presence. This way the interview emphasises her status as an example of the New Woman, but also the two sides of her star persona – the vamp and the girl (on the scale) – epitomised in her 'defining double role' in *Metropolis* (Weinstein 2012, 169).

However, Helm was also famous for her sense of fashion (Ganeva 2008, 141) and slim model looks (Weinstein 2012, 141). In the article she is, however, described as wearing a rather simple black dress, a dress that 'could have been worn by a small, handsome typist' ('Hos Brigitte Helm' 1929, 4). This slightly condescending description stresses the inappropriate ordinariness in her choice of clothing for a film star. Helm explains: 'I want to be myself not a fashion-model. Film and reality are two very different things' (4). Her argument taps into the paradoxical connection of the star image – the combination of the ordinary (the dress she wears in the photo) and the extraordinary (her on-screen glamourous look). Her current work is discussed in terms of her unsuccessful attempts to widen her acting portfolio and play other roles than the vamp.

The main reason for the journalist's visit to Berlin is that Helm has just lost a lawsuit against UFA. She was not happy with a particular clause in her contract stipulating that her body weight could not exceed 120 pounds (60kg). In Helm's view, moviemaking is hard work and she needs food to get through the long working hours. She also complained about not having spare time and the chance to go out like normal young people.

The need for 'the ordinary' functions as a revelation against the grain of what is generally perceived to be the star's persona. Helm does not particularly want to wear her 'vamp-costumes' at home and she is tired of having to dress up as a vamp for her roles. The piece ends with a brief biography containing Helm's rags-to-riches story: Fritz Lang allegedly offered her the role in *Metropolis* when he was 'walking the streets of Berlin' to find the right actress for his new film. However, as it turns out, the reason she was so thin when she got the part of Maria was because she was suffering from malnutrition. Now she is in a state of despair because she has lost the lawsuit, and she has to abide by UFA demands if she wants to keep her job. The interview presents her longing to play something other than a vamp and not to stay very thin as reasonable desires. Helm's problems with UFA are not presented as an expression of privilege or arrogance. Her wish to change the type of roles she plays is, however, not supported by the journalist, who concludes the article with the following statement: 'Those were the words of the vamp Brigitte Helm.' In terms of the celebrity matrix, she has a strong work ethic, it is addressed directly and the demands by UFA are presented as unfair. Her charisma is not shown in the article; instead, authentic details are reported by the journalist; for instance Helm's gait is described as 'trailing' and her eyes as 'funny'. Likewise, the description of her melodic voice is evidence that the journalist has spoken to Helm in person (at this point she had not yet starred in talkies). Conspicuous consumption is addressed since she prefers ordinary practical clothes when staying at home, reserving her fashion sense to her 'vamp-costumes' for her roles on-screen and in fashion magazines. The impression of authenticity is closely connected to communicated ordinariness – she wants to stay healthy rather than slim – and to her extraordinary fame as an actor with a successful career and access to fashion and an elegant home. Her lawsuit may strike the journalist as 'peculiar' but also testifies to the fact that the contracts offered to young female stars could be controlling.

In contrast to the previous two star portraits, which both might be a result of PR work by the film company, this article is surely not approved by UFA, because it provides an opportunity for Helm to tell her side of the story. Still the interview seems to confirm her star image and the story of her double role from *Metropolis*: the idealistic ordinary girl who the reporter meets in her Berlin flat, and the on-screen seductress Brigitte Helm in her vamp-costumes (Figure 6.5). This complexity seems to fascinate the reporter, and unfortunately it later turned out to be a problem for Helm in the remainder of her career (Weinstein 2012). Still, we are left with an impression of an unruly woman, as described by Kathleen Rowe, because Helm insists on taking back control over her own body, and having lost her lawsuit, at least insists on talking about it in public (Rowe 1995, 31).

Entangledness of Female German Stardom in Danish Film Culture

The three female stars of German cinema, and their portraits in two Danish magazines and a newspaper interview, all address the 'German-ness' of the stars, but with different foci.

For Asta Nielsen there is a complex dichotomy between her successful career in Berlin and her fame in Denmark, where her last eight films have been banned. Still her German films and skills as an actor are what set her apart from the 'saccharine' style of Hollywood cinema. Her cultural capital is exposed with her collection of art and literature. The title given to her as the 'high priestess of cinema' ('Asta Nielsen i sit hjem' 1925, 10) indicates that she is a grand old lady rather than fashion forward and skinny. The conclusion seems to be that she is still a major star, but her career is first and foremost in Germany now.

Figure 6.5 Brigitte Helm as the vamp in *Metropolis* on the cover of *Palads-Teatrets Films Nyheder. Sæson 1926–27*, no. 17. Danish Film Institute.

For Pola Negri it is stressed how her German films were better than her American ones and that because she is from Europe, she (like Asta Nielsen) can create European 'hygge' in a stately luxury Hollywood home. In this portrait, Negri's European origin is seen as a strength and a marker of quality, whereas Frymus, in her analysis of Negri's career in the US, finds that the opposite was generally the case. Negri's European descent was disqualifying for her star status and in the end proved to be detrimental to her career (Frymus 2020, 30). In contrast to her representation in Hollywood, it seems that the Danish representation, in *Vore Damer* at least, focuses on her 'Europeanness' as providing her with both relatability and ordinariness as well as cultural capital.

The Brigitte Helm article addresses her 'Germanness' implicitly as an indicator of a geographical closeness, because the journalist can easily travel to her private home in Schöneberg in Berlin. Likewise, the headline characterises her as a European film star in contrast to Hollywood. Helm was popular in Denmark, and she was both presented as 'The world's greatest film actress' ('Hos Brigitte Helm' 1929) and promoted in adverts as 'The confirmed favourite of the Copenhagen audience, Brigitte Helm' (*Morgenbladet*, 30 August 1929). The interview presents a contrast to her glamourous and fashionable image because it depicts her ordinariness and her legal battle with UFA.

Entanglement between Danish and German film culture can thus be detected in these three portrait-articles – shifting between celebrating 'Germanness' as a marker of film quality in contrast to Hollywood (Negri and Nielsen) or UFA as a demanding film production company (Helm). The differences between German and Danish film cultures are addressed in the Asta Nielsen portrait, with reference to her films in this period only being shown in Germany and rejected in Denmark by the state censorship.

Moreover, they all exemplify different aspects of the New Woman: Asta Nielsen as the powerful 'high priestess of cinema', with a career primarily in Germany and an unnamed husband playing ukulele in the background; Pola Negri with her transition to Hollywood demonstrating that her conspicuous consumption, 'the nice dollar' and her luxury villa come with an artistic compromise; Brigitte Helm as the German film star with a glamourous and international image who fights to maintain control of her own body and the way she is cast through her contract in the German film industry, giving a Danish reporter access to in her home in Berlin.

Concluding Remarks

German cinema was very present in Danish popular film culture, despite the dominance of Hollywood films, in a complex cultural exchange and an ongoing negotiation on different levels, often addressing questions of national identity (Meeuf 2016, 197).

The three female stars of German silent cinema, as represented in Danish media, had all achieved international fame and this was both recognised and applauded. However, even if they were understood as role models, there was also a sentiment that the exceptional success of a female film star was not a guarantee of trouble-free living. For Brigitte Helm, her physical well-being, and for Pola Negri, the quality of her artistic output, was questioned. Asta Nielsen's German films were banned by state censors in Denmark, which was disastrous for her connection to the Danish audience. Importantly, she remained successful in Germany and internationally. You could argue that one specific difference between the two national film cultures in this period was censorship policies, which had different standards in Denmark and Germany.

In contrast, Pola Negri and Brigitte Helm were both very successful in Denmark and in Germany, but both experienced difficulties, and both were forced to continually play vamps on screen. However, Pola Negri and Asta Nielsen, as well as Brigitte Helm, struggled with gaining or keeping control of their careers – Negri in Hollywood, and Nielsen and Helm in the German film industry.

When the audience engaged in film cultural practices, they could share a love for cinema as such, as seen in dailies as well as in ladies' magazines. Furthermore, the audience had become an integral part of how popular cinema was reported. It was not necessarily either German cinema or 'saccharine Hollywood'; it was both. This was evident in the dailies when the readers participated because they were fascinated by both German and Hollywood stars – and Danish ones – whether they were taking part in lookalike contests or sending letters to the editor. In contrast, the portraits and the interviews, as well as the critical reception, regularly framed stars in terms of specific nationalities (Danish/German/Polish), but oftentimes as a positive marker of cultural proximity and a contrast to Hollywood.

One could argue that there was a common film culture, shared between Denmark and Germany in the years of silent cinema, but it was complex and shifted focus depending on the film, the star and the media text, because as this analysis suggests: national identity was consistently deemed relevant to negotiate and reflect upon in the 1920s transmedia Danish film culture.

References

Allen, Julie K. 2012. *Icons of Danish Modernity*. Seattle: University of Washington Press.
Andersen, H. 1924. *Filmen i social og økonomisk Belysning*. Copenhagen: Komiteen til Belysning af Statsmonopoler.
'Asta Nielsen i sit hjem'. 1925. *Vore Damer* 13, no. 27 (2 July): 9–10.
Biltereyst, Daniel and Philippe Meers. 2020. 'Comparative, Entangled, Parallel and "Other" Cinema Histories. Another Reflection on the Comparative Mode within New Cinema History.' TMG *Journal for Media History* 23, no. 1–2, 1–9.

Dinnesen, Niels Jørgen and Edvin Kau. 1983. *Filmen i Danmark*. Copenhagen: Akademisk Forlag.
Dyer, Richard. 1979. *Stars*. London: BFI.
——. 1986. *Heavenly Bodies. Film Star and Society*. New York: St Martin's Press.
Elsaesser, Thomas. 2000. *Metropolis*. London: BFI.
'Enestaaende Asta, Den'. 1925. *Vore Damer* 13, no. 19 (7 May): 14.
Engberg, Marguerite. 1999. *Filmstjernen Asta Nielsen*. Aarhus: Forlaget Klim.
'Filmsleksikon Gratis, Et', no. 45. 5 November. 13 Aargang 1925: 1–40 (19).
Fiske, John. 2010. *Television Culture*. 2nd Edition. London: Routledge.
Frymus, Agathe. 2020. *Damsels and Divas. European Stardom in Silent Hollywood*. New Brunswick: Rutgers University Press.
Ganeva, Mila. 2008. *Women in Weimar Fashion. Discourses and Displays in German Culture, 1918–1933*. Rochester: Camden House.
Haastrup, Helle Kannik. 2021. 'Asta Nielsen: A Cosmopolitan Diva.' *Kosmorama* no. 276. Accessed 10 February 2023. https://www.kosmorama.org/en/kosmorama/en/asta-nielsen-cosmopolitan-diva
——. 2022. 'To be a Female Hamlet: Asta Nielsen's Star Image, Cross-Dressing Films, and Critical Reception.' *Kosmorama* no. 281. Accessed 10 February 2023. https://www.kosmorama.org/artikler/female-hamlet
Haskell, Molly. 1987. *From Reverence to Rape: The Treatment of Women in the Movies*. Chicago: University of Chicago Press.
Holmes, Su. 2017. '"Starring. . . . Dyer?": Revisiting Star Studies and Contemporary Celebrity Culture.' Westminster Papers in *Communication and Culture*. University of Westminster, London 2, no. 2: 6–21.
'Hos Brigitte Helm.' 1929. *Klokken 5*, 21 October 1929, 4.
Huyssen, Andreas. 1986. *After the Great Divide: Modernism, Mass Culture and Postmodernism*. Bloomington: Indiana University Press.
Jerslev, Anne. 1995. 'Asta Nielsen, kvindeligheden og de store følelser.' *Kosmorama* no. 213.
Kracauer, Siegfried. 2004 (1947). *From Caligari to Hitler: A Psychological History of the German Film*. Princeton: Princeton University Press.
Lee, Katja. 2016. '"What an elastic nationality she possesses!" Transnational Celebrity Identities in the Late Nineteenth and Early Twentieth Centuries.' In *Celebrity Cultures in Canada*, edited by Katja Lee and Lorraine York, 37–55. Waterloo: Wilfried Laurier University Press.
Loiperdinger, Martin and Uli Jung, eds. 2013. *Importing Asta Nielsen. The International Film Star in the Making 1910–1914*. New Barnet: John Libbey.
Lowenthal, Leo. 2006 (1961). 'The Triumph of Mass Idol.' In *The Celebrity Culture Reader*, edited by P. David Marshall, 124–52. London: Routledge.
Maltby, Richard. 2011. 'New Cinema Histories.' In *Explorations in New Cinema History. Approaches and Case Studies*, edited by Richard Maltby, Daniel Biltereyst and Philippe Meers, 3–40. Chichester: Wiley-Blackwell.
Marshall, P. David. 2006. 'Intimately Intertwined in the Most Public Way.' In *The Celebrity Culture Reader*, edited by P. David Marshall, 315–23. London: Routledge.

McCormick, Rick. 2020. *Sex, Politics, and Comedy. The Transnational Cinema of Ernst Lubitsch Book*. Indiana: Indiana University Press.

Meeuf, Russell. 2016. 'Transnational Stardom.' In *The Routledge Companion to Cinema and Gender*, edited by Kristin Hole, Dijana Jelača, E. Ann Kaplan and Patrice Petro, 195–202. London: Routledge.

Miskell, Peter. 2016. 'International Films and International Markets: the Globalisation of Hollywood Entertainment, c. 1921–1951.' *Media History* 22, no. 2: 174–200.

Mulvey, Laura. 1975. 'Visual Pleasure and Narrative Cinema.' *Screen* 16, no. 3 (autumn): 6–18.

Negra, Diane. 2001. 'Immigrant Stardom in Imperial America: Pola Negri and the Problem of Typology.' *Camera Obscura* no. 48 (16, no. 3): 158–95.

Palads-Teatrets Films Nyheder. Sæson 1926–1927, no. 17.

Petro, Patrice. 1989. *Joyless Street. Women in Weimar Cinema*. Princeton: Princeton University Press.

'Pola Negri og hendes Hollywood Hjem.' 1925. *Vore Damer* 13, no. 7 (12 February): 15–16.

Ponce de Leon, Charles L. 2002. *Self-Exposure: Human-Interest Journalism and the Emergence of Celebrity in America, 1890–1940*. Chapel Hill: University of North Carolina Press.

Rowe, Kathleen. 1995. *The Unruly Woman. Gender and the Genres of Laughter*. Texas University Press.

'Sport Cigarettes: Serie 1–7 (1923–26)'. n.d. Danish Movie and Pop Music Trading Cards (website). Accessed 24 June 2022. https://tohan.dk/samlemaerker/Filmstjerner.htm

Søland, Birgitte. 2021. *Becoming Modern. Young Women and the Reconstruction of Womanhood in the 1920s*. Princeton: Princeton University Press.

Thompson, Kristin. 1985. *Exporting Entertainment: America in the World Film Market 1907–34*. London: BFI Publishing.

Tybjerg, Casper. 2013. '1920–29: Et lille lands vagabonder.' In *100 års dansk film*, edited by Peter Schepelern, 63–89. Copenhagen: Rosinante.

'Vore Damers Filmsleksikon – Pola Negri.' 1925. *Vore Damer* 13, no. 47 (19 November): 2.

'Vore Damers Filmsleksikon – Asta Nielsen.' 1925. *Vore Damer* 13, no. 47 (19 November): 5.

Weinstein, Valerie. 2012. '10 January 1927: Brigitte Helm Embodies Ambivalence of the New Woman.' In *A New History of German Cinema*, edited by Jennifer M. Kapczynski and Michael D. Richardson, 166–72. Rochester: Camden House.

CHAPTER 7

Same Frame, Different Lens? Exporting Danish Film Style

Vito Adriaensens

What do you picture when you think of a Danish film?

Chances are it is an image of Mads Mikkelsen. Drunk. Dancing his tight behind off on a Copenhagen dock with a group of graduating students to the sounds of Scarlet Pleasure's *What a Life*, and then hurling himself freely off said dock, only to be captured forever in a freeze frame. His whole body is a blur and his black suit contrasts starkly against the overcast Danish skies – a naturalistic take on Wim Wenders' seminal angels in *Der Himmel über Berlin* (*Wings of Desire*; 1987). These iconic images come from director Thomas Vinterberg's Academy Award winning film *Druk* (*Another Round*; 2020). Behind the fluid, handheld, close-to-the-ground lensing of the sequence we find the unsung image taker, Norwegian cinematographer Sturla Brandth Grøvlen.

In hindsight, we might one day connect these images to a new age of Danish cinema, the 2020s, wont as we are to categorise film history by the decade. We might also view Vinterberg's visual and performative tactics as a return to the movement he helped found alongside Lars von Trier in 1995: Dogme 95. One of the few movements in film history that has been somewhat easier to categorise, what with the existence of a written manifesto and a self-declared 'Vow of Chastity' that bound films and filmmakers together. As Thomson points out, the more one investigates Dogme 95, 'the more one realizes that it is both deadly serious and playfully ironic' (2013, 25).

The general lack of manifestos is infuriating to the serious film historiographer. Dogme 95 trolled us before it was all the rage by demonstrating that an apparent insistence on negating style – by seeking to eliminate lights, controlled camera movements, optical effects, filters, props and even the idea of a director – only leads to a more recognisable and rigid style. Participants in the Dogme 95 experiment vowed to coax the truth out of its characters 'at the cost of any good taste and any aesthetic considerations' (von Trier and Vinterberg 2021, 203). Except, of course, for the long list of aesthetic considerations that preceded this final vow.

These stringent stylistic rules helped audiences recognise a Danish film. Its directors, credited or not, exploded onto the international scene. It initiated a second Golden Age of Danish Cinema, the 1990s. This chapter will investigate the first time audiences learned to recognise Danish films by their stylistic markers: the 1910s, the first Golden Age of Danish Cinema. I will focus on what made Danish films identifiably 'Danish' in the 1910s, and how this individuality – and lack thereof – was wielded and exported by Danish production companies, directors, actors and its unsung heroes, cinematographers.

In particular, I will highlight the journey of one pioneering cinematographer, Axel Graatkjær, from Denmark to Germany. Without any prior experience whatsoever, Graatkjær started shooting films for Ole Olsen and his Nordisk Films Kompagni in 1906, when the company first started producing films. Axel Graatkjær became Nordisk's top cinematographer and was responsible for lensing some of the most iconic Danish films of the 1900s and 1910s. His talents took him to Germany with Asta Nielsen and Urban Gad in 1913. In Berlin, he worked with Karl Freund, Ernst Lubitsch, Robert Wiene, Carl Froelich, F. W. Murnau and many more. He retired at the age of forty-five in 1930, having shot more than 300 films.

Figure 7.1 1914, Berlin Grunewald. From left to right: Karl Freund, Axel Graatkjær, Urban Gad. Danish Film Institute.

If a Danish national film style existed, Axel Graatkjær would technically have been best placed to help originate it, as he undeniably put his stamp on the Danish Golden Age of the 1910s. Moreover, Graatkjær arguably did the same for a national German style. By working with key German directors on career-defining films in the late 1910s and early 1920s, Graatkjær helped herald a Golden Age of Expressionist and Romanticist films that put the country on the map as a cinematic nation. The question that might be asked here, is how much visual 'Danishness' was Graatkjær able to imprint upon his new surroundings and collaborators?

Tableaux and Thespians

In keeping with the sentiments of Dogme 95, it was George Kubler who axiomatically posited that 'no human acts escape style' (1987, 167). When we examine the style of the films that Axel Graatkjær photographed – or any film for that matter – we will find that films are not merely boiled down to the sum of their visually identifiable parts, or 'shots'. Films and their style are rooted in a geography, in politics and in an economy. They are indebted to their art historical context, as part of a long history of visual arts. As David Bordwell put it in his seminal work, *On the History of Film Style*, when we investigate film style we are after answers to two key questions: 'What patterns of stylistic continuity and change are significant?' and 'How may these patterns be explained?' (2018, 4). Moreover, if style is 'any distinctive, and therefore recognizable, way in which an act is performed' (Gombrich 2009, 129), what exactly made a film a 'Danish' film in the 1910s?

Ironically, one thing that made Danish films 'Danish' in the 1910s was an attempt not to look Danish. The country's largest film company, the Nordisk Films Kompagni, had been oriented towards making films for the foreign markets since its inception in 1906 (Thorsen 2017, 30). This meant foregoing nation-specific tales, archetypes and architecture, in favour of a unified narrative and formal approach that could work anywhere in Europe, Russia or the United States, the prime markets at the time.

That a company such as Nordisk, or any company from a nation as small as Denmark, was able to compete on the international stage was nothing short of a miracle. From a film production standpoint, one of the biggest challenges will have been to consistently produce and deliver films to meet the growing demand created by their own marketing. With film production commencing at its Valby studio in 1906, Nordisk was on the cusp of entering a new age. All around the world, film had started being ratified as a form of entertainment worth everyone's time and business.

Permanent movie theatres were taking hold in the form of 'nickelodeons' and cinema palaces. Film trade journals were founded, becoming the site for marketing and discussions on the state of the art of film: *Der Kinematograph* (Germany, 1907), *Moving Picture World* (US, 1907) and *Ciné-Journal* (France, 1908) were three of the earliest and most influential, and many more quickly followed suit. And in 1908, a French film company named Le Film d'Art ('the art film') partnered with the storied theatrical acting institution La Comédie Française to produce the first branded art film, *L'Assassinat du duc de Guise* by André Calmettes and Charles Le Bargy, which set off the first wave of European art (house) films (Carou and de Pastre 2008).

Nordisk's founder Ole Olsen showed he had his finger on the pulse – and his eye on France – by taking advantage of both developments. The resulting stylistic approach has best been described as a 'tableau aesthetic'. 'Tableau' stands for 'picture' in the painterly sense, referring to the mostly static frame in which events unfurled for viewers in European cinema of the late 1900s and early 1910s. In a tableau-style film, the mise-en-scène, staging, lighting and performance come together to create a moving painting, or *tableau vivant*. Bordwell considers the action playing out in a 'single orienting view' in Europe to be a viable alternative to the much more editing-oriented American cinema, where actions would be more quickly broken up in a continuity of different shots (2005, 46–7). One could say that, to this day, the divide in perception between European and American cinema continues to be one of a mise-en-scène-based cinema versus an editing-based cinema.

As further explored by Bordwell (2006), Nordisk was able to adapt this approach into one that allowed them to make up to and over 100 films a year in their prime years (for figures see Engberg 1977), while retaining a sense of artistry that was recognised as 'quality' abroad. Nordisk's techniques and sensibilities were reminiscent of Dutch Golden Age genre painting, and their focus lay on contemporary subject matter in a middle and upper middle-class milieu, an approach I have previously explored in European cinema as 'bourgeois realism' (Adriaensens 2015 and 2016). Nordisk was also one of the first companies to heavily invest in narrative feature films, and the idea that one film could be the featured entertainment of the evening, as if one was seeing a play. As Sandberg has pointed out, the single-reel film had become an exception in Denmark by mid-1911, and Nordisk's Ole Olsen was quick to claim credit for having 'invented' the feature film (2005, 452–6).

The film in question was *Den hvide Slavehandel* (*The White Slave Trade*, 1910), and it has been documented that this film was entirely plagiarised from the competing Fotorama film of the same name – the latter came out in April, and Nordisk's version in August, but only Nordisk's survived (Engberg 2006). Cinematographer Axel Graatkjær remembered that the Nordisk team went to the premiere of this 'first' feature film, and that they came prepared:

> [Director August] Blom was present at the premiere and sat and took notes on every single scene point by point. The film was then shot, developed, and copied expressly so that Fotorama did not have the opportunity to sell quite so many copies of their film. After *Den hvide Slavehandel* we put the main emphasis on the long films. I remember that the first three-act film that we shot was *Ved Fængslets Port* (*Temptations of a Great City*, 1911). (Graatkjær in Olsen and Lauritzen 1969, 42)

In fact, it was an earlier film photographed by Graatkjær – back when he still went by Axel Sørensen – that was billed in its program as Nordisk's first single-feature three-acter: one of the company's first art films, *En Kvinde af Folket* (*A Woman of the People*, 1909). In Denmark, in keeping with newly minted practices in France, Nordisk had introduced beautifully designed accompanying programs, like playbills in a theatre. These usually told audience members what the plot of the film was going to be, who some of the players were and came with production stills. *En Kvinde af Folket* deals with love and class – a rich factory owner falls in love with one of his employees but quickly casts her off – and was thus an exponent of the bourgeois realist direction that Nordisk was taking.

The film played well abroad, most likely in no small part due to the efforts of Nordisk's communication teams. In the US, Nordisk had appointed Norwegian Ingvald C. Oes to represent their American counterpart, the Great Northern Film Company, and Oes maintained a close line of communication with trade journals. Interviewed by way of introduction in 1908, Oes was dubbed a 'pleasant and cultured gentleman' in *Moving Picture World*, and when asked about the company's thespians he stated that the 'artistical and dramatic side of the operations are led by artists of high standing, assisted by a staff of actors of recognized ability' (Anon. 1908, 261).

The advertising for *En Kvinde af Folket* showed the world how Nordisk wanted itself to be perceived, and Danish cinema by extension. A *Moving Picture World* advertisement led with the headline 'Quality Films', flanking the company's polar bear logo with 'manufacturers of meritorious productions' and 'photographic excellence unexcelled', before describing the film as a 'feature film of the highest order' (Anon. 1909b, 892). Normally, Nordisk took out half-page ads that incorporated several films, but this was a full-page ad for a single film. *Moving Picture World* writers seemed to agree or buy into the high quality of the pictures, for in the same number they sang the praises of the Great Northern's latest achievement, arguing that they excelled internationally thanks to their stellar (and stage-trained) actors:

> a good story, simply and clearly told and well photographed. Therein lies the secret of success; therein lies the secret of the creation of an international moving picture drama. In other words, the preparation and production of plays which are understood at a glance by people in all parts of the world. Think of it now! This Great Northern picture was made in far off Copenhagen, the capital city of Denmark, and, to us, in the ultra-modern metropolis of the New World, the action of the piece is as clear as daylight. [. . .] The photography of this picture is up to the fine standard which the Great Northern Company have set for themselves, the tints and tones being judiciously chosen. What we like about it, however, is the intense realism of the acting. Every word, every gesture of the principal characters in this piece is a masterpiece of carefully studied histrionics. This is another case where the illusion is so perfect that one seems, as it were, to be looking at scenes from life itself. Great Northern films, which are going from success to success, have a polish and finish about them which give them that distinction of quality which lifts the moving picture onto the plane of the pictorial. (Anon. 1909a, 871–2)

To elevate cinema to a painterly level was certainly a goal expressed by many for whom cinema was seen as the next of the classical arts, and it became the subject of many a piece in Danish film and theatre trades, such as *Masken* (see for instance Krag 1911, 98–9; Lindenborg 1912, 290–1; Rosenkrantz 1913, 272–4, to list just a few). On their end, Nordisk did a lot to close the perceived divide between theatre and film. Most directors at Nordisk came from the stage, a lot of them were former actors, like August Blom, and its actors continued to grace the Danish stages as they worked in film. Moreover, a number of high-profile Danish actors, like Asta Nielsen and Olaf Fønss, would also start working for German film studios, as would directors such as Urban Gad, Benjamin Christensen and Stellan Rye (Allen 2012, 147).

What Nordisk benefited from and acted upon in its marketing in the US was a general reverence for Scandinavian actors and playwrights. Scandinavia became synonymous with modern playwrights in the form of Norwegians Bjørnstjerne Bjørnson and Henrik Ibsen, the Swede August Strindberg and the Dane Holger Drachmann. These playwrights heeded Danish scholar Georg Brandes' 1871 call for a 'Modern Breakthrough' in Scandinavian literature – a call to focus on contemporary issues (Lisi 2011, 193). On the international stage, this move was embodied in the role of 'Nora' in Henrik Ibsen's *Et Dukkehjem* (*A Doll's House*), which premiered at Det Kongelige Teater in Copenhagen on 21 December 1879.

This exploration of the female psyche and a woman's place in a patriarchal society went on to dominate Scandinavian drama in the late-nineteenth and early-twentieth century and was inherited by a range of Scandinavian filmmakers (Haverty Rugg 2016, 352).

This strategy was made clear in another interview given by Oes to both *Moving Picture World* and *Moving Picture News* on 23 September 1911, promoting Nordisk's close relationship with the theatre industry (Anon. 1911b, 882 and Anon. 1911a, 11). The interview in the *Moving Picture News* was an extensive one, and it was followed by a two-page spread showcasing 'Some of the celebrated actors from the Denmark theatres who have helped to make the Great Northern films famous' (Anon. 1911b, 12–13). The actors were featured alongside their theatrical affiliation, and the standout was Mrs Betty Nansen, from the Royal Theatre.

A focus on performance in service of a mise-en-scène-based long-take aesthetic thus became a part of Nordisk's house style, and with the likes of Betty Nansen, one could even say that Nordisk was an early adopter of the 'famous players in famous plays' model. I have detailed elsewhere quite how far Betty Nansen's popularity and skill reached (Adriaensens 2018, 56–80), and it's worth pointing out again that Betty Nansen was Danish cinema's first real film star export, when she moved from Nordisk's 'Danish Hollywood' in Valby to Fox's studios in New York's 'Hollywood on the Hudson' in 1914. Nansen was seen as Scandinavian acting royalty, and news of her theatrical feats (in Danish) had started to reach New York as early as 1903 (Anon. 1903, 24). While Asta Nielsen is widely and correctly viewed as Denmark's first true film star, she was a middling theatre actor who nevertheless broke through on the silver screen in 1910 with *Afgrunden* (*The Abyss*). Nielsen became a historically key Danish export when she moved her star-unit to Germany, to the point of being mistaken for German, and Betty Nansen seemed to be more popular, or better advertised, in English-language territories. A detailed search on the Media History Digital Library's Lantern tool between 1910–1920 produces 242 hits for Asta Nielsen and 379 hits for Betty Nansen. In Germany, however, 'Die Asta' reigned supreme, with over 1000 combined hits in *Der Kinematograph* and *Die Lichtbild-Bühne* alone (most of them in the latter), with Betty Nansen reaching only in the dozens.

Identity Wars

This marked difference has everything to do with an event we might quickly overlook when compiling this type of correlative data; an event that defined everything in its path and compounded identities and alliances across Europe: World War I.

Before the war, Nordisk's biggest export markets in Europe were Germany, Russia and Austria-Hungary (Thorsen 2017, 101), three countries whose international standing changed drastically between 1914 and 1918. Since Denmark took a neutral position during the war, Nordisk continued to do business with Germany and the Central powers, as well as with the Allied powers, which not everyone was thankful for. As has been explored by Lars-Martin Sørensen and others in this volume as well, being mistaken for 'German' was not a good thing during the war, and especially not in its immediate aftermath. The challenge for Danish film companies like Nordisk was to maintain or strengthen their Danish identities, without cross-contamination from their Germanic neighbours.

A well-crafted public identity was an important marker for success, and one that might have separated Betty Nansen from Asta Nielsen in the US, for instance. In the case of Nielsen, Richard Abel has pointed out that before the war, perhaps American audiences were not sure exactly what to make of her (2013, 279). When the war started, Germany banned imports from Allied powers, and vice versa, preparing to strengthen a local market and leaving the door wide open for Nordisk to expand aggressively. The import ban was expanded beyond Allied powers in the spring of 1916, remaining in effect until almost two years after the war, on 31 December 1920 (Thompson 2005, 18).

Even in the 'good' times, however, Nordisk walked a tightrope. While Olsen courted Germany and appeased cautiously neutral Denmark with generous donations to both, his son-in-law Harald Frost was doing damage control in the UK, doubling down on making sure all titles included the word 'Copenhagen' to avoid any confusion between Danish films and German films (Thorsen 2017, 159). Meanwhile film companies in the US were ready to 'cash in on Europe' and abandon their relative isolationist stance (Thompson 1985, 49–50), laying the groundwork for a post-war domination that has persisted to this day.

So, what did this identity war mean for Danish and German film style in the 1910s? Was there even a pre-war German style? As Thomas Elsaesser put it so eloquently, the cinema before World War I mostly 'seems to exist only as preparation, pre-text and precursor. Emperor Wilhelm II's passion for the cinematograph is seen as symptomatic for a cinema of Führer figures [. . .]' (1996, 7). Indeed, stylistically, it is the 1920s that jumps out at us and grabs us by the throat. The cinema of the Weimar Republic (1918–1933): artificially cast shadows longer than one could imagine; expressionistically painted sets that would make Oscar Kokoschka and Georg Kaiser blush; camera masks, multiple exposures and split screens; and daring combinations of styles ranging from Wiener

Werkstätte to Dadaism, to the monumental Romanticism of Adolphe Appia and Caspar David Friedrich (see Elsaesser 2000 and Isenberg 2009). These masterpieces that we all know played out on a broad spectrum governed by underlying subtexts of post-war malaise, radical nihilism and despair that was palpable, and Siegfried Kracauer famously traced a straight line from the advent of films like *Das Cabinet des Dr. Caligari* (1920) to Hitler (1947).

For whatever lack of German style there seemed to be before the war, 1913 looked like a turning point. It was also the year in which we can most intently point to a clear stylistic influence between Danish and German cinema. In 1910, Danish directing pioneer Viggo Larsen had left Nordisk and led the way to Berlin, where he made films until 1921. In 1911, then, Urban Gad and Asta Nielsen left for Germany to set up their own 'Asta' subsidiary under PAGU and Deutsche Bioscop. Nordisk's star cinematographer Axel Graatkjær left to join them in 1913. Danish directors William Augustinus, Alfred Lind, Preben Rist, L. A. Winkel, Axel Breidahl and Einar Zangenberg also went to Germany in 1913. Stellan Rye, Danish stage director, playwright and one-time screenwriter, moved to Berlin one year before the other directors, in 1912, and made one of the classic German films of the 1910s: *Der Student von Prag* (1913). The film is a Faustian, Edgar Allan Poe-inspired doppelgänger tale, starring Paul Wegener, and was also known as *The Student of Prague*, but more widely discussed in the US as *A Bargain with Satan*. As Tybjerg has demonstrated, while Rye has been historiographically overshadowed in his authorship by the film's writer, the famed Hanns Heinz Ewers, there were plenty of reasons to consider Rye the most influential voice in the creation of the film. For one, Rye had already published a short story in 1905, *Teatrum Mundi*, that featured a doppelgänger. Foreshadowing German films such as *Die Puppe* (*The Doll*, 1919) by Ernst Lubitsch and *Das Wachsfigurenkabinett* (*Waxworks*, 1924) by Leo Birinsky and Paul Leni, the short story also featured mechanical waxworks (Tybjerg 1996, 156–7). Rye died at the front in 1914 after enlisting to fight for Germany. More recently, his authorship came into question again with the Munich Film Museum restoration, which credits him as an assistant director. Loew's research has indicated, however, that Rye already had a big stake in overseeing productions at Deutsche Bioscop before this film came along. She further cites a *Lichtbild-Bühne* interview with producer and cinematographer Guido Seeber from 1926, in which Seeber emphasised that while authors often received credit, it was Stellan Rye who directed the film (Loew 2021, 119).

Finally, then, 1913 was also the year in which Germany came up with its own response to the waves of art films that had washed over Europe, in the form of the 'Autorenfilm' (the author's film). The term was analogous to Pathé's SCAGL, or *Société cinématographique des auteurs et gens de lettres*, a director-unit subsidiary minted in 1908 to attract famous authors and adapt their works to film, hoping their prestige would rub off and draw bourgeois audiences, which it did (Abel 1998, 40). The German 'Autorenfilm' almost did not come to pass, had it not been for a big push by Nordisk.

As Engberg notes, the Danish precursor, or 'forfatterfilm', was systematised by Nordisk in 1912 when it started buying up copyrights and making deals for percentages with well-known authors like Sven Lange and Otto Rung. Moreover, they pursued the same strategy at their German branch, securing the rights to Gerhart Hauptmann's *Atlantis*, for which he had just won the Nobel Prize (1990, 128). The 1913 Nordisk film version by August Blom, with dazzling pictorial cinematography by Johan Ankerstjerne, remains one of the finest Danish films of all time. In a cinematic landscape that had become very competitive, Nordisk's managers knew that doubling down on the art film in all its guises was their biggest strength. This is evidenced by an August 1913 note from Harald Frost to Nordisk's London office, discussing that while the English market might not be ready yet for art films, it will be soon, because:

> We are quite sure that the Art Film is the only thing that can preserve the life force of moving images in the long run [. . .] In Germany and in several other countries, the naïve 'sensational films' are already unsaleable due to their overproduction [. . .]. We have been the first so far when new ground was to be broken, such as when the long films were introduced and we took the lead, and we believe that we have now also found the right direction. (Frost 1913)

In the wake of cinema's hands reaching successfully across the aisles towards those of theatre and literature, Michael Wedel describes how, counterintuitively, theatrical institutions in Germany waged a campaign against film producers, blaming movies for the slump in theatrical attendance. This campaign led to a May 1912 boycott against cinema that prevented theatre actors, directors and playwrights from working in film. Because Nordisk was able to reach deals with such prominent German writers as Hauptmann, Hugo von Hofmannsthal and Arthur Schnitzler, however, the path had been lighted and theatrical unions soon followed suit in deals with German companies (Wedel 2019, 47). This general attitude towards cinema may have explained why, relatively speaking, there were not many Danish actors active in Germany, because, as Engberg also confirms, 'they were neither highly estimated nor well paid during the early years of German film' (1990, 130). So, too, can it help explain the lack of German film stars on the international stage.

This move in the direction of a proper German art film, in keeping with what other European companies had been doing, was short-lived because of the war. Furthermore, as pioneering film sociologist Emilie Altenloh demonstrated, Germans were still overwhelmingly watching American films in 1912 (1914, 10). German identity naturally became an amplified point of discussion during the war, and the power of cinema was not lost on officials. In fact, one of the most important steps taken towards the creation of a truly 'German' film style happened in reaction against Danish influence in 1917. A letter dated 4 July 1917 from German General Erich Ludendorff to the Royal Ministry of War warned of Germany's lagging cinematic power, facing allies who had harnessed cinema and its propagandistic qualities. He called upon the German government to increase its output in neutral territories – that is, to make more films – and to standardise the German film industry so that films could have a 'methodic and insistent impact on the masses in the interest of the state' – to create a 'German' film style. On Danish influence, and the outsize influence of the Nordisk Films Kompagni in particular, Ludendorff's letter specified:

> An addition to the film industries of enemy peoples, the Nordische Gesellschaft enjoys a particular influence in the neutral territories. [. . .] The Nordic Company could thus pose a serious threat to German propaganda, should it appear hostile to Germany. Moreover, the Nordic Company currently has the ability to bring films to Russia. This influence, if it embraces a pro-German standpoint, is of nearly immeasurable worth for Germany [. . .]. Thus, our war duties indisputably require an immediate attempt to seek direct influence on the Nordic Company. The simplest and best means to accomplish this is bribery; most of the Nordic Company can be bought. If that fails, we will have to try another kind of affiliation, exploiting the Nordic Company's interest in the German film market. This sort of arrangement will be possible only if we can unify German film production to the extent that it can confront the Nordic industry as a cohesive contracting power. (Ludendorff 2016, 276)

The result of this powerful letter was a strengthening of the import ban and a consolidation of German companies into the behemoth that would come to be known as 'UFA', the Universum-Film Aktiengesellschaft, founded in December 1917. Isak Thorsen has explored just how drastic the impact of this decision was for Nordisk, which the government tried to force out of the German industry (2017, 191–232). For our purposes, the decision showed that Germany was finally ready to claim a style of its own. It did so by modelling itself after the factory studio model that had worked well in France, Denmark and the US in the 1910s. The studio grounds that would go on to become associated with UFA were Babelsberg, just outside of Berlin. German cinema thrived without much outside influence or competition. Kreimeier explains that the German government saw UFA as one of its most powerful weapons in the war, and so while all cultural institutions had to cut back, and even a theatrical icon like Max Reinhardt had to dial back the opulence of his sets, the money faucet was always open for UFA (1999, 39). After the war, with most of France and its film industry in ruins, Germany was suddenly a film giant and a force to be reckoned with.

The Dane behind the Dailies

With Germany's growing ambitions for a new cinematic approach as a backdrop, we return to the Dane who helped build a 'Danish Hollywood' in Valby, and who would later be one of the first people shooting on site at studio Babelsberg: cinematographer Axel Graatkjær. The cinematographer is the person who is ultimately responsible for the image, and when devising a production approach which would allow for the sheer magnitude of output that Ole Olsen and Nordisk first envisioned, their vision (and stamina) was indispensable.

Graatkjær – born Axel Sørensen in Velling in 1885 – liked to tell the story of how he answered an ad in 1905 to work at Ole Olsen's film theatre and was hired on the spot by Ole Olsen's wife – most likely because he stood out as a common sense farm boy amidst the Copenhagen lads (Graatkjær 1956). He was quickly at work turning the crank handle for the film projector, and his steady pace impressed Ole Olsen. He was promoted to sole cameraman when Nordisk started film production in 1906, alongside sole director, Viggo Larsen. There was little relief for Graatkjær in those first years, as he shot all fiction films between 1906 and 1909. Data compiled by Thorsen shows that with a team of just five to six people, Nordisk averaged sixty fiction films a year in this period, with 1909 topping off at eighty-two (2017, 45). As Graatkjær remembers it:

> For the first four years, I shot all the feature films. [. . .] I also shot [Valdemar] Psilander's films for the first four years – and I did that alone. Since we had two directors the first year, I filmed for both on the same day. When we got to 1913, Asta [Nielsen] and Urban Gad wanted a Danish cinematographer in Berlin. [. . .] I was the highest paid film worker at that time. (Graatkjær in Olsen and Lauritzen 1969, 41)

By 1910, then, Graatkjær already had over a hundred films under his belt. The art film wave was washing over Denmark. Ole Olsen was looking to expand production and hire more artistically-oriented helmers. It was around this time of expansion that Nordisk also started instating rules for directors and cinematographers. These directives would help keep Nordisk an efficient filmmaking machine, cranking out films at a ruthless rate, and they would also play a large part in dictating how its films were made.

As Thorsen notes, first, the director and cinematographer had to confer on the script, look at rehearsal and let Olsen know exactly how much film stock they thought they would need. Then, they would be allotted 100 metres at a time (around five and a half minutes of film at 16 fps). Thorsen hypothesises that this approach encouraged teams to continue to shoot in the popular long-take tableau style, and I would agree (2017, 136). Barry Salt has also noted that the average shot length of Danish films in this period was often more than twenty seconds – forty-three seconds even for *Ekspeditricen* (*In the Prime of Life* or *The Girl Behind the Counter*, 1911) (1996, 226). With their theatrical backgrounds, furthermore, Danish actors would have been used to the rehearsal process and to hitting their marks correctly as if 'live' on stage. This is also why some have referred to this tableau style as inherently theatrical, although its usage of depth of field, lighting and staging to maximise the optical playing field are clearly at odds with that.

While these directives seem quite spartan, they might make more sense if we know that film stock was hard to get and exceedingly expensive. A look at the Nordisk books in 1913 shows us that negative film stock had to be purchased for DKK 35 per metre, or almost $5 per metre (Nordisk Collection 1913, IX 21). This is the price without adjusting for inflation in 1913. In 2022, even in a time of global supply chain shortages and climate change, 35mm Kodak black and white negative film stock goes for only around $3 per meter. By comparison, in 1913, a kilogram of butter – one of the most expensive goods – cost DKK 2.36, and the average urban labourer only made DKK 3 per day (Khaustova and Sharp 2015, 19 and 22). Axel Graatkjær's 1912 contract shows that he made DKK 3000 per year, or DKK 8 per day (Nordisk Collection NF IV, Fotografer, IV 79). The numbers went up significantly every year, and, by his own admission and accounting for royalties, Graatkjær made around DKK 6000 per year by 1913, and the Cuban cigars that he would sometimes smoke with Ole Olsen cost DKK 25 each (1956). As if this life of wealth was not enough, Graatkjær's offer to join Asta Nielsen and Urban Gad in Berlin in 1913 was one for DKK 3000 per month, so it is no wonder he took it (Olsen and Lauritzen 1969, 42).

To return to the incredible cost of shooting, the film *Atlantis* (1913) survives at the Danish Film Institute in a 2280-metre version (114 minutes). The Nordisk books show us that the production spent DKK 222,250 on negative film stock (IX 21, No. 116, Conto 65). While this is an impressive number for the time, even more impressive is that they would have only shot 6350 metres of film, or less than three takes for every finished shot that is in the film. This shooting ratio of less than 3:1 is even more astounding when one accounts for the fact that *Atlantis* has big set pieces in the water, including a sinking ocean liner. (For contemporaries, it would have been very difficult not to think of the wreck of the *RMS Titanic* the year before; see Gunning 2011.) Shooting ratios have most likely gone up since the advent of digital, but even on the cusp of that in 2012, Kuhn and Westwell estimate shooting ratios ranging from 4:1 for low budget features, to anywhere as high as 50:1 or 100:1 for big budget feature films (237).

That Nordisk was able to issue this type of restraint and still end up with such a high quality output was impressive. When looking at behind-the-scenes pictures of the films that Graatkjær shot for them, we can see that the cameras must have often only held around thirty to sixty metres of film at a time. Furthermore, Nordisk's studio set-up was such that sets could consist of nothing more than two conjoined walls in the shape of an 'L', with a door in the back to add a layer of complexity. These sets would be reused, and they stood side by side on Nordisk's stages. Graatkjær and his colleagues would shoot into them from an angle, and often add mirrors, to maximise depth (see also Adriaensens 2015).

This can clearly be seen in Figure 7.2, taken in Nordisk's Valby studios on the set of an August Blom film c. 1910–1912. Natural light pours through the glass roof and windows, controlled and directed by large white and black curtains, acting as bounces for reflection and flags to block light, respectively. A mirror is on standby, and so are extra flats, which can be seen peeking out behind our L-shaped set. Set dressers are active to the left of the set, where we see plants, a sculpture and a man rolling out a carpet and another holding a painting, ready for a quick turnaround into the next scene. Axel Graatkjær mans the still camera on the far left, cinematographer Johan Ankerstjerne stands to Graatkjær's immediate right and instructs an unknown operator, and August Blom directs the scene in a bowler hat on the far right.

The challenge for cinematographers and directors would be to break the script down into shots that would fit the allotted film stock and allow them to shoot these films in the few days they were allotted. On average, 4 days were spent on films under 500 metres (27 minutes or less at 16 fps), and 13 days for feature length films (Thorsen 2017, 145). By comparison, a brisk turnaround time for features today would be seen as anywhere between 21 and 30 shooting days, let alone a cinematographer shooting more than 5 of those in a year.

Figure 7.2 Axel Graatkjær and Johan Ankerstjerne on an August Blom set at Nordisk's Valby studio. Danish Film Institute.

Regardless of how well it paid, the situation at Nordisk must have been like working in a pressure cooker. Graatkjær was not one to complain, but he photographed thirty-five films in 1910 (mostly shorts to mid-lengths), and twelve in 1911 (mostly mid-length to feature), so the offer to join Urban Gad and Asta Nielsen in Berlin to focus on making fewer films for more money must have sounded alright. There was the promise of bigger budgets, a bigger world and a chance to try new things and work for different companies and directors. Graatkjær would also be working on the Babelsberg studio site. Yet to become the storied lot, it was originally scouted and built to accommodate Asta Nielsen and Urban Gad, who inaugurated it in 1912 with the shoot for *Der Totentanz* (*Song of Death*) (Wedel 2012, 240).

In the Axel Graatkjær special collection at the Danish Film Institute, we find the cinematographer's own scrapbook. It consists mostly of newspaper and magazine articles written for the occasion of Nordisk's fiftieth anniversary in 1956, in which Graatkjær was an oft-interviewed guest, but in them he says remarkably little about his time in Germany. Most newspaper scraps focused on the juicy bits, such as the fact that upon retiring, Graatkjær raised pigs in Jutland, getting along with them so well because he was used to working with prima donnas; or the Bulgarian medal he received for making a film there about the Red Cross in 1916 (The film *Bogdan Stimoff*, directed by Georg Jacoby).

A few changes on the cinematographic front were imminent when Graatkjær moved to Germany in 1913. Artificial stage lighting had been used at Nordisk before, but for the most part studios were still built in glass and used muslin and various other scrims and devices to diffuse daylight. Asta Nielsen's Babelsberg studio in 1912, for example, was still a glass studio. As Keating points out, the process of changing the shooting process to rely fully on artificial lighting was gradual and did not happen fully until the 1920s, when studios gradually became darkened boxes. Moreover, the orthochromatic (and slow) film stock responded very well to the brightness and cooler colour temperature of daylight (c. 5000 Kelvin and up) (Keating 2010, 17).

While many of Graatkjær's German productions would rely on artificial lighting and effects, the change was indeed gradual. Robert Reinert's *Opium* (1919), for instance, showcased Graatkjær's mastery of daylight and plein air cinematography, playing with backlit compositions and natural shadows as if crafting a Pictorialist portrait. F. W. Murnau's *Phantom* (1922), though dotted with spotlight effects and artificial source light effects, clearly relies mostly on daylight cinematography. In Figure 7.3, the clever use of a camera mask creates an almost fully vertical frame to set up a thirty-second

Figure 7.3 Screengrab from *Phantom* (F. W. Murnau, 1922). Courtesy of Flicker Alley.

long take. This enhances the depth created by the doorways that guide our eyes towards the protagonist, Lorenz (Alfred Abel), as he slowly makes his way from the background towards the frontally posted camera. The minimalist flats, verging on abstract, cast shadows that contrast with the harsh daylight we can also see coming in over the prison façade. The soft magenta tinting of the print symbolises the promise of a new life for Lorenz.

I concur with Keating that daylight or artificial light makes no difference to a good cinematographer; they are merely tools used to craft a picture with, and indeed most photographers in the Pictorial movement used daylight to spectacular effect (2010, 18). Even in a more expressionist outing, like Graatkjær's Asta Nielsen film *Erdgeist* (*Earth Spirit*, 1923), we find this thematised, with the film opening on the type of north light studio that painters and photographers still prefer, as it avoids direct sunlight. This studio is the setting for most of the film's first act, in which Asta's Lulu falls for the painter who is painting her portrait (Carl Ebert as Schwarz). The rest of the film, too, favours long shots and close-ups that are evenly lit and often feature source windows. The expressionist feel is marked by painted walls and floors, and sets so monumental that they feel like a mid-century modernist home, or, thanks to thick black curtains that guard most entryways, a giant stage.

Graatkjær himself emphasised the importance of a good exposure when interviewed in the 1960s. Apart from the Swedes and the Southerners (presumably, the Italians), Graatkjær felt that most cinematographers simply closed down their aperture to make something feel moody, as opposed to carefully using lights and exposing to get detail even in the darkest shadows (Olsen and Lauritzen 1969, 42). To get the desired effects in the highlights, separate actors from the background, and even overexpose the slow stock a little, carbon arc lights were used more and more frequently. In New York, especially, as opposed to the perennially sunny West Coast, the visual continuity that carbon arc lamps provided was tempting for producers. A Media History Digital Library search confirms a boom in the use and advertising for the (theatrical) industry standard Klieg lights from 1914 onwards. A visit to Thomas Edison's new studio, for instance, revealed that it was outfitted entirely overhead with these lights, and the reporter describes that their 'flash and roar [sent] down a warm and dazzling light' (Petersen 1914, 118).

Lights today have come a long way, but on big productions one will note that the amount of electricity needed to keep them running is still astounding. This was no different then. And apart from the power needed, their noise and their warmth, people on set also had to contend with the inflammatory phenomenon known as 'Klieg eyes'. People's eyes would swell up and go pink after long periods of exposure. While this was believed for a while to be due to the carbon dust of the lights at the time (Brownlow 1989, 19), the *American Cinematographer* settled in 1923 that it was actually the lights' ultraviolet rays burning people's eyes (Anon. 1923, 9). This is why you would often see people on set wearing sunglasses or goggles in the silent era.

But perhaps the biggest change for Graatkjær was not keeping up with the technology. He had been brought up in the school of a pictorial, European tableau style, and had successfully mastered lighting effects as early as 1906 with *Fiskerliv i Norden* (Viggo Larsen) and fashioned them into a house style by 1911 – much like the house style at Louis Feuillade's Gaumont – with films such as *Ved Fængslets Port* (*Temptations of a Great City*, 1911), *Den hvide slavehandels sidste Offer* (*In the Hands of Impostors*, 1911), *Den farlige Alder* (*The Dangerous Age*, 1911), *Ekspeditricen* (*In the Prime of Life* or *The Girl Behind the Counter*, 1911 – the EYE Film Museum credits him as its cinematographer and that seems likely) and many more. The 1913 Asta Nielsen film *Die Filmprimadonna* (*The Film Primadonna*), which thematises the life of a film star, also presumably shows us the German studio that was built for Asta and Urban Gad. The slow opening pan shows us a studio with gigantic glass windows, but also rafters that could hold overhead lights, and freestanding arc lights. In the film within a film, lights also seem to be used to supplement daylight, although these could be very hot bounce boards reflecting the sun.

One change that Engberg noted is that it was not uncommon in Germany for two cinematographers to be working in tandem, operating two cameras side by side (2001, 44). It was in Germany that Graatkjær found himself shooting alongside Karl Freund, who had also started as a projectionist in 1906, and had been shooting Asta Nielsen's films in 1911 alongside Guido Seeber (Schmitt 2022, 6 and 11). *Die Filmprimadonna* lists Graatkjær, Freund and Seeber as cinematographers. Of the three, it seems likely that Graatkjær would have taken the lead, since he was by far the most experienced, after Seeber and then Freund, and since he had been expressly poached from Nordisk by Asta and Urban. It was Karl Freund, of course, who would go on to become the most renowned as a director and cinematographer, mostly because of his move to the US and the horror films he shot and directed there. In the Asta, Urban, Axel triangle, if Axel was not shooting alone, the partnership seemed to extend mostly to Karl Freund. Behind-the-scenes pictures show Axel and Karl working together on numerous occasions, like the time they were caught waist deep in water with their cameras for *Engelein*.

Figure 7.4 *Engelein* (Urban Gad, 1914). Axel Graatkjær (far left), Karl Freund (to Axel's right) and Asta Nielsen. Danish Film Institute.

Stepping into Focus

These are the types of changes in production we can glean from the scant visual evidence we have. We know that more time was taken to shoot these features and that the budgets rose higher and higher in Germany, until German productions were able to compete with Hollywood productions for scale in the 1920s, most notably through the work of Fritz Lang. The isolationism and the enormous financial investment in German films, initially to divest from Danish influence as we have seen, paid off in a big way when Robert Wiene's *Das Cabinet des Dr. Caligari* found its way to audiences abroad by 1921. The film was so individually and uniquely German that it effectively broke the ban on German films, coinciding with the end of the German moratorium on foreign films. The German film now had a face, that of somnambulist Cesare (Conrad Veidt), and a style: the angular, contorted, tortured and representational aesthetic of pre-war Expressionist painting and theatre, transformed by the moving image into a darkly moving fantasy that stunned the world. The opening issue of the French film journal *Cinéa* featured a two-page spread on German cinema that highlighted the importance of UFA for Europe as a studio capable of achieving the rare feat of commercial and artistic success. It went on to stress that the Expressionist movement was made for cinema, as its themes and characters exuded action, not dialogue (Goll 1921, 20–1).

Axel Graatkjær was certainly at the centre of this evolution towards a German cinematic identity, most notably in two works of science fiction: the aesthetically daring Weimar precursor *Der Tunnel* (*The Tunnel*; 1915), directed by visual artist and theatre director William Wauer and based on the successful novel by Bernhard Kellermann; and *Algol. Eine Tragödie der Macht* (*Power*; 1920) directed by Hans Werckmeister and co-photographed with Herrmann Kricheldorff.

In *Der Tunnel*, beautifully preserved in richly tinted and toned colours and shot in the finest tradition of European pictorial cinema, an architect teams up with a billionaire in the near future to build a tunnel and a high-speed rail connection between Europe and the US. The sets were designed by a young Hermann Warm, later of *Caligari* and Fritz Lang fame. The tunnel project is presented as a utopian connection that, surely, would be worth the lives and labour of thousands of faceless masses, and the villain is represented by the financial powers that be (represented as Jewish stereotypes) looking to sabotage the project. In the film, the world watches on screens, live broadcasting the final part of the journey. As Sprenger points out, the film is all the more interesting because it was used by the Nazi party in the 1930s as propaganda – Hitler was reportedly a fan of this megalomaniacal architect – but subsequently banned alongside its director and his 'degenerate' art later (2005, 354).

In *Algol*, a miner (Emil Jannings) is visited by an alien from the planet Algol, who gifts him a perpetual motion machine that can provide energy to the entire world. The machine looks a lot like a film projector, and Guerin has commented on the fact that Algol's alien is a fiendish Promethean force of light and life, symbolising technology and its dangers (2005, 79). *Algol* also foreshadows issues of climate change and, first and foremost, is a strong parable of how power corrupts. It shows how fine the line is between a utopia and a dystopia. The film's diegetic world cleverly (d)evolves along with its main character's journey to power, changing from a realistically set and pictorially photographed one to a distorted expressionist and Wiener Werkstätte-inspired realm of the dark. The same holds true for Emil Jannings, whose character turns into a poster child for the Expressionist body. In Figure 7.5, for instance, we meet Jannings as humble coal miner Robert Herne, embraced by his partner Maria (Hanna Ralph). Herne indicates that he is doomed never to see the light of day again. Graatkjær's careful sculpting with harsh light and negative fill successfully captures the gloom of the moment while also literally foreshadowing that Herne is a man marked by darkness.

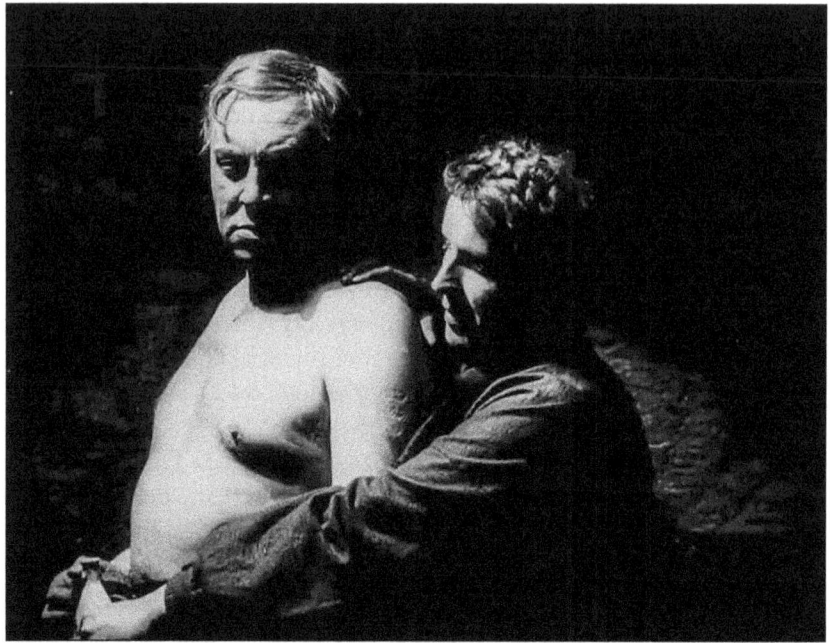

Figure 7.5 Screengrab from *Algol. Tragödie der Macht* (Hans Werckmeister, 1920). Courtesy of Filmmuseum München.

The films mentioned above are only scratching the surface of the body of work that Axel Graatkjær was involved in, as he photographed more than 300 films over a period of twenty-four years. He remained very steadily active in Germany until the advent of sound film in 1930. The overwhelming majority of these films is currently lost, but every new rediscovery offers us clues as to their role in the geopolitical and cinematic landscape that they and Graatkjær inhabited. As a young farmer's son, Graatkjær walked into Nordisk's offices looking for an additional income to supplement his studies, or perhaps even fund a trip to the US, to seek his fortune there. Instead, he became a part of the very fabric of Danish cinema, from the inception of its largest and most influential film studio, the Nordisk Films Kompagni, through a Golden Age that he definitively put his stamp on. Graatkjær was there to map out the visual strategies and house style alongside Ole Olsen and Viggo Larsen, and to define what the Danish version of an art film should look like with August Blom. The success of these films was felt both critically and commercially. In spite of the fact that a large number of them were made according to a formula of sorts – a pictorial tableau style, focusing on bourgeois realist subject matter, approached in director-units, on large stages that were set up to shoot interiors in the most efficiently interesting way possible, with a set amount of film stock – one can never discount the personal nature of every single film project, and the difference that a script, a director, an actor or the circumstances can make.

Moreover, by the end of 1913, the departure of quite a few important Danish talents made clear that certain individuals had differentiated themselves from others, and that bigger and bolder challenges awaited. Here again, Graatkjær was at the cradle of a national cinematic identity waiting to be established fully. Asta Nielsen and Urban Gad's Babelsberg studio provided the location and the talent hub that would make for a storied German history. Graatkjær landed right under the wire, benefiting both from the good standing that Denmark and the Nordisk Films Kompagni had in Germany, and by the relative isolationism and means that he was able to work in during and after the war. He was able to share his talent and exchange best practices with the likes of cinematographer colleagues Karl Freund, Guido Seeber and Herrmann Kricheldorff, and to work with Ernst Lubitsch, Robert Wiene, William Wauer and F. W. Murnau, to name a few, in establishing a style and approach that suited them. He grew alongside them, although he was usually the most experienced person on set, and went on to shoot at UFA at a time when filmmakers from all around the world, such as one Alfred Hitchcock, cut their teeth there, in the German Hollywood. Unlike some of his Danish and German peers, Graatkjær never did make it to the actual Hollywood, but he was undeniably an influential part in the creation of two national styles, and that was probably more than enough.

References

Abel, Richard. 1998. *The Ciné Goes to Town. French Cinema 1896–1914*. Updated and expanded edition. Berkeley and Los Angeles: University of California Press.

———. 2013. 'Asta Nielsen's Flickering Stardom in the USA: 1912–1914.' In *Importing Asta Nielsen. The International Film Star in the Making 1910–1914*, edited by Martin Loiperdinger and Uli Jung. New Barnet: John Libbey, 279–88.

Adriaensens, Vito. 2015. 'Kunst og kino: The Art of Early Danish Cinema.' *Kosmorama* no. 259.

———. 2016. 'Malerei in Bewegung: Bürgerlicher Realismus und Piktoralismus im europäischen Kino (1908–1914).' In *Film Bild Kunst. Visuelle Ästhetik des vorklassischen Stummfilms*, edited by Jörg Schweinitz and Daniel Wiegand. Marburg: Schüren Verlag, 151–75.

——. 2018. 'The Bernhardt of Scandinavia: Betty Nansen's Modern Breakthrough.' *Nineteenth Century Theatre and Film* 45, no. 1 (2018): 56–80.
Allen, Julie K. 2012. *Icons of Danish Modernity. Georg Brandes & Asta Nielsen*. Seattle and London: University of Washington Press.
Altenloh, Emilie. 1914. *Zur Sociologie des Kino. Die Kino-Unternehmung und die Sozialen Schichten ihrer Besucher*. Jena: Eugen Diederichs.
Anon. 1903. 'Transatlantic Topics.' *The New York Times* 53, no. 16: 793 (1 November 1903), 24.
Anon. 1908. 'Ingvald C. Oes – Of the Great Northern Film Company.' *Moving Picture World* 2, no. 13 (28 March 1908): 261.
Anon. 1909a. 'A Woman of the People.' *Moving Picture World* 4, no. 26 (26 June 1909): 871–2.
Anon. 1909b. 'A Woman of the People.' *Moving Picture World* 4, no. 26 (26 June 1909): 892.
Anon. 1911a. 'Interesting Facts from Abroad, Gleaned from an Interview with Mr. I. C. Oes, Manager of the Great Northern.' *The Moving Picture News* 4, no. 38 (23 September 1911): 11.
Anon. 1911b. 'Oes returns.' *Moving Picture World* 9, no. 11 (23 September 1911): 882.
Anon. 1911c. 'Some of the Celebrated Actors from the Denmark Theatres Who Have Helped to Make the Great Northern Films Famous.' *The Moving Picture News* 4, no. 38 (23 September 1911): 12–13.
Anon. 1923. 'The "Klieg Eyes" Question.' *American Cinematographer* IV, no. 7 (October 1923): 9.
Axel Graatkjær Collection. Danish Film Institute.
Bordwell, David. 2005. *Figures Traced in Light. On Cinematic Staging*. Berkeley and Los Angeles: University of California Press.
——. 2006. 'Nordisk and the Tableau Aesthetic.' In *100 Years of Nordisk Film*, edited by Lisbeth Richter Larsen and Dan Nissen. Copenhagen: Danish Film Institute, 80–95.
——. 2018. *On the History of Film Style*. 2nd ed. Madison: Irvington Way Press.
Brownlow, Kevin. 1989. *The Parade's Gone By. . . .* London: Columbus Books.
Carou, Alain and Béatrice de Pastre, eds. 2008. 'Le Film d'art et les films d'art en Europe (1908–1911).' *1895 – Revue d'Histoire du Cinéma* 56 (Special issue, December 2008).
Elsaesser, Thomas. 1996. 'Preface and Acknowledgements.' In *A Second Life. German Cinema's First Decades*, edited by Thomas Elsaesser and Michael Wedel. Amsterdam: Amsterdam University Press, 7–9.
——. 2000. *Weimar Cinema and After. Germany's Historical Imaginary*. London and New York: Routledge.
Engberg, Marguerite. 1977. *Dansk Stumfilm: De store År I-II*. Copenhagen: Rhodos.
——. 1990. 'The Influence of Danish Cinema on German Film 1910–1920.' *Griffithiana – La Rivista della Cineteca del Friuli/Journal of Film History* 38/39 (October 1990): 121–34.

———. 2001. 'Drej en Se – Film. Danske stumfilmstjerner: Axel Graatkjær.' *Objektiv* (April 2001): 42–5.
———. 2006. 'Plagiarism, and the Birth of the Danish Multi-Reel Film.' In *100 Years of Nordisk Film*, edited by Lisbeth Richter Larsen and Dan Nissen. Copenhagen: Danish Film Institute, 2006, 72–9.
Frost, Harald. 1913. 'Brev 18. Aug. 1913 fra Frost til N.F. i London.' August Blom collection, Danish Film Institute.
Goll, Ivan. 1921. 'Le Cinéma allemand. Films Cubistes.' *Cinéa* 1, no. 1 (6 May 1921), 20–1.
Gombrich, Ernst. 2009. 'Style.' In *The Art of Art History. A Critical Anthology*, edited by Donald Preziosi. Oxford and New York: Oxford University Press, 129–40.
Graatkjær, Axel. 1956. 'Radio Interview DR.' Danish Film Institute. Accessed 13 February 2023. https://www.stumfilm.dk/en/themes/film-pioneersGuerin, Frances Jane. 2005. *A Culture of Light. Cinema and Technology in 1920s Germany*. Minneapolis and London: University of Minnesota Press.
Gunning, Tom. 2011. 'Literary Appropriation and Translation in Early Cinema: Adapting Gerhardt Hauptmann's *Atlantis* in 1913.' In *True to the Spirit. Film Adaptation and the Question of Fidelity*, edited by Colin MacCabe, Kathleen Murray and Rick Warner. Oxford: Oxford University Press, 41–58.
Haverty Rugg, Linda. 2016. 'A Tradition of Torturing Women.' In *A Companion to Nordic Cinema*, edited by Mette Hjort and Ursula Lindqvist. Chichester: John Wiley & Sons, 351–70.
Isenberg, Noah. 2009. *Weimar Cinema. An Essential Guide to Classic Films of the Era*. New York: Columbia University Press.
Keating, Patrick. 2010. *Hollywood Lighting from the Silent Era to Film Noir*. New York: Columbia University Press.
Khaustova, Ekaterina and Paul Sharp. 2015. 'A Note on Danish Living Standards through Historical Wage Series, 1731–1913.' *EHES Working Papers in Economic History* 81 (July 2015): 1–25.
Kubler, George. 1987. 'Toward a Reductive Theory of Visual Style.' In *The Concept of Style*. Revised and expanded ed., edited by Berel Lang. Ithaca and London: Cornell University Press, 163–73.
Kuhn, Annette and Guy Westwell. 2012. *A Dictionary of Film Studies*. Oxford: Oxford University Press.
Kracauer, Siegfried. 1947. *From Caligari to Hitler. A Psychological History of the German Film*. Princeton: Princeton University Press.
Krag, Thomas. 1911. 'Teater-Films.' *Masken* 2, no. 13 (24 December 1911): 98–9.
Kreimeier, Klaus. 1999. *The UFA Story. A History of Germany's Greatest Film Company 1918–1945*. Berkeley and Los Angeles: University of California Press.
Lindenborg, P. 1912. 'Kino-Kunst.' *Masken* 2, no. 38 (16 June 1912): 290–1.
Lisi, Leonardo. 2011. 'Scandinavia.' In *The Cambridge Companion to European Modernism*, edited by Pericles Lewis. Cambridge and New York: Cambridge University Press, 191–203.

Loew, Katharina. 2021. *Special Effects and German Silent Film. Techno-Romantic Cinema*. Amsterdam: Amsterdam University Press.
Ludendorff, Erich. 2016. 'The Ludendorff Letter.' In *The Promise of Cinema. German Film Theory 1907–1933*, edited by Anton Kaes, Nicholas Baer and Michael Cowan. Oakland: University of California Press, 275–7.
Nordisk Collection. NF IV, 74–80. Fotografer, IV 79.
———. 1913. *Films Conto, IX 21*. Danish Film Institute.
Olsen, Claus Ib and Philip Lauritzen. 1969. 'Cand. Film Axel Graatkjær,' *Kosmorama* no. 94 (December 1969): 40–2.
Petersen, Cecilie B. 1913. 'A Visit to the Edison Studio.' *Motion Picture Magazine* VII, no. 5 (19 May 1914): 118–20.
Rosenkrantz, Palle. 1913. 'Film og Fremtid.' *Masken* 3, 46 (17 August 1913), 272–4.
Salt, Barry. 1996. 'Early German Film: The Stylistics in Comparative Context.' In *A Second Life. German Cinema's First Decades*, edited by Thomas Elsaesser and Michael Wedel. Amsterdam: Amsterdam University Press: 225–36.
Sandberg, Mark B. 2005. 'Multiple-Reel/Feature Films: Europe.' In *Encyclopedia of Early Cinema*, edited by Richard Abel. London and New York: Routledge, 452–6.
Schmitt, Gavin. 2022. *Karl Freund. The Life and Films*. Jefferson: McFarland & Company.
Sprenger, Veit. 2005. *Despoten auf der Bühne. Die Inszenierung von Macht und ihre Abstürze*. Bielefeld: Transcript Verlag.
Thompson, Kristin. 1985. *Exporting Entertainment. America in the World Film Market 1907–1934*. London: British Film Institute.
———. 2005. *Herr Lubitsch Goes to Hollywood. German and American Film after World War I*. Amsterdam: Amsterdam University Press.
Thomson, C. Claire. 2013. *Thomas Vinterberg's Festen (The Celebration)*. Seattle: University of Washington Press.
Thorsen, Isak. 2017. *Nordisk Films Kompagni 1906–1924. The Rise and Fall of the Polar Bear*. East Barnet: John Libbey.
Tybjerg, Casper. 1996. 'The Faces of Stellan Rye.' In *A Second Life. German Cinema's First Decades*, edited by Thomas Elsaesser and Michael Wedel. Amsterdam: Amsterdam University Press, 151–9.
von Trier, Lars and Thomas Vinterberg. 2021. 'Dogme '95 Manifesto and Vow of Chastity (Denmark, 1995).' In *Film Manifestos and Global Cinema Cultures. A Critical Anthology*, edited by Scott Mackenzie. Berkeley: University of California Press, 201–3.
Wedel, Michael. 2012. 'The Beginnings 1912–1921.' In *100 Years Studio Babelsberg. The Art of Filmmaking*. Kempen: teNeues, 232–57.
———. 2019. *Pictorial Affects, Senses of Rupture. On the Poetics and Culture of Popular German Cinema, 1910–1930*. Berlin and Boston: De Gruyter.

CHAPTER 8

'Die Deutsch-Nordische-Film-Union marschiert!': the Entangled Relations between Nordisk Films Kompagni, UFA, and DNFU 1918–1928

Isak Thorsen

In May 1928 attorney Svend Aage Funder could report from Berlin, that if Nordisk Film Kompagni's German subsidiary 'should collapse then Nordisk Film would definitely be dragged down too' (NF, I, 8, no. 96). Less than a month later Nordisk Film suspended its payments, and this meant the temporary end of a company which had belonged to the big players on the world market and had been a major force in the golden age of Danish silent cinema. The letter testifies that in terms of business, the entanglements between Danish and German cinema were probably never closer than in the post-World War I years and the entanglements came to have far reaching consequences for the companies involved. In the decade following the armistice, Nordisk Film interacted on various levels with the German film industry, first and foremost with the newly established Universum Film Aktiengesellschaft (UFA) and later through the company Deutsch-Nordische-Film-Union (DNFU).

This article will lay out and discuss these entanglements in the light of the overall question of this volume: how and to what extent did Denmark and Germany constitute a common film culture during the silent era? But what actually constitutes a common film culture between two nations? This is a challenging task to define. In addressing this question, Stephan Michael Schröder asks: 'does the very idea of being or becoming a common culture not presuppose the existence of both a Danish and a German film culture, separately from each other?' (Schröder 2020). Schröder's question points at a fundamental and much debated issue in film studies concerning nationality and transnationality, because the presumption of two separate national film cultures forming a common one takes place in a culture which is fundamentally transnational (e.g. Vitali and Willems, 2006, Shaw, 2017). Andrew Higson states that 'filmmaking and film exhibition have been transnational since the first public film shows in the 1890s' (Higson 2010, 70), while Tom Gunning writes 'cinema was international before it was national'

(Gunning 2016, 11). Cinema was born with an inherent transnationality, entailing entanglements across borders on all levels of the film business from script to exhibition, thus from the outset challenged the idea of a national film culture. Furthermore, the years from 1918 to 1928 coincide with what has been labelled the 'Film Europe' movement, characterised by a high degree of collaboration, co-production and itinerancy of filmmakers between the European film industries. The Film Europe movement was mainly a response to the competition from American films, which had found a strong foothold in Europe as well as on the world market after World War I (Higson and Maltby 1999). Though the following study will focus on the entanglements between entities situated in Denmark and Germany, it would be misleading not to include those coming from elsewhere, for instance the United States, the Soviet Union and Japan.

Nevertheless, nationality is the basis of the research perspectives in this volume, and the idea of nationality can at first seem to clash with cinema's underlying transnationality. Malte Hagener has elaborated on this issue: 'it is a misunderstanding to see a transnational approach as antithetical to regional, national or global histories; instead it complements the latter by understanding the reciprocity and interaction of developments at different speeds and in different places' (Hagener 2014, 4). In this sense, the transnational and national aspects of the Danish-German relations can complement each other, and nation will be a key frame of reference in the analysis of the entanglements.

Andrew Higson's works on national and transnational cinema, as well as his writings on 1920s European cinema, have influenced this study (Higson 1999; Higson 2000; Higson 2010). Akin to Hagener, Higson writes: 'We cannot [. . .] simply dismiss the category of the nation altogether, but nor should we assume that cultural specificity is best understood and addressed in national terms' (Higson 2000, 65). Cinemas can be national in a variety of ways, Higson writes; faced with such a variety, a single all-encompassing grand theory may be less useful than more piecemeal historical investigations of specific cinematic formations (Higson 2000, 57). The following can be seen as a piecemeal study, or a study following a 'middle-level-research strategy' (Bordwell 1996, 26–30), of transnational cinematic formations with nationality as a framework. Higson argues that border crossings since the 1920s have taken place on two broad levels: first, the level of production and the activities of filmmakers, including co-productions bringing together resources and experience from different nation-states as well as the itinerancy of filmmakers moving from one production base to another; second, the level of distribution and reception of films (Higson 2000, 61).

These two levels will guide this study. Production and the activities of filmmakers as well as distribution are all aspects of the cinema business or industry, and this study thus proceeds from an underlying assumption that, in the words of Vitali and Willemen, 'the developmental engine of cinema is driven by industrial, rather than cultural, forces' (Vitali and Willemen 2006, 2). However, I will also attend to cultural forces at the end of the chapter by analysing some of the films produced and co-produced by Nordisk Film and the German companies with which it was entangled in the decade after the end of World War I.

Thus far, the term 'entangled' has been purposefully used in accordance with the overall approach of the research project underlying this volume, which is influenced by *histoire croisée*/entangled historiography as suggested by Werner and Zimmerman (see Tybjerg, this volume). The concept of transnationality is central to any entangled history, but in contrast to a strictly comparative analysis, the entangled history approach is open to an analysis attentive 'in particular to various forms and phases of connection, interrelation, diffusion, flow, transfer or exchange in history' (Cronqvist and Hilgert 2017, 131). The approach thus opens up a multitude of perspectives based in empirical findings and emphasises some basic considerations that have shaped my analytical and methodological framework (Werner and Zimmerman 2006). A diachronic point of view is present emphasising the interaction among the objects of the comparison. It is evident that the objects analysed not only interrelate, but also modify one another reciprocally. As I will show, this is very much the case in the entangled history between Nordisk Film, UFA and DNFU, and importantly these entities were not stable from 1918 to 1928, as they underwent fundamental changes in the decade.

Werner and Zimmerman's approach does not offer a particularly concrete methodology and therefore leaves room for different interpretations: and perhaps it is rather what one could call a 'reflexive toolbox'. Their suggestion of a reflexive 'pragmatic inductive' methodology, in which the research is 'subject to continual readjustments in the course of empirical investigation', seems a bit vague (Werner and Zimmerman 2006, 47). Because this is a study based on archival research, the analytical schemes have obviously been continually adjusted during the research, and in this perspective the entangled history approach encompasses a sensitivity to the 'messiness' of the surviving sources contrary to a strict comparative methodology. The main sources in the research are the Nordisk Film Collection, the surviving business archive of the company, documents from the German *Bundesarchiv* and accessible articles from Danish newspapers and volumes of the German trade magazines *Der Kinematograph* and *Die Lichtbild-Bühne*. Werner and Zimmermann emphasise the position of the observer (Werner and Zimmerman 2006). My position is Danish, and this influences the research perspective in the sense that while the study traces a variety of entanglements, it is centred on the Danish company Nordisk Film.

Why were there so many entanglements between Danish and German film companies after the end of World War I? To understand these interactions between 1918 and 1928, I will begin by outlining the historical context.

'Schreckgespenst' from Denmark

Of the more than 2000 fiction films produced in Denmark in the silent era (Christensen and Richter Larsen 2021, 108), Nordisk Film stood behind approximately 1160 of them, and the amount is telling for the position the company held in Denmark. Established in November 1906 by Ole Olsen as the first film company in Scandinavia, the international market was the goal from the very beginning. At the time Berlin was one of the two film trade capitals in Europe, London being the other, representing an open market-system, in which films could be traded freely between producers, distributors and cinema-owners (Blom 2003, 29–30). Nordisk Film's first sales office in Berlin was established the very same month as Nordisk Film, and in the following years offices were opened in London, Vienna and New York. On average, Nordisk Film produced sixty short fiction films per year and numerous non-fiction films. More than ninety per cent of those films were exported to foreign markets, Germany being the main market from the very beginning (Thorsen 2017, 30; 63).

In 1910–1911 Nordisk underwent a major change. The company was the first in the world to reorganise its production around multiple-reel films, which lifted the Danish company up to become one of the big players in the world market (Bordwell 2006, 81). Multiple-reel films became the new standard, and Nordisk Film was able to deliver the new attractive commodity. The transition to longer films was a tremendous change, and Nordisk Film was re-organised into a departmentalised mode of production, anticipating the mode adopted by Hollywood to great success in the late 1910s.

When World War I broke out in July 1914, the neutrality of Denmark represented a golden opportunity for Nordisk Film, especially as its main competitors on the world market – the French companies Pathé Frères and Gaumont – withdrew from the important German market. With Olsen at the helm Nordisk Film began an aggressive expansion strategy buying and investing in film production and distribution companies in Germany, Central Europe, Scandinavia and Russia. The German film industry reacted to this intrusion with protest meetings appealing for help from the German Government, and hard accusations that Nordisk Film was expanding with the aid of foreign and possibly even hostile capital. In the German trade press, the Danish company was written about as an intruding 'Schreckgespenst' (bogeyman) (*Lichtbild-Bühne*, 15 April 1916, 12).

In a decade or so, Olsen had built Nordisk Film up to being one of the largest European film companies during World War I. From having three offices in Germany before the war, Nordisk Film was now a vertically integrated company with eight branches and thirty-three cinemas in Germany and Central Europe, and investments in other film companies and cinemas in Europe and Russia. The highly efficient film-factory worked at high speed, and production peaked in 1915, with a total of 174 films, of which ninety-six were multiple-reel films.

According to Kristin Thompson, 'As of 1917, the USA had essentially gained control of most world markets outside Central and Eastern Europe, the USSR and the Middle East' (Thompson 1999, 56). With the exception of the Middle East, Nordisk Film was highly influential on the markets not yet controlled by the American film industry. With backing from Copenhagen-based banks, Olsen and Nordisk Film had the capital and ideas for further expansion, among them a plan of establishing a grand pan-European film distribution company (Thorsen 217, 185–7).

But in late 1917 Olsen returned from Berlin, reporting to the company's board of directors that he had received an offer from a group of German businessmen who wished to buy the Danish company's business network in Germany and Central Europe. Olsen recalls: 'We had no choice – as foreigners in a country at war, we had to make the most of the deal' (Olsen 1940, 139). The German businessmen were acting as puppets for the German military high command, who wanted to establish a national propaganda organisation, including film. Nordisk Film was seen as a powerful organisation in Germany, but also represented a threat: there were concerns that Nordisk might show films from enemy countries, particularly Russia, in the cinemas in Germany that the company controlled. In late 1917 Nordisk Film's branches and cinemas in Germany and Central Europe were taken over by the new German company Universum Film Aktiengesellschaft (UFA). Nordisk Film's organisation and network became the backbone of UFA. The share capital of UFA was 25 million German marks, and by possessing 8.4 million worth of the shares, Nordisk Film gained a substantial influence in the newly founded company.

Figure 8.1 Ole Olsen in Nordisk Film's main office in Berlin. Danish Film Institute.

Nordisk Film and UFA

Seen from the outside, the collaboration between the two companies seems quite asymmetrical, as Nordisk Film came from a small country with approximately three million inhabitants in 1918 and had lost its international position. How could UFA benefit from the collaboration? The German home market consisted of nearly sixty-five million people, and with support from influential industrialists and the German State, UFA was one of the most powerful entities in the 1920s European film industry (Higson 2010, 70). Details of a confidential meeting in the German Foreign Ministry held in August 1918 shed light on what UFA hoped to gain. At the meeting it was agreed that Olsen's knowledge, his access to capital and his connections within the film industries of the entente powers could be used for propaganda purposes (Goergen 1994, 38). Olsen's knowledge and connections were considered valuable assets, and the transfer agreement between Nordisk Film and UFA therefore stipulated that Olsen should carry on as Director General of Nordisk Film for five years after the UFA takeover (BArch, R109–39). Another area where UFA could draw on Olsen's knowledge was in the organisation of the German company. Bock and Töteberg emphasise the way the newly established UFA represented a new and modern production mode in German cinema. German production companies had been family-run enterprises organised around an individual star or an entrepreneurial personality. UFA was a joint-stock company that created a German studio system with directors, cinematographers, art directors and so on, using modern marketing, cross-media and promotion campaigns prioritising a corporate identity (Bock and Töteberg 2020, 285). In this organisation of the film production, a lot could be learned from Olsen and Nordisk Film's efficient departmentalised mode of film production.

By the end of the war, Nordisk Film had lost most of its foreign investments, and the lucrative contracts according to which the films were pre-sold had expired; moreover, the company had gained a dubious reputation among the victorious allies. Olsen must have been aware of the new conditions Nordisk Film had to navigate because during the negotiations with UFA in November 1917, before signing an agreement, Olsen imposed the condition that UFA would buy films from the Danish company. This secured distribution of the company's films in Germany and Central Europe. UFA had to buy at least sixteen prints of each film, although the annual quantity of negatives should not exceed 50,000 metres (BArch, R109–39). From Nordisk Film's perspective, the agreement with UFA secured distribution of films, and to emphasise Nordisk Film's exceptional position, the company was granted a special import licence by the German Foreign Office at a time when a general import ban was in effect in Germany. In return, Nordisk Film gave up the rights to own or run cinemas as well as to produce films in Germany.

In purely industrial terms, the companies could benefit each other through distribution agreements, through knowledge transfer of efficient production practices and through access to international film business networks. But a fundamental asymmetry concerning nationality is traceable in the collaboration between Nordisk Film and UFA.

UFA was conceived as a national entity, with the backing of the German government, the military and influential businessmen. For instance, UFA bought Skandinavisk Films Union in the spring of 1918 to distribute German propaganda films in Scandinavia, and acquired the majority of the shares in the Copenhagen cinema Kinografen. A total of 60 per cent of the films shown in the cinema had to come from Skandinavisk Films Union and should mainly be German (Goergen 1994, 37). In this case, business considerations were subordinated to national interests. Nordisk Film on the other hand was a private limited and purely commercial company, with no connections to the Danish state. It had been an advantage to be situated in a neutral country during the war, but nationality as part of the promotion of the films was generally absent

(Schröder 2020). In the films from Nordisk Film, national traits were deliberately diminished or erased. Specific rules for avoiding the national and highlighting the international were formalised through the company's 'Guidelines for scriptwriters', rules and memos. Producing alternative endings for the films to suit different foreign markets as a production standard is another example of adapting the films for international sale (Thorsen 2017, 103–17).

The contrast between national and economic interests is clear in the case of the company Deutsche Lichtspiel Gesellschaft (DLG). Founded in 1916 by the German military, DLG can be seen as a precursor of UFA. Within the UFA organisation, DLG would promote propaganda and public information. In Olsen's view, DLG had no commercial potential whatsoever and should be sold off. From the minutes of the board of Nordisk Film, a recurrent complaint in the early collaboration with UFA was the bad management of the German company, with Olsen referring to the economic and industrial dispositions of UFA as 'The German Chaos' (NF: I,25 10 July 1919). The asymmetrical economic and political goals of UFA and Nordisk Film came to play an important role in the companies' entanglements.

DAFCO and Famous Players

In 1919, Nordisk Film and UFA formed the Copenhagen-based company Danish American Film Corporation (DAFCO). Looking back, influential German film merchant Lothar Stark described this in 1924 as 'the biggest deal ever in the movie world' (Østsjællands Folkeblad, 4 November 1925, 3). (Stark was a key figure in the German distribution of the films of Pat and Patachon; see Chapter 9, this volume.) The aim of this ambitious deal was to buy American films that had not been shown in Europe due to the war, and to use the distribution network and cinemas of UFA to circulate the films in Germany and Central Europe. For $3.7 million, DAFCO bought 955 first-class American films, with UFA and Nordisk Film each paying half – and Nordisk Film acting as the guarantor for the full amount. Part of UFA's management were very unhappy with the DAFCO deal because it violated 'a management resolution "to avoid under any circumstances" making contracts in foreign currencies' (Kreimeier 1996, 63, quoting the minutes of the UFA executive committee meeting, 30 December 1919). When the deal was closed in June 1919, one dollar was worth fourteen marks. By the end of the year, inflation had increased the value of the dollar to forty-two marks (Saunders 1994, 71). Even worse, the deal was based on the prediction of experts that the German government was about to end its ban on the import of foreign films, introduced in 1916, but the ban was kept in place. Because of UFA's close links to the German government, the company had hoped for an exemption, but the German film industry knew that the foreign company Nordisk Film was involved in the DAFCO deal, and because of this it was hard to justify an exemption. UFA and Nordisk Film were now stuck with 955 films they could not distribute on the scale they had hoped. UFA had borrowed the money, and as inflation rose, UFA's debt from the DAFCO deal increased to forty-seven million marks (Saunders 1994, 70). Because Nordisk was guarantor for the films, the DAFCO deal lay as a heavy burden on both companies. The import ban was partly lifted in December 1920 and a fair profit was gained on a few of the films, but the other films – now five to six years old – were no longer commercially attractive.

Concurrently with the DAFCO deal, Olsen had worked on a larger plan that caused a stir in the German film industry. Olsen was seen as solely responsible for the dangerous decisions that nearly took UFA into the abyss and was accused of signing the DAFCO deal as part of a bigger plan to take control of UFA with the aid of the American company Famous Players (*Lichtbild-Bühne*, 2 May 1921, 11). 'If the name Ole Olsen is associated with any business in the film industry, from that moment on that business is under sentence of death', *Lichtbild-Bühne* wrote in 1921. This resentment against Olsen and Nordisk Film was partly based on old animosity towards the Danish company's expansion on the German market during the war, but *Lichtbild-Bühne* was right: Olsen had indeed hoped to create a grand new transatlantic film coalition between UFA and Famous Players, with Nordisk Film in the middle.

Judging from the minutes of the board of directors, Olsen and Nordisk Film still dreamt of regaining a position as one of the most important film companies in the world, and in 1919 Olsen presented the board with a new plan. UFA had continuously asked Nordisk Film for loans and credits, which Olsen had refused. Instead, he worked on taking over the majority of shares in UFA in collaboration with Adolph Zukor, the head of Famous Players. Well into the spring of 1920 Olsen continued to work on this plan, and he was personally chosen by Adolph Zukor to oversee the negotiations with UFA (NF: I, 25 31 March 1920). Several of UFA's shareholders, including the German Ministry of Finance, were willing to sell their shares, but instead Deutsche Bank bought the shares and even expanded the capital to 100 million marks in 1921. Deutsche Bank had a clear national-political ambition of upholding a strong German film production (Kreimeier 1996, 72) and did not want to share influence in the company with either Nordisk Film or Famous Players.

Emerging from the episode with only 8.4 million marks' worth of the total of 100 million marks of shares, Nordisk Film lost its influence in UFA. Nordisk Film sold off the shares for 11 million marks, and as the Danish company was bound by a non-competition clause, the company could not start any new business on its own in Germany. The company chose to pull the money out of the country, but because of inflation, Nordisk obtained only a paltry 993,000 kroner for the 11 million marks (NF: I, 25 19 August 1921). The formal ties between UFA and Nordisk Film ended in March 1921, but Ole Olsen kept a seat on UFA's supervisory board (*Aufsichtsrat*), and Felix Kallmann from UFA got a seat on the board of directors of Nordisk Film.

Deutsch-Nordische-Films-Union

The separation sent the two companies in very opposite directions. Creative producer Eric Pommer joined UFA in late 1921, and with films like Fritz Lang's *Die Nibelungen* (*The Nibelungs*, 1924), F. W. Murnau's *Der letzte Mann* (*The Last Laugh*, 1924) and E. A. Dupont's *Varieté* (*Variety*, 1925), the German company set new artistic standards in European cinema. UFA expanded with distribution offices and subsidiaries in several European countries as well as in New York (Bock and Töteberg 2020, 287–8). While UFA moved into an artistic heyday, Nordisk Film licked its wounds. The losses on the DAFCO deal and the sale of the shares in UFA were visible in the annual accounts, showing a loss of 4.5 million kroner, half of Nordisk Film's share capital. From being a secure investment with good returns, Nordisk Film shares were now losing their value. By 1923, the debts had grown to 5.2 million kroner and constituted an unsustainable situation in the long run. The board considered the option of liquidating Nordisk Film altogether, but instead decided – on Kallmann's advice – to reduce the share capital from nine million kroner to three, and write off 778.678,49 kroner, primarily in old negatives (NF: I, 25. 6 February 1923). Among the shareholders, dissatisfaction spread, leading to the formation of a group headed by stockbroker Christian Bencard. The group began to buy up shares in Nordisk Film, eventually gaining enough influence on the board of Nordisk Film to change the management and board of directors. In 1924 Ole Olsen stepped down as Director General, which coincided with his earlier agreement with UFA to stay on for five years. Olsen had disposed of his shares in Nordisk Film prior to the war and was able to retire as one of the wealthiest men in Denmark.

Though the ties between Nordisk Film and UFA were cut, entanglements between Danish and German cinema continued. The UFA production *Der Mann ohne Namen – 1. Der Millionendieb* (*The Man Without a Name*, Georg Jacoby, 1921) was shot in Copenhagen (*Folkets Avis*, 26 October 1921). Norwegian actor Gunnar Tolnæs, who had been the major male star at Nordisk Film since Valdemar Psilander left the company in 1916, alternated between working for Nordisk Film and playing parts in German films. Danish directors like Robert Dinesen, Carl Th. Dreyer, A. W. Sandberg, Holger-Madsen and Benjamin Christensen, as well as cameraman Frederik Fuglsang and scriptwriter Harriet Bloch – all of whom except Christensen were former employees of Nordisk Film – went south to work in Germany.

The finances of Nordisk Film were in a sad state in the early 1920s, and the lack of operating capital prevented the company from making competitive films. The basis for distribution to the important German and Central European markets had disappeared with the break with UFA, and this is traceable in Nordisk Film's own production (Table 8.1). On average less than a handful of feature films were produced each year from 1921.

Table 8.1 Nordisk Film's film production 1918–1928

1918	1919	1920	1921	1922	1923	1924	1925	1926	1927	1928
65	52	12	11	3	4	7	5	3	2	1

Source: Thorsen 2017, 30.

In the meetings of the board of directors, the possibility of using foreign directors for future projects was discussed as well as the idea of making actual international co-productions. Negotiations in April 1925 with an English company did not lead to anything conclusive, but in May Nordisk Film was invited to enter a collaboration with the German distribution company Deutsch-Amerikanische-Films-Union (DAFU). DAFU was a minor stock company founded in Dresden in 1921 and was mainly connected to smaller firms like Kultur-Film AG and Humboldt GmbH, companies that specialised in making documentaries. DAFU enlarged and reorganised in January 1923 when it commenced a collaboration with Internationale Arbeitershilfe (IAH), originally formed by the German Communist Party in 1921, to gather and disperse funds and goods for famine relief in the Soviet Union. IAH extended its activities under the leadership of Willi Münzenberg to include import and distribution of Soviet films as well as providing aid to film production in the Soviet Union (Thompson 1992, 32–3). IAH formed its own distribution company *Prometheus* in 1925, which was probably the reason that IAH and DAFU separated.

DAFU was now on the lookout for potential partners, and the minutes of the board of Nordisk Film give a fairly detailed account of the company's early collaboration with the Danish company. In July 1925 Nordisk Film obtained half of the shares in DAFU for 60,000 gold marks, and DAFU became Deutsch-Nordische-Films-Union (DNFU). The managers of the German part of DNFU were Dr Oscar Horney and Edmund Herms, who had previously helped Nordisk Film with business in Germany. The expectation was to produce good average films, which would earn approximately 175,000 gold marks per film. With a deduction of 15,000 gold marks for copying and marketing, the profit would be shared equally between DNFU and Nordisk Film (NF I, 26, 11 May 1925). From a national perspective, the collaboration with DNFU opened new possibilities for Nordisk Film. Since the break with UFA, Nordisk Film had distributed its films in Germany through the UFA subsidiary company Deulig, but it had been an ongoing hassle for the Danish company to collect its payments. This was a general problem; other distributors in Europe were also slow to pay Nordisk Film. This may have been the result of a general economic downturn in Europe at the time, but it also bears witness to the fact that Nordisk Film was far from its former strength (NF I, 26, 27 January 1925).

Figure 8.2 'Die Deutsch-Nordische-Films-Union marschiert!' Full page advertisement in *Der Kinematograph*, 6 November 1925, 39.

Quotas and taxes on film to protect national interests were a common condition for the European film industries of the 1920s. As early as 1916 the German government introduced a general ban on the import of luxury goods, including film, and in January 1921 Germany introduced a quota on imported film, which meant that one company could only import the equivalent of 15 per cent of the negative film produced in Germany (Thompson 1985, 106). This quota system was known as 'Kontingentfilme' (quota films), and basically meant that if you wanted to export films to Germany, you needed either someone producing films in Germany to import your films, or to produce films in Germany yourself to obtain the 'Kontingent' to import. Siegfried Kracauer writes that many of the quota films were never released; their sole reason of existence was the acquisition of a 'Kontingentschein' (quota certificate) to be able to get films into Germany. 'In the cafés where the film agents met, these certificates were traded like stocks', Kracauer writes (2019, 133).

The collaboration with DNFU opened a path for the export of films from Nordisk Film to Germany, because DNFU possessed a quota Nordisk Film now could use. From the few surviving contracts and memos from DNFU concerning co-productions, it is clear that the 'Kontingent' belonged to DNFU, not to Nordisk Film (e.g. NF I, 5:75, NF I,4:65). The distribution ledgers of Nordisk Film also reveal that it was mostly a negative of the company's films that was sent to Berlin. This was because only the actual length of film counted in the quota, and DNFU was then able to print additional positive copies for distribution in Germany (NF XXII, 39).

The films imported and distributed by DNFU came from a variety of European countries. Naturally some of the films were produced by Nordisk Film, like the Dickens adaptation *Lille Dorrit* (*Little Dorrit*, 1924) and *Maharajahens Yndlingshustru* (*Oriental Love/The Favourite Wife of the Maharadja*, 1926). Among the others were films such as the German production *Die Biene Maja und ihre Abenteuer* (*The Adventures of Maya*, 1926) and the Soviet director Lev Kuleshov's *Dura Lex* (*By the Law*, 1926), two titles linking to DAFU's former ties with German film companies producing documentaries and the IAH.

In October 1925, DNFU wished to begin shooting its first feature film, but the company's working capital was too small to complete the shooting, and Nordisk Film lent DNFU 15,000 kroner. In December, manager Dr Horney had to put up his shares of DNFU as a guarantee for yet another loan. Nordisk Film continuously bought shares in DNFU, and by March 1926 Nordisk Film owned five-sixths of DNFU. The following month Dr Horney left the company and Herms became the new manager

(NF I, 26, 13 October 1925, 16 December 1925, 3 March 1926, 9 April 1926). Nordisk Film now possessed the majority of shares in DNFU, and in both the Danish press and the German trade papers, DNFU was described as a German subsidiary of Nordisk Film (*København*, 20 June 1927, 2). With the formation of DNFU a new trademark was introduced. Nordisk Film's familiar trademark with the polar bear roaring triumphantly on top of the globe was used as a template, but the polar bear was now walking arm in arm with a man in a German folk costume, signalling fraternisation and brotherhood between the Danish and German film industries (*Der Kinematograph*, 6 November 1925, 39). However, the trademark was soon changed back to Nordisk Film's familiar logo with the polar bear on the top of the globe, but with the name Deutsch-Nordische-Film-Union instead of Nordisk Films Kompagni.

Figure 8.3 The trademarks of DAFU and DNFU.

Nordisk Film entered twelve co-productions through DNFU from 1926 to 1928 (see Table 8.2), and it is noticeable that the agreements were made directly between Nordisk Film and the co-production companies, circumventing DNFU, confirming that the German firm was financially subordinate to Nordisk Film.

The DNFU co-productions will be discussed in more detail in the next section, but it is worth noting here that DNFU had not been satisfied with the quality of the first productions from 1926. This is evident from a memo about DNFU's production for the 1927/1928 season. The memo urges everyone to put in their strongest efforts during the forthcoming season because the competition was going to be even harder, especially from America, given the Parufamet deal (NF I, 5:75). The Parufamet agreement between Paramount, MGM and UFA resulted from UFA having had to turn to the American film industry for a loan due to financial trouble in 1925. UFA obtained a loan of $4 million and was guaranteed distribution of ten of the company's films annually in the US. In Germany, the three companies set up a joint rental company, which would distribute twenty Paramount and twenty MGM films a year. If the Parufamet agreement was a means of raising capital for UFA and securing some sort of outlet for their films in the US, from an American perspective it was basically a means of gaining import certificates to release films in Germany (Thompson 1999, 61).

The agreements between DNFU and their co-production partners reveal at what markets the films were aimed. In general, the rights for distribution in Germany and Scandinavia belonged to DNFU, the rights to the rest of Europe including Turkey sometimes went to the co-production partner, and in other cases were divided equally between the partners with a 10 per cent provision to the company that did the actual sale. Only in one case is an overseas (non-European) market mentioned: South America (e.g. I, 5:75, I,4:65). The division of the markets is telling for which markets were considered lucrative, and at no time is the US mentioned as a potential market.

Table 8.2 Deutsch-Nordische-Film-Union's co-productions

Year	Title	Director(s)	Co-production company
1926	*Bushidô: Das eiserne Gesetz*	Karl Heiland/ Zanmu Kako	Heiland Film/Toa Tojin (Japan)
1926	*Das Rätsel von Borobudur*	Karl Heiland	Heiland Film
1926	*Die weisse Geisha*	Karl Heiland/ Valdemar Andersen	Heiland Film
1927	*Eine tolle Nacht*	Richard Oswald	Richard Oswald Produktion
1927	*Funkzauber*	Richard Oswald	Richard Oswald Produktion
1927	*Gehetzte Frauen*	Richard Oswald	Richard Oswald Produktion
1927	*Das Geheimnisse des Abbé X*	Julius Brandt/ William Dieterle	Charha Film
1927	*Ich habe im Mai von Liebe geträumt*	Franz Seitz	Charha Film
1927	*Da hält die Welt in Atem an*	Felix Basch	Lothar Stark Film
1927	*Ein schwerer Fall*	Felix Basch	Max Sperling & Ossi Oswalda Film-Produktion
1927	*Das brennende Schiff*	Constatin J. David	Sascha Goron Paris
1927	*Ich hatte einst ein schönes Vaterland*	Max Mack	Aco Film-Althoff-Film

The years of 1927 and 1928 were turbulent ones for Nordisk Film, where finances were still strained, and in the late summer of 1927, DNFU directors Edmond Herms and Heinrich Graf joined the board of Nordisk Film (*Folkets Avis*, 17 August 1927). In the Nordisk Special Collection at the Danish Film Institute, there are very few documents from the early months of 1928, when Nordisk was approaching bankruptcy. But regardless of the difficult financial situation, further entanglements between Nordisk and DNFU were added. Dr Rudolph Becker, the director of DNFU and the former head of foreign sales at UFA, became the new General Director of Nordisk Film on 21 April 1928. Becker was now in charge of both Nordisk Film and DNFU, and most of the decisions were made in Berlin. DNFU seems to have become the economic basis of Nordisk Film, and a staff list from 1928 gives an impression of the size of DNFU. The company had 78 employees in 6 offices across Germany: 27 in the main office in Berlin, 8 in Munich, 9 in Hamburg, 10 in Düsseldorf, 14 in Leipzig and 9 at a Berlin branch office (NF I, 8:91).

Member of Nordisk Film's board Svend Aage Funder could report from a visit to the German capital that Becker 'possessed a speed and energy which for a slow Dane like me is entirely admirable' (NF I, 8:96). Becker was highly engaged in putting together a programme for DNFU's 1928/1929 season. The plan was to acquire and co-produce around fifteen films, at an expected cost of 1.4 million Reichsmarks, and hopefully gain a return of 2.5 million Reichsmarks. However, this proved to be nearly impossible as no one would give the company credit (NF I, 8:96). But in May 1928 the company placed a full-page advertisement in *Lichtbild-Bühne* proclaiming the countdown to the disclosure of the company's films for the season, which would happen on 2 June (*Lichtbild-Bühne*, 26 May 1928, 15). It seems like the wealthy stockbroker Carl Bauder, who had been Nordisk Film's secret benefactor from the mid-1920s, once again put up the capital to accomplish the plans of DNFU. On 2 June Becker announced that DNFU would have twenty '*Grossfilmen*' ('big movies') ready for the 1928/1929 season, and *Lichtbild-Bühne* gave a detailed account of the coming films, their directors and stars (*Lichtbild-Bühne*, 2 June 1928, 20). The same day, just after the Copenhagen stock exchange had opened, the board of Nordisk Film reported that the company had suspended its payments. An explanation for the action was given in a later message. The new Director General Rudolph Becker had worked hard with promising results, but an indictment against the former director of Nordisk Film, Christian Bencard, had caused the termination of all the company's credit in Germany (*Børsen*, 3 June 1928). Bencard was accused of spreading rumours about Nordisk Film to increase the value of the company's shares.

In a detailed statement of the financial situation of Nordisk Film, issued less than a month after the firm had suspended payments, the assets were estimated at 308.890,02 kroner and the debts at 2.871.639,07 kroner. DNFU's share of the debts was 1.209.127,94, which was considered irrecoverable claims (NF I, 8:195, 1, 5–7).

DNFU went into receivership and closed in October 1928. Rudolph Becker travelled to London and became General Manager of the British Associated Sound Film Industries in 1929 (Low 1985, 183). The production of *Metropolis* (1927) brought UFA into a severe economic crisis, and the company was bought by Alfred Hugenberg. In 1929, Bauder once again lent money to Nordisk Film, this time some hundreds of thousands of kroner, and re-established the company.

Film Europe and the DNFU Co-productions

The development of co-productions and migration of film workers coincides with a general movement in the 1920s European film production, often referred to as 'Film Europe'. Andrew Higson has written about the movement:

> The argument was that, through such collaborations, the strongest and most ambitious European film companies might be able to establish the sort of critical mass, industrial integration, and market-size that the Hollywood studios enjoyed. The hope was that this would enable European companies to compete on more equal terms with Hollywood, and especially to regain a greater share of the various European markets. (Higson 2010, 71)

In the middle of World War I, Ole Olsen had argued in a similar way when explaining why Nordisk Film was buying cinemas and film companies in Germany, Central Europe, Scandinavia and Russia. According to Olsen, Nordisk was preparing for the end of the war, when, as Olsen correctly foresaw, the American film industry would flood the markets, spelling the death of the European film industry ('Interview' 1916, 25–6).

By 1925, the share of American films shown in Danish cinemas was around 64 per cent, and in Germany it was approximately 42 per cent (Thompson 1985, 107, 129, based on Canty 1928, 4, Bureau 1928, 7). This relatively modest share is indicative of Germany's unique position on the European film market. For years, Germany was one of the only countries in Europe resisting the American takeover by imposing embargos and quotas on imports (Thompson 1985, 106). The fear and resentment of American dominance is traceable in the Danish press, where a certain discourse emerged surrounding the films from UFA. When the Danish distribution company Fotorama began distributing films from UFA, a newspaper commented that it was a small step in the fight against 'the Americans' parasitizing of the European film market' (*Klokken 5*, 8 January 1926, 2). Another newspaper reported on the German film industry's 'hopeless fight against the American film's dictatorial dominion' (*Holstebro Dagblad*, 31 August 1925, 3). German film and particularly UFA were seen as a last defence against the American film industry.

In his analysis of the Film Europe trend, Higson has summarised:

> The goal was not to produce 'European' films that stood above national interests. On the contrary, the goal was to produce films that were carefully tailored to the perceived interests of audiences in different national or language markets: films that might appear to those audiences as national films, thereby effectively undermining any pretensions towards internationalism. Films could be further 'localised' or 'nationalised' at the point of distribution, through re-titling the film, through producing a new set of intertitles, or through promoting one particular, familiar star rather than another. (Higson 2010, 77)

The co-productions between Nordisk Film and DNFU can be seen as part of the Film Europe movement. How the first productions came about is unclear. Apparently German, traveller, writer, cameraman, producer and director Heinz Karl Heiland had continuously shot footage on a lengthy journey through Japan, China and India between 1924 and 1926 (Haukamp 2021, 29). On his return to Europe, some of this footage was used in three fiction films co-produced with DNFU and Nordisk Film. *Bushidô: Das eiserne Gesetz* ('Bushido: The Iron Law', 1926), co-produced with the Japanese company Toa Tojin and directed by Heiland and Japanese director Zanmu Kako, is considered 'Japan's first international co-production' (Haukamp 2021, 29). *Die Weisse Geisha* ('The White Geisha', 1926) was co-directed with Valdemar Andersen, co-produced with Toa Tojin, and partly shot on Nordisk Film's lot with Danish actors. In Denmark *Die Weisse Geisha* was advertised as 'The season's fourth Danish film from Nordisk Film Co.' (*Roskilde Avis*, 22 March 1927, 5). Nordisk Film only produced two films the year *Die Weisse Geisha* was released, and by calling it the fourth production of the year the German film promotion localises the film to a Danish national context.

The third Heiland film, *Das Rätsel von Borobudur* ('The Riddle of Borobodur', 1926), was shot on Java. The attraction of the three Heiland films was the exotic locations of the Far East. In Germany an interest in Japanese culture in the mid-1920s was fuelled by theatre, literature and lectures (Haukamp 2021, 30), and the Heiland films connect to this current. In *Der Kinematograph*'s review, *Bushidô: Das eiserne Gesetz* was labelled 'primitive' and 'not first class'. The film included exotic scenery, hara-kiri, a lance-fight and a storm on a castle, and it was interesting to watch 'the yellow sons of heaven', but the right venue for the film should have been a cinema club (*Der Kinematograph*, 15 May 1927, 19). The Danish reception of *Das Rätsel von Borobudur* was not generous either: 'There was every reason to "shoot the piano player" – this film was extremely naïve, bereft of artistic taste, endlessly boring and poorly directed' (*Nationaltidende*, 4 May 1927, 3).

The three Heiland films offered exotic stories from the other side of the world, whereas DNFU's scheduled productions for the following season seemed to go in two directions: productions aimed at a local German audience and films made in the international Film Europe trend.[1] DNFU engaged in three co-productions with the highly productive German director Richard Oswald and his production company. Oswald's 'Ein Rundfunkfilm', later known as *Funkzauber* (*Radio Magic*, 1927), had to be ready for a grand radio exhibition in the Berlin Beba Palast in September 1927. The promotion of the film was free of charge as the German Reichs-Rundfunk would promote it through the radio to every part of the country, accompanied by a competition of coming up with a proper title for the film (NF I, 5:75). Though the big-name German star Werner Krauss played the lead in the episodic film, *Der Kinematograph* considered *Funkzauber* below the normal standard of an Oswald film. The journal thought of the film as a 'Werbefilm', an advertisement, for the new radio medium and wondered if its propaganda-like message was suited for cinemas at all (*Der Kinematograph*, 2 October 1927, 20). *Funkzauber* was a film made for and aimed at a German public. The same was possibly the case with the patriotic war film *Ich hatte einst ein schönes Vaterland* ('I Once Had a Beautiful Fatherland', 1927), directed by Max Mack, and *Ich habe im Mai von Liebe geträumt* ('I Dreamt of Love in May', 1927), a rural romance directed by Franz Seitz about a young woman and her two suitors, one the son of a miller and the other a musician. The latter film was compared with the novels of the popular German author Ludvig Ganghofer, presenting an idyllic depiction of village life (*Der Kinematograph*, 21 August 1927).

Ich habe im Mai von Liebe geträumt seems like a story which could also be 'localised' in markets outside of Germany, and a way of making films appear local, national or familiar, and thereby waking the interests of audiences in different national or language markets, is to refer to already known and familiar stories and genres. This can be found in some of the DNFU productions. *Eine tolle Nacht* (*A Crazy Night*, 1927) was a comedy with Harry Liedtke and Ossi Oswalda a about a naïve businessman who arrives in the metropolis of Berlin in search of a variety dancer he fancies. In *Das Geheimnis des Abbé X* (aka *Der Mann, der nicht lieben darf; Behind the Altar*, 1927), Wilhelm Dieterle (who also co-directed the film with Julius Brandt) played an abbot secretly in love with the widow of his dead brother. Both are familiar stories which could easily be localised in other nations. A recurrent critique in *Der Kinematograph*'s reviews of the films from DNFU was their stereotypicality and lack of inventiveness. *Da hält die Welt den Atem an* (*Make Up*, 1927) draws on 'the already established template of the backstage film', wrote the journal (*Der Kinematograph* 13 March 1927, 27). The plot of *Le bateau de verre* (*The Glass Boat*, German title: *Das brennende Schiff*, 1927) was nothing new, according to the review in *Der Kinematograph* (18 December 1927, 22). The same was said about *Das Geheimnis des Abbé X* (*Der Kinematograph* 11 December 1927, 18).

A characteristic of the Film Europe trend was films with a mixed cast of European stars. Felix Basch's *Da hält die Welt den Atem an* (*Make Up*, 1927) was a '*Revuefilm*', a variety show picture produced by Lothar Stark. It was shot at the Moulin Rouge in Paris and featured the peripatetic Italian star Marcella Albani, who also made films in Italy, France and Czechoslovakia, the Russian-born French star Sandra Milovanoff, and the German Werner Krauss. Another was *Le bateau de verre*, co-produced with the French company Sascha Goron and featuring French, German and Swedish actors.

Comparing the films produced by DNFU in Germany with the ones shot by Nordisk Film in Denmark reveals certain similarities. The company's prestigious Dickens adaptations, which were clearly situated in Britain, show a sensibility open to national settings, and perhaps to the possibility of export. Other productions, such as *Kærligheds-Øen* (*Honey-Moon Island*, 1924), are set in familiar but decontextualised settings transcending the national. Nordisk Film also made use of European actors in their non-co-production films, like the German actresses with the anglicised names, Mary Kid and Mary Parker. *Klovnen* (*The Golden Clown*, Sandberg, 1926) is perhaps the best example of a film made as an international production during the Film Europe trend. It had a mixed cast of Europeans, including the Swedish star Gösta Ekman and the famous French actor Maurice de Féraudy, and was partly shot in France.

Nordisk Film's big gamble in 1928 was *Jokeren/Der Faschingskönig* (*The Joker*, 1928), based on a British play by Noel Scott and directed by German Georg Jacoby. The cast was an international mixture of British actors Henry Edwards and Miles Mander, French actors Gabriel Gabrio and Renée Héribel, the German actress Elga Brink and the Danish actors Philip Bech and Aage Hertel. Shot in Copenhagen, Berlin and

'DIE DEUTSCH-NORDISCHE-FILM-UNION MARSCHIERT!' 203

Figure 8.4 The last feature produced by Nordisk Film in the silent era, *The Joker*. Danish Film Institute.

Nice, this was indeed a European film intended to have an international appeal. The cost of *The Joker* was 342.252,97 kroner, making the film very expensive compared with the company's two prior productions: *Den sørgmuntre Barber* ('The Tragi-Comic Barber', 1927) cost 46.305,85 kroner and *Dydsdragonen* ('The Plaster Saint', 1927) 57.870,11 kroner (NF I, 8:195, 9).

In some places the film is credited as a co-production between DNFU and the German company Horwa-Goron, though in Nordisk Film's numbering of its own production *The Joker* received no. 1880. The reason is probably because the finances of Nordisk Film and DNFU were now so entangled that it was hard to distinguish which of the companies stood behind the film. During the filming of the spectacular carnival interior scenes, which were shot in Berlin, problems arose with payments of the salaries, and Danish cameraman Poul Eibye even threatened to leave the production and ride all the way from Berlin to Copenhagen on his bicycle if he didn't get his payment (Nielsen 1976). *The Joker* became the last film produced by Nordisk Film before the company suspended its payments in June 1928.

A Common Culture?

The entanglements between the Danish and German film industry were numerous in the years from 1918 to 1928. This study has focused on Nordisk Film's interconnections with the company's most important export market in the silent era, Germany. The underlying assumption has been that the engine of the collaborations between Nordisk Film and UFA, and later DNFU, was partly economic and industrial necessity, partly economic opportunity. The intentional formation of a common Danish-German film culture did not play a part to the same degree.

When Nordisk Film lost its business network in Germany and Central Europe in 1918, one of the company's main goals was to survive as a business, upholding a continuous transnational distribution of films. UFA could help in achieving this goal. However, this did not stop Olsen and Nordisk Film's dreams of returning to the company's former glory on the international film market. The entanglements with UFA made it possible to enter the DAFCO deal as well as paving the way for the attempt to take control of UFA together with American film mogul Adolph Zukor. After the break with UFA, Nordisk Film needed to engage in a company with a quota license in Germany. DAFU had lost its agreement with IAH and needed a new business partner, and together Nordisk Film and DAFU formed DNFU. The entangled history approach takes into consideration the diachronic point of view stressing the non-stability of the compared entities. In the post-World War I years, Nordisk Film and UFA as well as DNFU developed and changed considerably, in some cases even in their interactions with each other. Instead of comparison, the entangled history perspective focuses on the relations, contrasts and reciprocities of the involved film companies.

Transnationality is a keyword in entangled history, and Higson argues that border crossings take place on two overall levels: on the level of production and activities of filmmakers and on the level of distribution and exhibition. The entanglements between Nordisk Film, UFA and DNFU unfolded on these two levels and are expressions of this fundamental transnationality in cinema. The entanglements between Nordisk Film and UFA and DNFU demonstrate that cinema's underlying transnationality is not just something abstract and ideal. It was in the economic interest of both large and small businesses to build links with other companies. Building up businesses, growing economic trade and expanding markets are all parts of the transnationality of cinema. We cannot, however, simply dismiss the category of the nation altogether. UFA was imbedded in a national context, and import limitations and quotas were obstructions in border crossings connected to nationality.

Do these entanglements then constitute a common film culture between 1918 and 1928? The character of 1920s European cinema, including the Danish and German film industries, is difficult to separate from the major industrial shift as American companies entered Europe. Perhaps the film culture of Nordisk Film's entanglements with Germany rather connects to general transnational trends in post-war European cinema than constituting a specific Danish-German film culture. There is no evidence that anyone tried to create a certain Danish-German culture through their films. Comparing the films co-produced between Nordisk Film, DNFU and other European companies with Higson's characteristics of films made within the Film Europe movement, they resemble films made in other European countries. In this sense a specific Danish-German common film culture seems absent. In Higson's opinion, the goal of the Film Europe movement was not to produce film that stood above national interests. Elaborating on this, the Danish-German films produced by DNFU do in a few cases connect to a specifically German cultural context, but the Danish national context is absent. Due to the overall nature of the films produced by Nordisk Film, where nationality was subdued to enhance the potential of export, it is difficult to isolate a particular national culture in the films from Nordisk Film. In this sense, neither do the films produced by Nordisk Film in the 1920s nor those produced by DNFU point to a particular Danish-German common film culture, but rather to the overall trends in European film production during the decade.

Note

I am grateful to Andrew Higson for comments and suggestions in the writing of this chapter.

1. Unfortunately, it has not been possible for me to watch the films co-produced by DNFU. Apparently, *Die Weisse Geisha*, *Eine tolle Nacht*, *Da hält die Welt in Atem an*, *Bushidô: Das eiserne Gesetz* and *Ich hatte einst ein schönes Vaterland* have all survived in Gosfilmofond in Russia. Cinémathèque royale de Belgique has a print of *Das Geheimnis des Abbé X*. A 217-meter nitrate fragment of *Funkzauber* in bad condition is held by Deutsche Kinemathek in Berlin, and the Bundesarchiv and British Film Institute hold copies of *Da hält die Welt in Atem an*. *Eine tolle Nacht* has been digitised but is not available for private viewing; an eight-minute fragment of the film is available on YouTube: https://www.youtube.com/watch?v=qft4pI1Udw0 (Accessed 27 June 2022).

References

BArch, R109-139. Bundesarchiv-Filmarchiv R109-139. Deutscher Besitz, Nordisk Kopenhagen. Bundesarchiv, Berlin-Lichterfelde.

Blom, Ivo. 2003. *Jean Desmet and the Early Dutch Film Trade*. Amsterdam: Amsterdam University Press.

Bock, Hans-Michael and Michael Töteberg. 2020. 'A History of UFA.' In *The German Cinema Book*, edited by Tim Bergfelder, Erica Carter, Deniz Göktürk and Claudia Sandberg, 285–96. London: Bloomsbury.

Bordwell, David. 1996. 'Contemporary Film Studies and the Vicissitudes of Grand Theory.' In *Post Theory. Reconstructing Film Studies*, edited by David Bordwell and Noël Carroll, 3–36. Madison: University of Wisconsin Press.

Bordwell, David. 2006. 'Nordisk and the Tableau Aesthetic.' In *100 Years of Nordisk Film*, edited by Dan Nissen and Lisbeth Richter Larsen, 80–95. Copenhagen: Det Danske Filminstitut.

Bureau of Foreign and Domestic Commerce, Motion Picture Section. 1928. *Market for Motion Pictures in Scandinavia and the Baltic States*. Trade Information Bulletin no. 553. Washington, DC: United States Department of Commerce.

Canty, George R. 1928. *The European Motion-Picture Industry in 1927*. Trade Information Bulletin no. 542. Washington, DC: United States Department of Commerce.

Christensen, Thomas C. and Lisbeth Richter Larsen. 2021. 'Film Heritage Streaming at the Danish Film Institute.' *Journal of Film Preservation*, no. 104 (April): 105–12.

Cronqvist, Maria and Christoph Hilgert. 2017. 'Entangled Media Histories. The Value of Transnational and Transmedial Approaches in Media Historiography.' *Media History* 23, no. 1: 130–41.

'Interview med Ole Olsen.' 1916. *Filmen* 5, no. 3 (15 November): 25–6.

Goergen, Jeanpaul. 1994. 'Neue Filme haben wir nicht erhalten. Die deutsche Filmpropaganda 1917/18 in Dänemark.' In *Schwarzer Traum und weisse Sklavin: deutsche-dänische filmbeziehungen 1910–1930*, edited by Manfred Behn, 30–40. München: edition text+kritik.

Hagener, Malte, ed. 2014. *The Emergence of Film Culture. Knowledge Production, Institution Building, and the Fate of the Avant-garde in Europe, 1919–1945*. New York: Berghahn Books.

Haukamp, Iris. 2021. *A Foreigner's Cinematic Dream of Japan. Representational Politics and Shadows of War in the Japanese-German Co-production*. New Earth (1937). London: Bloomsbury Academics.

Higson, Andrew. 2000. 'The Limiting Imagination of National Cinema.' In *Cinema and Nation*, edited by Mette Hjort and Scott Mackenzie, 57–68. London: Routledge.

———. 2010. 'Transnational Developments in European Cinema in the 1920s.' *Transnational Cinemas* 1, no. 1: 69–82.

Higson, Andrew and Richard Maltby, eds. 1999. *'Film Europe' and 'Film America'. Cinema, Commerce and Cultural Exchange, 1920–1939*. Exeter: University of Exeter Press.
Kracauer, Siegfried. 2019. *From Caligari to Hitler. A Psychological History of the German Film*. Princeton: Princeton University Press.
Kreimeier, Klaus. 1996. *The UFA Story. A History of Germany's Greatest Film Company 1918–1945*. New York: Hill and Wang.
Low, Rachael. 1985. *The History of British Film*. Vol. 7. London: George Allen & Unwin.
NF. Nordisk Film Collection, Danish Film Institute, Copenhagen.
Nielsen, Joachim, II. 1976. Interview with Joachim Nielsen II, conducted by Arne Krogh and unknown, 7 October 1976. The Danish Film Institute.
Olsen, Ole. 1940. *Filmens Eventyr og mit eget*. Copenhagen: Jespersen og Pios Forlag.
Saunders, Thomas J. 1994. 'Von Dafco zu Damra.' In *Das Ufa-Buch. Kunst und Krisen, Stars und Regisseure, Wirtschaft und Politik*, edited by Hans-Michael Bock and Michael Töteberg, 70–1. Frankfurt am Main: Zweitausendeins.
Schröder, Stephan Michael. 2020. 'On the "Danishness" of Danish Films in Germany until 1918.' *Kosmorama* no. 276 (www.kosmorama.org).
Shaw, Deborah. 2017. 'Transnational Cinema: Mapping a Field of Study.' In *The Routledge Companion to World Cinema*, edited by Rob Stone, Paul Cooke, Stephanie Dennison and Alex Marlow-Mann, 290–8. London: Routledge.
Thompson, Kristin. 1985. *Exporting Entertainment. America in the World Film Market 1907–1935*. London: BFI Publishing.
———. 1999. 'The Rise and Fall of Film Europe.' In *'Film Europe' and 'Film America'. Cinema, Commerce and Cultural Exchange, 1920–1939*, edited by Andrew Higson and Richard Maltby, 56–81. Exeter: University of Exeter Press.
———. 2003. 'Government Policies and Practical Necessities in the Soviet Cinema of the 1920's.' In *The Red Screen. Politics, Society, Art in Soviet Cinema*, edited by Anna Lawton, 19–41. London: Routledge.
Thorsen, Isak. 2017. *Nordisk Films Kompagni 1906-1924. The Rise and Fall of the Polar Bear*. East Barnet: John Libbey Publishing.
Vitali, Valentina and Paul Willemen, eds. 2006. *Theorising National Cinema*. London: BFI Publishing.
Werner, Michael and Bénédicte Zimmermann. 2006. 'Histoire Croisée and the Challenge of Reflexivity.' *History and Theory* 45, no. 1: 30–50.

CHAPTER 9

Pat and Patachon as Transnational Film Stars

Jannie Dahl Astrup

The comedy double act Pat and Patachon ('Fyrtaarnet og Bivognen' in Danish) starred in forty-eight films between 1921 and 1940. The Danish production company Palladium produced most of these, thus becoming the only other film company in Denmark – besides Nordisk Films Kompagni – to maintain a steady production throughout the 1920s. The films quickly reached large audiences outside Denmark, conquering screens in Scandinavia, across the European continent, Russia and many other places. Particularly important were Germany and Austria, where the cinemagoing audience became acquainted with the Danish duo under the character names 'Pat' and 'Patachon' in 1923. Excluding the debut film, *Landsvägsriddare* (*Love and Burglars*) from 1921, and the Danish sound film *Med fuld Musik* (literally: 'With Full Music') from 1933, the characters of Pat and Patachon were played by actors Carl Schenstrøm and Harald Madsen in the forty-six remaining films. Alongside the Palladium productions (thirty-five in total), actors Schenstrøm and Madsen were also loaned out to film companies making Pat and Patachon films outside of Denmark. These foreign Pat and Patachon films account for thirteen productions in total from 1925 through 1937. All the films – both those produced by Palladium and by other companies – enjoyed wide international success. Spanning well into the era of sound film, Pat and Patachon were not just a silent film phenomenon. Eleven out of the entire body of work of forty-eight films are sound films, thus underlining the Danish film duo's longevity as a popular act in both the silent and the sound era in a wide array of countries.

Which factors best explain the popularity of Pat and Patachon outside of Denmark? In this chapter, I will examine two threads in connection to their fame in Germany and Austria. First, I will examine the films produced in these countries starring the Danish double act (five in Austria and three in Germany). Second, I will look at the different entanglements of business partners, production companies, film consortiums and the press discourse on Pat and Patachon in Germany and Austria.

The research literature often emphasises Germany as a main market for Pat and Patachon films. Moreover, it was where Palladium's primary foreign distributor from 1923 and onward, Lothar Stark, was situated, and the production country of three of their foreign films. As Joseph Garncarz describes in *Medienwandel* (2016, 134), films with Pat and Patachon were very popular with German cinemagoers in the latter part of the 1920s, consistently ranking high in annual polls conducted among German cinema owners by the trade press publication *Film-Kurier*. In other words, Germany makes an interesting case for examining all sorts of transnational entanglements and cross-border interconnections in relation to Palladium and their two stars.

Austria provides other perspectives, since this was where a legal case on the rights to the German character names 'Pat' and 'Patachon' took place from 1925 to 1927. Furthermore, Austrian film companies produced both silent and sound films with Pat and Patachon, while also being the main country of interest for Palladium, when directors Svend Nielsen and Lau Lauritzen considered re-locating the entire film company in both 1924 and 1926.

When film stars Carl Schenstrøm and Harald Madsen travelled from city to city throughout the 1920s and 1930s, enormous crowds in Germany and Austria greeted them. Mayors and ambassadors welcomed them, and the duo appeared on the covers of magazines. The Danish press was virtually brimming with bold headlines and lengthy articles on the phenomenal 'World success' of Denmark's very own 'Fy og Bi' (as the duo is affectionately nicknamed in Danish). A professional journalist was hired to accompany Palladium's two stars on a promotional tour through Germany and Austria on their way to a shoot in Vienna, and the sensational headline from Berlin read: 'Pat and Patachon Stop Traffic on Potsdamer Platz' (*Politiken*, 24 March 1925). Palladium's international sales agent Arthur G. Gregory also played a significant role in promoting Pat and Patachon outside of Denmark. After the advent of sound, the English-born Gregory signed on as the duo's international agent, striking deals with foreign film companies to produce Pat and Patachon films. The films made in Germany and Austria in the mid-1930s are thus the result of Gregory's connections in the film industry.

Palladium, Pat and Patachon and the actors portraying them, their German distributor and their English sales agent all played significant roles in connection with establishing and maintaining the films' high level of success in Germany and Austria. Through an examination of these entangled issues, this article illuminates the interconnectedness of the agents and interests at work in the film industry, both during the silent era and after the transition to sound.

Pat and Patachon's Place in Film Historiography

Before examining the productions in detail, I will call attention to Pat and Patachon's place in film historiography, zooming in on the international, non-Palladium films featuring the Danish double act and exploring the degree to which they feature in academic publications and books on film history. Excluding the publications written in Danish, where silent film scholar Marguerite Engberg's *Fy & Bi* (1980) ranks as the most comprehensive study and a series of articles by Carl Nørrested (1991; 1996; 1996a) draws attention to issues of distribution and Palladium's border-crossing activities, the German-language *Pat und Patachon. Dokumentation* (1979) written by Hauke Lange-Fuchs (in co-operation with Engberg) is the only monograph published detailing both actors, Palladium director Lau Lauritzen and the full filmography of the duo – including Austrian and German productions. Lange-Fuchs summarises his points in a short, English-language article (2014), stressing the popularity of Pat and Patachon in Germany. Much along this line, Engberg recapitulates in English in an article focusing on Palladium and the silent films with Pat and Patachon in the anthology *Nordic Explorations. Film Before 1930* (Fullerton and Olsson 1999). As Engberg primarily covers the silent era, she only calls attention to the two Austrian silent films; *Zwei Vagabunden im Prater* ('Two Vagabonds in the Prater', 1925) and *Schwiegersöhne* ('Sons-in-Law', 1926): 'Two Austrian directors also tried their hands with Long and Short [the duo was called Long and Short in England]. But only a fragment from one of these films has survived. The film was too compressed and somewhat inept' (Engberg 1999, 61). Not belonging to what Engberg labels the 'typical' (Enberg 1980, 52–89) Pat and Patachon films, and what director Lauritzen in 1925, in a somewhat derogatory term, calls an 'Extra film' in the Danish newspaper *Klokken 5* (28 March 1925), the foreign Pat and Patachon productions seem almost destined to a life in the shadows of film history.

Previous research into Austrian film history in the period in focus here, 1925–1937, shows little or no interest in the films produced in the country featuring Pat and Patachon. Even Robert Dassanowsky's *Screening Transcendence* (2018), which deals specifically with the period 1933–1938 in Austrian film, does not include discussions on any of the Pat and Patachon films made during these years. There are numerous mentions of E. W. Emo and Carl Lamac; the directors behind *Zirkus Saran* ('Circus Saran', 1935) and *Pat und Patachon im Paradies* ('Pat and Patachon in Paradise', 1937). The producers Arnold Pressburger and Gregor Rabinowitsch also feature on numerous occasions in Dassanowsky's volume. Their production company Cine-Allianz Tonfilm made the 1932 sound film *Lumpenkavaliere*

Figure 9.1 *Schwiegersöhne* (1926, Hans Steinhoff). Danish poster by Sven Brasch. Danish Film Institute.

('Cavaliers in Rags'). It was directed by the German Carl Boese but shot in Vienna.

Despite the prevalence of Pat and Patachon films in German cinemas during the 1920s and 1930s, the Danish duo rarely appears in literature exploring German/Weimar film and film culture. Mentions in passing best describes the way film historiography – when dealing with Germany in this period – handles Pat and Patachon. In this vein, Corinna Müller (2003, 47) includes a very brief discussion of a silent Pat and Patachon film, *Hr. Tell og Søn* (*William Tell and Son*), directed by Lau Lauritzen in 1930, in her work on the transition from silent to sound film in Germany. Citing a contemporary review in *Der Film*, Müller points to the fact that even though sound film was prevailing in Germany in October 1930, both audience members and film reviewers were enthusiastic in their response to the still silent Pat and Patachon comedies produced by Palladium. As mentioned, Joseph Garncarz (2004, 57–64; 2016, 131–7) also highlights the popularity of Pat and Patachon in Germany in the context of a broader discussion of the producers Arnold Pressburger and Gregor Rabinowitsch and their knack for choosing the right stars and making films with a broad appeal to the European audiences through their Berlin-based production company Cine-Allianz Tonfilm. This exploration also considers the aforementioned *Lumpenkavaliere*, thereby connecting the dots between Denmark, Germany and Austria. In his biography of German director and infamous Nazi propagandist Hans Steinhoff, Horst Claus (2013) writes about the Pat and Patachon film *Schwiegersöhne* (1926). Like Garncarz, Claus stresses the fact that the duo's films, including this one directed by Steinhoff (but shot in Austria), were popular with audiences: 'Pat and Patachon films were crowd favourites that could be sold in other countries for a lot of money' (Claus 2013, 118). Writing about the production and distribution strategy of the German company Prometheus Film-Verleih und Vertriebs-GmbH, Bruce Murray calls attention to how one of the titles of the films produced by Prometheus in 1926, *Kladd und Datsch, die Pechvögel* ('Kladd and Datsch, The Jinxes'), 'evoked an association with the very successful Pat und Patachon film series' (Murray 1990, 122).

Anne Bachmann (2013) explores inter-Scandinavian silent film culture in her doctoral thesis. In a chapter dedicated to the 'joint proprietorship' (Bachmann 2013, 181–218) of Pat and Patachon in Sweden and Norway in the 1920s, she tracks various transnational negotiations in relation to the two Danish film comedians. For example, similarities and differences in character names, film titles, audience reception and press discourse. Bachmann focuses primarily on the silent era and Scandinavia, so German and Austrian films with Pat and Patachon are mostly discussed as instances where the Scandinavian countries seem to agree that these films were inferior to the Danish Palladium productions:

> In the discourse, noses were collectively turned up at the foreign-made films featuring Fy and Bi *outside* of Scandinavia. Within the Scandinavian countries, there

was a nearly joint or more exactly strongly overlapping sense of who was entitled to use and understand the Fy and Bi format, and who was not. (Bachmann 2013, 182)

Bachmann concludes by challenging the notion that the series of films with Pat and Patachon only fits within a framework of Danish national cinema (Bachmann 2013, 217). She specifically argues for the advantages of 'a historiographic approach' when looking to uncover the transnational nature of the Pat and Patachon phenomenon.

Answering Bachmann's call, this author (Astrup 2020; 2022), alongside Braae and Ruedel (2022), has mapped and discussed various issues in connection to the transnational business relations of Palladium, archival holdings and foreign Pat and Patachon films. In close alignment with the historiographic approach suggested by Bachmann, this article further seeks to uncover the blind spots of film historiographies and map out the entangled, transnational connections of the German and Austrian Pat and Patachon films produced between 1925 and 1937.

The Films Produced in Austria 1925–1937

From 1920 to 1925, Palladium produced fifteen films in their Pat and Patachon series. Lau Lauritzen, who also ran the company together with the economic manager Svend Nielsen, directed them all. In 1925, the Danish film company adapted their mode of production to include foreign-based companies also making films starring the popular double act. First in line was a Swedish company, AB Svensk Film Industri. Actors Carl Schenstrøm and Harald Madsen shot *Polis Paulus påskasmäll* (*The Smugglers*, 1925) from January to March 1925 mainly at the Råsunda studio lot outside Stockholm, and then travelled to Austria almost immediately after the shoot.

In Vienna, Palladium had signed a contract with the production company Hugo Engel-Film and shooting commenced in the newly constructed Vita-Film studio at Rosenhügel. The Danish Film Institute's Palladium collection contains a draft of the contract between Palladium and an undisclosed Austrian company drawn up in 1925 but not signed. The contract, written in German, merely mentions 'the company' in the different clauses and stipulations. It states specifically that 'Palladium places the actors Schenstrøm and Madsen, known as Pat & Patachon, at the Company's disposal free of charge for the recording of a film in Vienna or other locations in Austria where the Company so decides' (Contract draft, Palladium collection, DFI). Further, it is stated that the film is to be shot between 1 February and 1 May 1925, as the two actors are due back in Copenhagen by May. Carl Schenstrøm and Harald Madsen seem to have been delayed by the Swedish production, however, and the filming in Vienna did not begin until 25 March 1925 (*Klokken 5*, 19 March 1925).

Based in Vienna, Hugo Engel-Film distributed and produced films. Palladium and the popular double act were on their radar already the previous year. In October 1924, representatives from the company visited Copenhagen in connection with the big premiere of Palladium's latest Pat and Patachon film, *Raske Riviera Rejsende* (*At the Mediterranean*, 1924). However, it was not only the distribution and sale of films with the Danish comedians that interested the Austrian company; Hugo Engel-Film's first venture into production became *Zwei Vagabunden im Prater* with Pat and Patachon. Accompanying the two Danish stars from Copenhagen to Vienna was also the actor Lili Lani, who had just married Palladium director Svend Nielsen in the spring of 1925. Lani starred alongside Schenstrøm and Madsen in the Austrian production directed by Hans-Otto Löwenstein. Löwenstein was both a seasoned and well-known director in Austria at this point. In fact, just one year later, the Austrian film publication *Mein Film* ('My Film') published an article titled

Figure 9.2 Behind the scenes of *Zwei Vagabunden im Prater* in Vienna (1925, Hans-Otto Löwenstein). Danish Film Institute.

'The Man who made 350 films', which celebrated Löwenstein's 350th film (*Mein Film*, no. 34, 1926, 2). His Pat and Patachon film, *Zwei Vagabunden im Prater*, was in production from 25 March to early May. Schenstrøm and Madsen arrived back in Copenhagen on 11 May (*Social-Demokraten*, 12 May 1925).

The presence of the two Danish actors, alongside their co-star Lili Lani, prompted considerable attention from the press in both Germany and Austria during the months of shooting. Before even setting foot in Vienna, 'Pat' and 'Patachon' appeared in articles describing their trip and pit stop in Berlin along the way. A close reading of the Danish discourse around this production and the Berlin visit uncovers that Palladium hired a Danish journalist, the foreign correspondent Andreas Vinding, to wire home news with sensationalist headlines like the already mentioned 'Pat and Patachon Stop Traffic on Potsdamer Platz' (*Politiken*, 24 March 1925). In his memoirs, Carl Schenstrøm even described how Vinding assisted him writing autographs upon arrival in Vienna (Schenstrøm 1943, 93). Another Danish newspaper bluntly called Schenstrøm and Madsen's foreign production a 'promotion trip' (*Social-Demokraten*, 1 April 1925), criticising the film agents working with the company for having hired a journalist to 'write bombastic telegrams in the style of Barnum' on the endeavours of the two Danes. Nevertheless, Palladium's promotion stunt clearly worked, and newspapers happily wrote about all things related to the Danish duo. This incident highlights how Palladium dealt with matters concerning press and promotion, and how the entanglement of those areas often proved advantageous in the star-making process surrounding Pat and Patachon.

Once in Vienna, though, the Austrian press – as well as the public – appear to have had a genuine interest in the visiting actors. Numerous front pages and enthusiastic headlines featured Pat and Patachon in the spring of 1925 (*Die Filmwelt*, 7. 1925; *Neue Illustrierte Wochenschau*, 4 April 1925; *Illustrierte Kronen Zeitung*, 29 March 1925), and a huge crowd welcomed the actors upon arrival at the Westbahnhof train station.

Even though film was still silent at this point, the Austrian press took an interest in the language skills displayed by the two Danes. At the press conference held at their hotel, *Die Filmwelt* reported on Madsen's formidable German pronunciation, while Schenstrøm was slightly ridiculed (*Die Filmwelt*, 7. 1925, 9). Nothing along this line seems to have occurred when the duo shot their film in Sweden, where the similarity of the languages is much more pronounced. *Die Filmwelt* reported that 'Mr. Madsen speaks German quite well, while Mr. Schenström tries to make himself understood in German with 90% Danish, Danish with 25% English and English with 10% German' (*Die Filmwelt*, 7. 1925, 9).

Pat and Patachon's first Austrian film was shot in the newly constructed Vita studio. It was the country's most modern studio, equipped with the latest technology (*Die Filmwelt*, 27. 1923, 3). Nevertheless, a large part of *Zwei Vagabunden im Prater* was filmed in and around Vienna, both at the Prater amusement park and in the area around Schönbrunn Castle, firmly situating the two Danes in a distinctly Austrian setting. Even the original, Austrian title of the film, which translates to 'Two vagabonds in the Prater', evokes the unique 'Austrianness' of the production. In Denmark, the film did not premiere until April 1926, almost an entire year after completion. The reviews were lukewarm, pointing to the fact that it was Palladium and its directors, Lau Laurtitzen and Svend Nielsen, who were to blame for the mediocrity of this foreign production. Writing on the new line of production, where Palladium signed deals with foreign companies to produce films with Pat and Patachon, *Social-Demokraten* (12 April 1926, 5), the leading left-wing newspaper in Denmark, scolded Palladium. They accused company directors Lauritzen and Nielsen for having sold Schenstrøm and Madsen off without consulting the two actors in the matter. All for the sake of profit. To make matters worse, in the eyes of the left-wing newspaper, Palladium was also working on setting

Figure 9.3 Director Hans Steinhoff (middle) with Carl Schenstrøm (left) and Harald Madsen (right) on the set of *Schwiegersöhne* (1926).
Internationale Filmschau, 5 February 1926.

up a permanent business in Paris 'to evade taxes', as *Social-Demokraten* (12 April 1926, 5) bluntly stated. Apparently, this part of the Danish press did not approve of the transnational mode of production initiated by Palladium in 1925 with the Swedish film and then this first Austrian effort. Regardless, Palladium continued successfully along this line throughout the 1920s and well into the 1930s.

Both the Austrian production company Hugo Engel-Film and the German distributor Emelka were also involved in the next film Schenstrøm and Madsen shot in Austria: *Schwiegersöhne* (1926). Helmed by German director Hans Steinhoff, filming began on 11 January 1926 in the Listo studio (Claus 2013, 118) located in the middle of Vienna at Gumpendorferstrasse 132 (*Die Filmwelt*, 6, 1923). The Listo studio was equipped with a glass roof structure in 1922, making it the city's largest rooftop studio among the six functioning film studios in Vienna in this period (*Die Filmwelt*, 25, 1924, 11). When production started, the first Austrian Pat and Patachon film had not yet premiered in Denmark.

According to Horst Claus (Claus 2013, 117), *Schwiegersöhne* was produced as a so-called 'contingent film'; a fast and not too expensive production, the primary purpose of which was to fill a certain quota of film productions – very similar to the so-called 'quota quickies' from England (Ward 1989, 100). This was primarily a tool utilised to protect a national film production and, at the same time, ensure that cinemas were not flooded with foreign (mainly American) films. The Pat and Patachon film was one of Steinhoff's three quota films (Claus 2013, 118). The other two were *Frau Sopherl vom Naschmarkt* ('Mrs. Sopherl from the Naschmarkt', 1926) and *Der Herr des Todes* (*The Master of Death*, 1926). Once again, Schenstrøm and Madsen's return to Vienna made headlines in Austrian, German and Danish media. Not least due to all the people who gathered at the Franz-Josefs-Bahnhof in the city to welcome the two actors and the tumult that ensued. Upon arrival, where the press noted that the stars were wearing their civilian clothes, Schenstrøm and Madsen were greeted by Paul Engel and Alois Weil of the Engel/Emelka team and Steinhoff himself (*Mein Film*, 3, 1926, 8). In addition to Schenstrøm and Madsen, the two Danish actors, Agnes Petersen and Gorm Schmidt, also appeared in Steinhoff's film. They had both previously starred in Palladium's Pat and Patachon films.

In addition to the Listo studio in Vienna, *Schwiegersöhne* was also filmed in the winter sports town of St Moritz. The shoot was actually postponed for a few days in early March because the entire crew was held up in Vienna waiting for snow in Semmering before continuing to St Moritz. Eventually, the snow fell, and Schenstrøm and Madsen could

Figure 9.4 Harald Madsen and Carl Schenstrøm as Pat and Patachon on the cover of the Austrian film magazine *Mein Film*, no. 52, 1926.

shoot the film's last scenes in Switzerland. Having completed Steinhoff's film in Switzerland, they travelled directly on to Spain, where Palladium's prestige production of *Don Quixote* – starring Schenstrøm and Madsen in the roles of Don Quixote and Sancho Panza – was lined up.

From Denmark to Austria and Switzerland under the direction of a German, on to Spain to shoot a world classic helmed by a Dane, Pat and Patachon exemplified the transnational tendencies at work in the film industry during this period. Only after the coming of sound did the Danish double act return to Austria for another non-Palladium film. German director Carl Boese headed the production of *Lumpenkavaliere* (1932), their third Austrian film. Arnold Pressburger and Gregor Rabinowitsch's company Cine-Allianz Tonfilm GmbH produced it. During the six intermediate years, Schenstrøm and Madsen had already made two sound films: the part-talkie *Alf's Carpet* (1929) in England and the German *1000 Worte Deutsch* ('1000 Words in German', 1930). According to Distelmeyer (2004, 7–8), Cine-Allianz was one of the most successful German production companies in the 1930s due to its ability to collaborate across borders and with other companies. Pressburger and Rabinowitsch, both Jewish, had many years of experience in film production when, in 1932, they joined forces to found Cine-Allianz. Pressburger served as head of the Sascha Filmindustrie in Vienna from 1918, where he spearheaded several of the company's major films. The Russian-born Rabinowitsch, who had worked both as a lawyer and in the financial sector (Weniger 2011, 403; Klapdor 2007, 409), began his career in the film industry in 1920s Paris. Following his career in Paris, he moved to Germany. In 1927, he was hired as a production manager by UFA. At UFA, Pressburger and Rabinowitsch began their collaborative efforts, finally establishing their own production company, Cine-Allianz Tonfilm in Berlin in 1932. One of their first productions, *Lumpenkavaliere*, began filming on 21 May 1932 in the Sascha studio in Vienna and was completed in seventeen days. The production was a collaboration between Cine-Allianz, the distributor Südfilm and Danish Palladium. In addition to Schenstrøm and Madsen, Lau Lauritzen, Jr (son of Palladium owner and director Lauritzen) and Alice O'Fredericks also assisted with script and editing work (*B.T.*, 15 June 1932, 4) both during and after the shoot. It is also possible to link Carl Boese to Palladium through Danish cinematographer Frederik Fuglsang. Fuglsang primarily worked in the German film industry, but he was also one of two cinematographers on the Danish Pat and Patachon film *Hallo! Afrika forude!* (*Clever Cannibals*, 1929, Lau Lauritzen). Additionally, Fuglsang shot Boese's German production *Grock* (1931) the year before Boese made *Lumpenkavaliere* in Austria. Here we clearly see the various transnational entanglements at work in the European film industry – both in the silent era and after the coming of sound.

Palladium was also connected to Arnold Pressburger through Arthur G. Gregory, a mutual business partner. Gregory, a film agent, who had handled world sales for Palladium since 1923, was thus involved in the production of *Die singende Stadt* (*The Singing City*, 1930), starring Brigitte Helm and Jan Kiepura (*B.T.*, 24 April 1930). The musical, set in Capri, was produced by Pressburger's company Allianz Tonfilm, which by March 1932 had merged into Cine-Allianz Tonfilm with Gregor Rabinowitsch on the board (Fuchs 2004, 35).

For Oscar Glück's Vienna-based Projectograph-Film, Schenstrøm and Madsen appeared once again as Pat and Patachon in the 1935 comedy *Zirkus Saran*, directed by E. W. Emo. Hans Moser, who was widely considered a distinctly Viennese actor and singer due to his dialect and numerous appearances in so-called 'Wiener films', starred. Pat and Patachon were thus reduced to Moser's sidekicks in their fourth Austrian film.

As a tie-in to the film, songs featured in the film were released in both German and re-recorded Danish versions. In German, Carl Schenstrøm sang 'Ein bisschen Singsang' ('A Bit of Singsong', released on Polydor 25685) while the Danish version, written by Schenstrøm himself, was called 'En smule Syng-Sang' (Polyphon XS 50453). The b-side of the Danish release featured another song from the film, also performed and written by Schenstrøm: 'Bror – du skal le' ('Brother – You Must Laugh'). The Danish release on Polyphon was produced and distributed with the entire Scandinavian market in mind (*Vendsyssel Tidende*, 27 July 1935). The aforementioned Arthur G. Gregory, who initially served as Palladium's sales agent, now handled the interests of Schenstrøm and Madsen as their manager (*Demokraten*, 28 January 1935, 3). Gregory was behind the deal with Projectograph-Film's *Zirkus Saran* as well as the other foreign Pat and Patachon films produced between 1935 and 1937. The role of the English-born film agent based in Denmark was thus significant in the latter part of the Danish film duo's career. On the general tendency of loaning out Schenstrøm and Madsen, Gregory noted that E. W. Emo's film, along with other German and Austrian Pat and Patachon films of the period, were made outside of Denmark due to German sound film patent considerations (*Politiken*, 27 January 1935). Furthermore, there were no available studio slots in Denmark at the time (*Social-Demokraten*, 13 January 1935). Thus, *Zirkus Saran* was filmed at the Tobis-Sascha studio in Vienna. On Austrian director E. W. Emo, Robert Dassanowsky noted that he 'would become the comedy expert for Vienna's productions after 1938' (Dassanowsky 2018, 80). Much like Steinhoff, who worked fast and efficient in the mainstream on so-called mid-budget 'Mittelfilme' (Claus 2003, 118) for a large part of his career, Emo also belonged in the mainstream. His films were 'technically well-made, slickly produced, and German-friendly entertainment' (Dassanowsky 2018, 181).

In many ways, the very last film Schenstrøm and Madsen made together outside of Denmark, *Pat und Patachon im Paradies* (1937), epitomised the transnational and entangled film culture at play in Europe in the 1920s and 1930s. The director Carl Lamac (née Karel Lamač) was born in Prague in the Austro-Hungarian Empire. Lamac's career was defined by cross-border productions in Germany, Austria, the Netherlands and England. He also served as producer on the German crime comedy *Der Doppelgänger* ('The Doppelganger', 1934) directed by *Zirkus Saran*'s E. W. Emo. When the Danish press discussed Lamac in connection with *Pat und Patachon im Paradies*, it was mainly as 'Anny Ondra's Director' (*Isefjordsposten*, 30 May 1938), the Czech actress with whom he, in addition to directing and starring opposite, also established a film company in 1930. The Ondra-Lamac connection also points to Gregory once again, as he was known in Denmark for importing a range of different Ondra films for distribution (*Aftenbladet*, 11 October 1938). Thus, it is likely that Gregory and Lamac had past business ties before he helmed a Pat and Patachon film in 1937.

Lamac's Pat and Patachon film, although Austrian by way of Vienna-based production company Atlantis-Film, was actually shot in Hungary in the Hunnia studio located in Budapest. The shoot started late December 1936 and continued into the first weeks of January 1937. In his memoir, Schenstrøm recalls the break-neck production in these words:

> It was shot in Budapest with Carl Lamac as director. Regarding days spent, it became a record-breaking film. Having pushed through during the last five days, where I did not go to bed before 4 a.m. upon returning from the studio, the pain was over in just seventeen days. (Schenstrøm 1943, 146)

Schenstrøm and Madsen were back in Denmark on 13 January, where several newspapers reported that the two Danish stars had shot the film with 'a series of German artists' in Budapest. Numerous sources point to the fact that the production of *Pat und Patachon im Paradies* should have started already in 1936 – initially in July, then in November (*Svendborg Avis*, 11 July 1936; *Social-Demokraten*, 8 November 1936). Perhaps due to these delays, the film ends up being a 'record-breaking film' – shot in just seventeen days as described by Schenstrøm.

In an interview with a Danish newspaper on the day of his and Madsen's return from Budapest, Schenstrøm offered his thoughts on this as well as other German-language films with Pat and Patachon:

> Hopefully, we will make a big film in Denmark this summer. Our German films have not been overwhelming successes here, so we think we owe it to the audience.

> However, one thing to keep in mind is that our films are seen by 3½ million people in Denmark, who may not like that we speak German. Then again, the films are first and foremost intended for Germany and the surrounding countries, where they truly have become great successes. (*Herning Avis*, 13 January 1937, 2)

Schenstrøm's prediction for the summer of 1937 did not hold up. And in spite of the German-language films being big hits outside of Denmark, Lamac's Austrian/German/Hungarian Pat and Patachon film marks the last foreign production in which the Danish double act starred together.

The Films Produced in Germany 1930–1936

Contrary to Austria, where Schenstrøm and Madsen made both silent and sound features, they only worked on sound films in Germany. These were *1000 Worte Deutsch* by Georg Jacoby, together with *Mädchenräuber* (*Girl Kidnappers*, 1936) and *Blinde Passagiere* (*Stowaways*, 1936), both directed by Fred Sauer.

Jacoby's German Pat and Patachon film represents the duo's full transition into sound filmmaking, as the British production *Alf's Carpet* (1929) was made as a so-called part-talkie and with cockney actors voicing Schenstrøm and Madsen's characters. The duo did not make a Danish sound film until the 1932 remake of the 1922 hit *Han, Hun og Hamlet* (*He, She and Hamlet*), directed by Lau Lauritzen. Thus, their departure from Denmark, arrival in Berlin, production and premiere events of the German sound film garnered substantial coverage in the press.

The German production and distribution company Deutsches Lichtspiel-Syndikat AG (DLS) signed a contract with Palladium to produce Pat and Patachon's first sound film. Initially DLS planned to produce more Pat and Patachon films (*Der Kinematograph*, 10 March 1930), but only ended up making the one directed by Georg Jacoby. Another Dane, Lilian Ellis, also appeared alongside Palladium's double act in the German film. Both the shoot and post-production were swift, as the film had its world premiere on 5 December 1930 in Berlin's newly built Universum cinema on Kurfürstendamm, not even two months after Schenstrøm and Madsen first arrived in the German capital. The Danish audience had to wait until 7 February 1931 before Pat and Patachon's first talkie premiered in Denmark. Up until that point, readers were able to follow the footsteps of the two actors in all matters related to the production of *1000 Worte Deutsch*, from Schenstrøm and Madsen's scheduled arrival time at the Stettiner Bahnhof in Berlin, to a story from a football match between teams Hertha BSC and Viktoria, where the two Danes watched the game from the stands while enjoying a 'Berliner Salzstangerl' snack

(*Tempo Berlin*, 21 October 1930). Prior to sending his two valued players off to Berlin, Palladium director Lau Lauritzen shared his plans for the upcoming production with Danish newspaper *B.T.*:

> No matter what language the films are recorded in, I have decided that Pat and Patachon must remain Danish. This will result in them speaking with an accent, yes, but as long as they are associated with Palladium, they shall stay Danish. I think this is a very good solution to the language problem. (Lau Lauritzen, *B.T.*, 17 September 1930)

One month earlier, the same newspaper reported that the film was going to be shot in both German and Danish (*B.T.*, 18 August 1930). Making multiple language versions of films was not uncommon during these transitional years (Distelmeyer, ed., 2006), but *1000 Worte Deutsch* was eventually only shot in German, with Schenstrøm and Madsen's sparse dialogue including Danish words and phrases as part of the plot of the film. The same article also stated that an ongoing silent Pat and Patachon production at Palladium would be synchronised with sound and music by Tobis Klangfilm in Berlin. The film in production at Palladium's studio in Hellerup outside of Copenhagen was *Hr. Tell og Søn* (1930). It did in fact end up being synchronised and was released in Germany by DLS in both a silent and a sound version (*Reichsfilmblatt*, 11 October 1930). In Denmark, it was only shown as a silent film. As mentioned, DLS also served as the production company on Jacoby's Pat and Patachon film *1000 Worte Deutsch*. The film was shot at the EFA studio on Cicerostrasse 2–6 in Berlin, newly equipped for sound film production. In charge of the production was Leo Meyer, who worked on G. W. Pabst's *Westfront 1918* (1930) the same year. German director Georg Jacoby was already a well-known name in a Danish context at this point. Jacoby directed the lavish *Jokeren* (*The Joker*, 1928); a Danish-German-British co-production between Nordisk Films Kompagni, Deutsch Nordischen Film-Union and Horwa-Goron-Film. It was the very last silent film produced by the former very successful Nordisk Films Kompagni before it went bankrupt. The company was re-established as Nordisk Tonefilm ('Nordic Sound Film') in 1929.

Jacoby finished the production on *1000 Worte Deutsch* around 20 November 1930. The world premiere took place a few weeks later on 5 December at the Universum cinema in Berlin. In anticipation of the premiere later that day, German trade magazine *Lichtbild-Bühne* referred to Pat and Patachon as an 'international film brand' and a 'trademark' in an article (*Lichtbild-Bühne*, 5 December 1930). A month earlier, *Der Filmspiegel*, another trade publication, published a story on the upcoming

Pat and Patachon talkie. The article tried to imagine how the voices of the two actors would sound: 'Pat hums in the deepest bass while Patachon whistles in the highest treble' (*Der Filmspeigel*, 1 November 1930). There was no mention of the nationality of Pat and Patachon, nor did the reporter infer anything about accents. This underlines the idea of Pat and Patachon being true transnational film stars; a brand or trademark, if you will, not affected by the coming of sound and dialogue in different tongues.

The German reviews, however, were somewhat lukewarm. Several commented that the script by Wassermann and Schlee dragged along and failed to put Pat and Patachon to proper use (*Neue Berliner Zeitung*; *Lichtbild-Bühne*, 6 December 1930). Nevertheless *1000 Worte Deutsch* proved a hit with audiences across Germany, making headlines in the trade papers on record sales and number of copies in distribution. *Der Film* (6 December 1930) reported that *1000 Worte Deutsch* was distributed in more than forty copies in Germany during Christmas. The number of copies was increased to sixty when Christmas box-office sales proved solid (Engberg 1980, 103). *Der Kinematograph* (3 January 1931) marvelled that the film secured the year's largest box-office revenue for the Turma-Palast cinema in Berlin's Schöneberg district. The German headlines on record sales for Pat and Patachon also made it to the Danish press prior to the film's wide release in Denmark in February 1931, while the actual reviews upon release were less enthusiastic. Nevertheless, *1000 Worte Deutsch* ran for nearly three consecutive weeks in Copenhagen's large World Cinema. The audience did not seem at all bothered by the somewhat indifferent reviews in the Danish press.

Palladium, however, was not entirely pleased with Jacoby's German sound film featuring their two stars. According to the Danish daily *Morgenbladet* (8 February 1931), the company decided that this was to be the last film with Pat and Patachon helmed by a German director. Still, Schenstrøm and Madsen appeared in another six foreign films after *1000 Worte Deutsch*, two of which were produced in Germany.

Schenstrøm and Madsen returned to Germany in 1935 to shoot *Mädchenräuber* (1936), and in 1936 *Blinde Passagiere*; both for the Majestic Film company. The duo's manager, Arthur G. Gregory, was responsible for the two-film deal with Majestic Film and the Austrian director Fred Sauer. Sauer had previously recorded films for Messtro-Film GmbH (Gandert 1993, 1). Other Pat and Patachon directors with ties to Messtro-Film include Carl Boese, Hans Steinhoff and Georg Jacoby, who worked as head of production (Claus 2013, 230). Once again, transnational entanglements and interconnections present themselves as cornerstones in the foreign business relations of Pat and Patachon. Furthermore,

Messtro-Film co-produced a film in 1930 in consortium with companies Orplid-Film and Arnold Pressburger's Allianz-Tonfilm (Fuchs 2004, 35), after which Pressburger and Rabinowitsch's Cine-Allianz Tonfilm made *Lumpenkavaliere* (1932) in Austria.

Majestic Film, to which Schenstrøm and Madsen had now been hired out, was founded in 1930 in Berlin (*Der Kinematograph*, 17 March 1930). In 1935, the film producer Christoph Mülleneisen Jr became a shareholder in Majestic Film. The following year he was appointed director of the company; this was a result of the Nazi policy of placing Aryans in charge of German companies, including film businesses. Mülleneisen and Gregory had previous ties from an attempted Danish-Swedish film consortium in 1932, where Mülleneisen was going to inject German capital into the company. The deal with Majestic Film here in 1935/36 thus re-established business ties between Mülleneisen and Gregory, starting with the 'Berliner film' *Mädchenräuber* (*Fredericia Social-Demokrat*, 19 September 1936).

Carl Schenstrøm's memoirs once again prove a good source on production history:

> We started in the dark December days with location shots in Mecklenburg. It was cold and rainy, and we were convinced that we would have to do re-shoots, as no portable lighting had been at hand. Luckily, the light-sensitive film stock sufficed and was perfectly usable. On the third day of Christmas, filming began in Johannisthal's Atelier, and it progressed briskly under the direction of Fred Sauer. (Schenstrøm 1943, 145)

The Johannisthal studio mentioned by Schenstrøm was taken over by Tobis Atelier GmbH in 1933. *Mädchenräuber* was thus produced using Tobis-Klangfilm's sound system, which Johannisthal had been equipped with. Filming took place the second week of January 1936. As usual, the Danish press wrote on all things related to Pat and Patachon. On this production, reporters highlighted the use of the traditional Danish folk song, 'Det var en Lørdag Aften' ('It was a Saturday Night') in the film. In both *1000 Worte Deutsch* and *Lumpenkavaliere*, the Danish origin of Pat and Patachon was incorporated into the bits of the film's story and dialogue. Catering to both a German and Danish audience, Sauer also employed Danish elements strategically. Not only by using a well-known folk song, but also in the final scene of the film, where Pat and Patachon cross the border from Germany to Denmark while singing the aforementioned song (*Aalborg Stiftstidende*, 14 April 1936). Another Danish newspaper wrote that part of the duo's dialogue consisted of Danish phrases and distinct 'Copenhagen-slang' (*Aarhus Stiftstidende*, 11 June 1936). Ads promoting the film emphasise, in even larger writing than the film's title, that 'Pat and Patachon speak Danish' (*Aalborg Stiftstidende*, 14 April 1936), while the review in *Aalborg Amtstidende* (14 April 1936) stated that 'It might as well have been filmed in Valby as in Berlin'.

A blatant Nazi propaganda film initially accompanied the Danish release of Sauer's Pat and Patachon comedy *Mädchenräuber*. Several newspapers (*Fyns Venstreblad*; *Fyens Social-Demokrat*, 5 May 1936) reported that it caused distress and uproar in the audience and *Fyens Social-Demokrat* demanded the propaganda film be removed from the program. In 1936 – three years into Nazi rule – Pat and Patachon's German filmmaking excursions were still tolerated in Denmark. However, being force-fed Nazi propaganda in the cinema as an appetiser to the main course did not go down well.

On 23 May 1936, Schenstrøm and Madsen once again headed for Berlin to star in another Majestic production directed by Fred Sauer; *Blinde Passagiere*. This would be their last German film. Shooting commenced in the Terra studios (*Mein Film*, 545, 1936) equipped with the Tobis Klangfilm system. A large portion of the film was shot on location in Hamburg and on board the ocean liner *SS Königin Luise* in mid-June. According to Schenstrøm (1943, 146), the duo were in a rush to get back home, as Gregory had arranged for them to star in a Swedish film in the fall of 1936 and the Swedes were 'waiting for them'. Upon the two actors' return to Copenhagen in July, *B.T.* interviewed Schenstrøm. He disclosed that *Blinde Passagiere* was set to premiere in Germany 'in conjunction with the Olympics' (*B.T.*, 11 July 1936). Sauer's film opened simultaneously in Berlin's Primus-Palast and Titania-Palast on 21 August 1936, just about a week after the Olympics closed. In Denmark, the film had a limited opening about a month later, while the nationwide premiere and audiences in Copenhagen had to wait until 9 November 1936. Reading between the lines of the advance press coverage, one senses a burgeoning hostility towards the popularity of the two Danes in Germany:

> In Germany, the two fellows are more popular than ever, and their autographs are almost on a par with Hitler's and Göring's. The two Danish comedians have become a good asset to German film production. The German Pat and Patachon films have become big hits throughout Central Europe, paving the way for quite a comeback. (*Berlingske Tidende*, 24 July 1936)

The quote from *Berlingske Tidende* encapsulates how closely film, fame and politics were intertwined in Nazi Germany during this period, and how this spilled over into popular culture in other countries as well. Being labelled 'a good asset to German film production' was not positive for popular stars with an international career towards the end of the 1930s. Perhaps this explains why Pat and Patachon manager Gregory and Schenstrøm himself were careful to point out that the contract between Majestic Film and the two Danish actors explicitly stated that they must speak Danish in every film produced (*Randers Dagblad*, 27 August 1936). True or not, the evasive tactic succeeded. Danish newspapers seemed content to report on the Danes' supposed contractual demand to remain Danish, even in a German film produced on the brink of the nationalisation of the German film industry that was put into effect in 1937. *Blinde Passagiere* is thus one of the last productions made in the transitional period in German film (Hales, Petrescu and Weinstein 2016, 12) from the end of the Weimar Republic to the imposition of complete state control. A film reviewer in the Danish newspaper *Social-Demokraten* also weighed in on the matter by way of ridicule. The reviewer noted that German actor Rudolf Platte, one of Schenstrøm and Madsen's co-stars in *Blinde Passagiere*, 'looks like Goebbels and is not much funnier' (*Social-Demokraten*, 10 November 1936). The dislike is not targeted directly at Schenstrøm and Madsen. Still, one does sense how public opinion towards Nazi Germany and the films produced within that system is changing, evident through small, satiric side notes like this.

The transnational mode of film production popular throughout Europe in the 1920s and the early 1930s falls victim not only to the coming of sound, but also to the nationalisation of industries, as is the case in Nazi Germany and the *Anschluss* of Austria to the German Reich in 1938. Collaboration with production and distribution networks with strong ties to Germany and Austria was no longer advantageous or perceived in a positive light. The silent comedy double act Pat and Patachon managed the transition to sound by travelling around Europe on loan to various production companies and directors. Returning home just before nationalisation and overt ideological filmmaking became predominant, they remained popular with their Danish audience.

The Transnational Entanglements of Palladium

The Austrian and German films featuring Danish stars Pat and Patachon are tangible examples of the transnational ties and entanglements at work in the European film industry. In films like *Zwei Vagabunden im Prater* (1925) and *1000 Worte Deutsch* (1930), Danish, German and Austrian interests intersected. These productions were, however, the result of Palladium's deliberate business strategy, constantly seeking to expand areas of distribution and capacity of production.

Zooming out from the individual films, looking instead to the connections at work on a more general level, this part of the chapter will map out some of the links between Palladium's business partners and the different production companies that made the German and Austrian Pat and Patachon films. Additionally, the negotiations in 1924–1925, between Palladium and the transnational film consortium Westi (Thompson 1985, 113), are discussed as an attempt at pan-European co-production that failed.

Denmark-Germany-Austria

German distributor and producer Lothar Stark became Palladium's strongest link to Germany from 1923 onwards, when he and Arthur G. Gregory signed with the Danish company as distributor and sales agent, respectively. By 1923, Stark had made a name for himself in the German film industry as a valued and esteemed professional (Astrup 2020, n.p.). Having either been employed by or collaborated with a range of production companies like PAGU, Cines and Richard Oswald Film, and eventually setting up his own company in 1914 (*Der Kinematograph*, 2 December 1914), Stark had an ever-growing network within the business. He was also involved in the trade organisation Club der Filmindustrie, serving as its president from 1923. Before venturing into film, Stark worked as a journalist and editor on newspapers in Breslau, Frankfurt am Main and Copenhagen. During one period, from 1902 to 1904, he even lived in Copenhagen. On several occasions during this period, Stark spoke at meetings in the 'Danish Zionist Association' (Dansk Zionistforening) founded by Louis Herman Frænkel. Judging from letters Stark sent asking Frænkel for advice in relation to a dispute between him and Palladium in the 1930s, the two men remained close friends throughout their lives. Marriage tied Stark to Denmark as well; with Etta Meyer in 1903 and with Else Oda Pedersen (date unknown). Lothar and Else Stark remained married until his death in 1944. German-born Lothar Stark's close ties to Denmark are also evident from the fact that he lived in exile in Denmark after the Nazis seized power in Germany in 1933. It is, in other words, difficult to separate the professional network and entangled business connections of Stark from his personal life, as Danish relations are notable throughout his life.

While Palladium and Stark were close collaborators, Germany thus seemed the obvious choice when the Danish company was looking to move and reorganise production to another country in 1924, and again in 1926. Nevertheless, company directors Lau Lauritzen and Svend Nielsen initially set their eyes on Austria instead. A Danish newspaper reported

Figure 9.5 German distributor and producer Lothar Stark (seated) with actors Harald Madsen and Carl Schenstrøm. Year unknown. Danish Film Institute.

that Palladium might shoot a Danish film in Vienna during the spring of 1924 (*Aalborg Stiftstidende*, 3 February 1924, 7). Further details were disclosed in a lengthy article in *Ekstrabladet* a month earlier (3 January 1924). The headline stated: 'Pat and Patachon are heading to Austria. Lau Lauritzen will shoot a film in Vienna and its surrounding area.' The full article shines a light on Palladium as a transnational operation in several ways. For instance, economic manager and director Svend Nielsen is off to Paris to meet with director Lau Lauritzen. Lauritzen has just arrived from Rome, where he attended the Italian premiere of a Danish Palladium film with Pat and Patachon, *Mellem muntre Musikanter* (*Among Merry Musicians*, 1922). In Paris, Palladium's two directors will meet up with distributors from the Netherlands and France. Nielsen and Lauritzen will also discuss the possibility of shooting a Pat and Patachon film in Vienna under Lauritzen's directorial watch. Moreover, German distributor Lothar Stark is also included in the discussion of a possible Austrian production:

> On behalf of the Austrian film company 'Pan Film', German film tycoon Lothar Stark, Palladium's representative for Germany, Romania, Czechoslovakia, Bulgaria, Yugoslavia, and Turkey, has expressed wishes that a Lau comedy be filmed in Vienna and the surrounding area. (*Ekstrabladet*, 3 January 1924)

Stark appears to play an active role in establishing the connection between Palladium and key players in the Austrian film industry, thus paving the way for *Zwei Vagabunden im Prater* (1925), one of the first foreign productions starring Pat and Patachon. However, while assisting Palladium in this case, Stark thwarted the Danish company's collaboration plans with the film consortium Westi (Nørrested 1991, 56).

Negotiating with Westi Film 1924–1925

International co-productions were in vogue in the 1920s (Abel 1984, 35). Palladium, always looking to expand its market and strike up new and even more lucrative deals, was also eager to join in. One of its first stabs at such a deal appeared in late 1924, when the newly established film consortium Westi Film was shopping around Europe looking for production companies and stars to sign (Thompson 1985, 113).

Westi Film, a project led by the German industrialist Hugo Stinnes and the wealthy, Russian émigré Vladimir Wengeroff, was short-lived but illustrated several of the initiatives that shaped the film industry of the 1920s. It was established in Berlin in 1923 as a defence against the American films flooding the European market; this was done through co-operations with strong affiliated producing partners (Abel 1984, 29) and by hiring already established and marketable stars, like Danes Carl Schenstrøm and Harald Madsen in the roles of Pat and Patachon. On these grounds, Wengeroff visited Copenhagen in November 1924 to negotiate with Palladium in a bid for the duo. As Hugo Stinnes died on 10 April 1924, just a year into setting up Westi and co-operations across Europe, Wengeroff was in charge of the consortium by the time Westi and Palladium finally met. The possible collaboration was already rumoured in the Danish press in August 1924. Describing Westi's plans to expand into the Scandinavian market, the local newspaper *Horsens Social-Demokrat* wrote:

> Director Wengeroff will be here in a few days. So far, one million dollars has been raised for the work in Scandinavia. The intention is to establish a Scandinavian office in Copenhagen. Based on current estimates, it is fair to assume that the company will also assert its power in the three Nordic countries in the near future. Due to the success of Pat and Patachon in many European countries, special attention is directed at the Danish company Palladium. (*Horsens Social-Demokrat*, 25 August 1924, 1)

The story of the European film trust Westi trying to gain foothold in the Nordic countries had even made it to the front page of the paper, underlining the significance of the renewed interest in Denmark as a film-producing country with international stars. Palladium and Westi, however, did not meet up until 2 November 1924. Present at the negotiations in Copenhagen we also find Lothar Stark (*København*, 3 November 1924) and a Mr Givatovsky, a secretary to Wengeroff (*Nationaltidende*, 4 November 1924). A great deal of press attention was paid to the negotiations in Copenhagen; *Berlingske Tidende* interviews 'the German [*sic*!] movie mogul' Vladimir Wengeroff, who is 'out to bag the two stars' (4 November 1924), while *Aftenbladet* talks to Palladium director Lau Lauritzen. Under the headline 'Pat and Patachon as Denmark's biggest export opportunities' (*Aftenbladet*, 4 November 1924), Lauritzen discloses that nothing is set in stone yet. According to Lauritzen, three possible scenarios are on the table: either Westi buys Palladium's entire production, hires Schenstrøm and Madsen for a few individual films, which would have to be shot by Westi, or rents the two stars once a year. Much on par with the late Hugo Stinnes' way of doing business, Westi's initial plan was to buy stocks in the Palladium production company. According to a Danish newspaper, shareholders were not interested in selling (*Næstved Tidende*, 4 November 1924). When the two parties met in Copenhagen in November 1924, they failed to close a deal once again (Nørrested 1991, 56). Having already signed a deal for the forthcoming Palladium films, Lothar Stark stood his ground as distributor. The newspaper *København* wrote:

> For the time being, the German movie mogul Lothar Starc [*sic*] has put a stop to director Wengeroff's plans to adopt our darling Pat and Patachon for half a year at a time. Having bought Palladium's production for Central Europe long ago, he is now demanding 10,000 dollars per film to renounce the deal. (*København*, 13 November 1924)

The article further reported that Wengeroff was most likely going to turn down Stark's offer, causing the whole deal to fall apart. Stark's show of force in this case demonstrates the German distributor's entangled role in relation to Palladium's business dispositions. Despite being unable to close a deal with Palladium on future Pat and Patachon productions, Westi remained interested in Denmark and the Nordic countries. In January 1925, the consortium opened a Scandinavian branch with head office in Copenhagen. Arthur G. Gregory, Palladium's sales agent and close collaborator, was hired to run Westi's operations from the office located at Købmagergade 67 in central Copenhagen. This was also the address of Gregory's own business (*Kraks Vejviser*, 1925). With the addition of its Copenhagen office, Westi now had branches in Berlin, Vienna, London, Paris, Zürich, Riga, Warsaw, Stockholm, Cairo, Kobe and Tokyo

(*Der Kinematograph*, 3 May 1925). The Danish press frequently mistook Gregory for a German due to his close association with the German film industry. This was also the case when the trade magazine *Kinobladet* (15 January 1925, 104) wrote about Westi's new office in Copenhagen. *Kinobladet* interviewed Gregory, who had just returned from a meeting with the Westi consortium in Berlin. Gregory spoke about the different films Westi was going to release in Scandinavia and the countries and film production companies they were already co-producing with; for instance, Pathé in France and Richard Oswald-Film in Germany. They were also closing a deal with Sascha-Film in Austria. There was, however, no mention of Palladium in the article. Gregory closed the interview by stating that Westi would have 'no shortage of money for the realisation of the big plans' (*Kinobladet*, 15 January 1925, 104). Despite this claim, Westi soon found itself in a financial bind. The Stinnes corporation was deeply in debt (Abel 1984, 34) and its Westi Film consortium was ultimately dissolved in August 1925, with UFA acquiring the company shares (*Berlingske Tidende*, 22 August 1925). A Danish newspaper summed up the short-lived Westi endeavour: 'Stinnes wanted the entire European film industry to join forces against America. But Stinnes died – and with him Westi-Film' (*Holsterbro Dagblad*, 31 August 1925).

Even though Palladium's grand plans of co-production with Westi fell through, Pat and Patachon managed to navigate the European film industry with great skill. The duo remained on-screen and top of mind with production companies and exhibitors throughout the 1920s and well into the 1930s. Distributor Lothar Stark and manager Arthur G. Gregory made sure of that by using their networks all over Europe. In 1924, the Westi-Palladium plan was to have Pat and Patachon make two to three films in Denmark with the usual production values, plus two to three films with bigger budgets in Germany or other countries (*Aarhus Stifts-Tidende*, 5 November 1924, 3). From 1925 to 1937, Carl Schenstrøm and Harald Madsen appeared in thirteen foreign productions (five in Austria and three in Germany), while also shooting three to four films regularly at Palladium until the beginning of the 1930s. As it turned out, the production mode suggested by the Westi deal, should that have come into being, was more or less adopted by Palladium.

Conclusion

By loaning out Pat and Patachon to production companies in Austria and Germany (as well as Sweden and England), Palladium was able to meet contractual agreements already made with distributors while also maintaining the status of their stars in these markets. Palladium's alternation between its own production and 'outsourcing' of activities was its way of tackling the increasingly protective film industry of the late 1920s and early 1930s. Zooming very specifically in on the Pat and Patachon films made in Austria and Germany (as examples of both the popularity of the duo and the praxis of the stars-on-loan), this chapter has offered a perspective on the European film industry during this period. In the many Pat and Patachon films produced outside of Denmark – both in the silent era and after the coming of sound – we see transnational entanglements at work. Pat and Patachon, although inherently Danish according to the general discourse of their time, also signify an essential part of Film Europe (Higson & Maltby 1999). In Carl Schenstrøm and Harald Madsen's cross-border career, zigzagging between Palladium's studio in seaside Hellerup outside Copenhagen, Berlin, Vienna, London and Stockholm, transnational film production is exemplified. Tracing the interconnections of business partners and co-producing companies without the restrictions that national film historiographies tend to subscribe to, a more nuanced picture emerges. One of a Danish slapstick double act becoming transnational stars; easily marketable to a wide, international audience and an asset to a range of production companies throughout Europe. A true testament to their enduring popularity and border-transcending stardom is the substantial number of German-language talkies produced well into the 1930s – every so often featuring Pat and Patachon speaking Danish.

References

Abel, Richard. 1984. *French Cinema. The First Wave, 1915–1929*. Princeton: Princeton University Press.

———. 2015. *Menus for Movieland. Newspapers and the Emergence of American Film Culture, 1913–1916*. Oakland: University of California Press.

———. 2019. 'Reading Newspapers and Writing American Silent Cinema History.' In *The Routledge Companion to New Cinema History*, edited by Daniel Biltereyst, Richard Maltby and Philippe Meers. Abingdon and New York: Routledge, 68–82.

Allen, Robert C. and Douglas Gomery. 1985. *Film History. Theory and Practice*. New York, McGraw-Hill.

Arnau, Frank, ed. 1932. *Universal Filmlexicon*. Berlin: Universal-Filmlexicon GmbH.

Astrup, Jannie Dahl. 2020. 'World Agents and Mighty Filmmakers – The Transnational Business Relations of Palladium.' *Kosmorama* #276 (www.kosmorama.org).

———. 2022. *Fy og Bi: Et transnationalt filmfænomen. En undersøgelse af grænsekrydsende entanglements i produktions-, distributions- og modtagerperspektiv*. Ph.d.-dissertation. Copenhagen: University of Copenhagen.
Astrup, Jannie Dahl, Mikael Braae and Ulrich Ruedel. 2022. 'Towards Preserving a Transnational Comedy Phenomenon: The World of Pat and Patachon.' *Kosmorama* #281 (www.kosmorama.org).
Bachmann, Anne. 2013. *Locating Inter-Scandinavian Silent Film Culture. Connections, Contentions, Configurations* (Acta Universitatis Stockholmiensis). Stockholm: Stockholms Universitet.
———. 2017. 'The Press Cutting, Film Studies and the Digital Age.' *Journal of Scandinavian Cinema* 7, no. 2 (2017): 149–54.
Biltereyst, Daniel, Richard Maltby and Philippe Meers, eds. 2019. *The Routledge Companion to New Cinema History*. Abingdon and New York: Routledge.
Biltereyst, Daniel and Lies Van de Vijver, eds. 2020. *Mapping Movie Magazines. Digitization, Periodicals and Cinema History*. London: Palgrave Macmillan.
Bock, Hans-Michael and Tim Bergfelder, eds. 2009. *The Concise Cinegraph. Encyclopaedia of German Cinema*. New York and Oxford: Berghahn Books.
Braae, Mikael and Ulrich Ruedel. 2019. 'Slapstick Scandinavian Style.' *Catalogue. Pordenone Silent Film Festival 5–12 ottobre 2019*. Pordenone: Associazione Culturale 'Le Giornate del Cinema Muto', 104–6.
Claus, Horst. 2003. 'Commerce, Culture, Continuity: Hans Steinhoff's "Mittelfilm" Production of Stefan Zweig's *Angst* (1928).' *German Life and Letters* 56, no. 2 (April): 117–31.
———. 2013. *Filmen für Hitler. Die Karriere des NS-Starregisseurs Hans Steinhoff*. Wien: Verlag Filmarchiv Austria.
Dassanowsky, Robert. 2018. *Screening Transcendence. Film under Austrofascism and the Hollywood Hope, 1933–1938*. Bloomington: Indiana University Press.
Dick, Rainer. 1999. *Lexikon der Filmkomiker*. Berlin: Lexikon Imprint Verlag.
Distelmeyer, Jan, ed. 2004. *Allierte für den Film. Arnold Pressburger, Gregor Rabinowitsch und die Cine-Allianz*. Munich: edition text + kritik.
———, ed. 2006. *Babylon in FilmEuropa. Mehrsprachen-Versionen der 1930er Jahre*. Munich: edition text+kritik.
Eddy, Robert. 1928. *Fyrtaarnet og Bivognen*. Copenhagen: Zinklar Zinglersen.
Engberg, Marguerite. 1968. *Den danske stumfilm 1903–1930: et index*. Copenhagen: Det Danske Filmmuseum.
———. 1977–1982. *Registrant over danske film 1896–1930, Bind I–V*. Copenhagen: Institut for Filmvidenskab/C.A. Reitzels Forlag.
———. 1977. *Dansk stumfilm. De store år*. Copenhagen: Rhodos.
———. 1980. *Fy & Bi*. Copenhagen: Gyldendal.
———. 1987. *Dansk Filmhistorie 1896–1985: et kompendium*. Copenhagen: C.A. Reitzels Forlag.
———. 1999. 'Palladium and the Silent Films with "Long and Short".' In *Nordic Explorations. Film Before 1930*, edited by John Fullerton and Jan Olsson. Sydney: John Libbey, 56–62.

——. 1994. 'Zwischen Kopenhagen und Berlin. Ein Überblick.' In *Schwarzer Traum und Weisse Sklavin. Deutsch-dänische Filmbeziehungen 1910–1930*, edited by Manfred Behn. Munich: edition text + kritik, 7–14.
Feld, Hans. 1982. 'Jews in the Development of the German Film Industry. Notes from the Recollections of a Berlin Film Critic.' In *The Leo Baeck Institute Year Book* 27, no. 1, January 1982, 337–65.
Fuchs, Christoph. 2004. 'Im Labyrinth der Allianzen.' In *Alliierte für den Film. Arnold Pressburger, Gregor Rabinowitsch und die Cine-Allianz*, edited by Jan Distelmeyer. München: edition text+kritik, 34–45.
Fullerton, John and Jan Olsson, eds. 1999. *Nordic Explorations. Film Before 1930*. Sydney: John Libbey.
Gandert, Gero. 1993. *1929. Der Film der Weimarer Republik. Ein Handbuch der zeitgenössischen Kritik*. Berlin: Walter de Gruyter.
Garncarz, Joseph. 2004. 'Produzenten von europäischen Ruf. Zur Produktionsphilosophie von Arnold Pressburger und Gregor Rabinowitsch.' In *Alliierte für den Film. Arnold Pressburger, Gregor Rabinowitsch und die Cine-Allianz*, edited by Jan Distelmeyer. München: edition text+kritik, 57–64.
——. 2016. *Medienwandel*. Stuttgart: utb.
——. 2021. *Begeisterte Zuschauer. Die Macht des Kinopublikums in der NS-Diktatur*. Köln: Herbert von Halem Verlag.
Hales, Barbara, Maichala Petrescu and Valerie Weinstein, eds. 2016. *Continuity and Crisis in German Cinema, 1928–1936*. Rochester: Camden House.
Hales, Barbara and Valerie Weinstein, eds. 2021. *Rethinking Jewishness in Weimar Cinema*. New York and Oxford: Berghahn Books.
Hampicke, Evelyn and Christian Dirks. 2004. 'Paul Davidson: Die Erfindung des Generaldirektors.' In *Pioniere in Celluloid. Juden in der frühen Filmwelt*, edited by Irene Stratenwerth and Hermann Simon. Berlin: Henschel, 49–55.
Heinke, Ralf Heiner and Christoph Ziener. 2016. 'Globale Kinoexpansionen: Transnationale Filmgeschichte der Zwischenkriegszeit.' *MEDIENwissenschaft* 04/2016, 409–24.
Higson, Andrew and Richard Maltby, eds. 1999. *'Film Europe' and 'Film America'. Cinema, Commerce and Cultural Exchange 1920–1939*. Devon: University of Exeter Press.
Hochscherf, Tobias. 2011. *The Continental Connection. German-Speaking Émigrés and British Cinema, 1927–45*. Manchester: Manchester University Press.
Jacobsen, Wolfgang and Heike Klapdor, eds. 2013. *In der Ferne das Glück. Geschichten für Hollywood*. Berlin: Aufbau Verlag.
Klapdor, Heike. 1997. 'Erforschung des Filmexils.' In *Recherche: Film. Quellen und Methoden der Filmforschung*, edited by Hans-Michael Bock and Wolfgang Jacobsen. München: edition text+kritik, 37–46.
——, ed. 2007. *Ich bin ein unheilbarer Europäer. Briefe aus dem Exil*. Berlin: Aufbau.
——, ed.. 2021. *Mit anderen Augen. Exil und Film*. München: edition text+kritik.
Lange-Fuchs, Hauke. 1979. *Pat und Patachon. Dokumentation*. Schondorf/Ammersee: Programm Roloff & Seesslen.

——. 1984. *Die Filme der Nordischen Filmtage. Filmografie*. Lübeck: Senat der Hansestadt Lübeck.
——. 2014. 'Pat and Patachon: A "German" Comedy Couple on the Screen.' *Journal of Scandinavian Cinema* 4, no. 3 (2014): 209–14.
Loacker, Armin. 1993. 'Die österreichische Filmwirtschaft von den Anfängen bis zur Einführund des Tonfilms.' *Maske und Kothurn* 39, no. 4, 1993, 75–124.
——. 1999. *Anschluss im 3/4-Takt. Filmproduktion und Filmpolitik in Österreich 1930–1938*. Trier: WVT - Wissenschaftlicher Verlag Trier.
Loacker, Armin, and Martin Prucha. 1999. 'Österreichisch-deutsche Filmbeziehungen und die unabhängige Spielfilmproduktion 1933–1937.' *Modern Austrian Literature* 32, no. 4, Special Issue: Austria in Film, 1999, 87–117.
Loacker, Armin and Martin Prucha, eds. 2000. *Unerwünschtes Kino. Deutschsprachige Emigrantenfilme 1934 bis 1937*. Wien: Verlag Filmarchiv Austria.
Maltby, Richard, Daniel Biltereyst and Philippe Meers, eds. 2011. *Explorations in New Cinema History. Approaches and Case Studies*. Malden: Wiley-Blackwell.
Murray, Bruce. 1990. *Film and the German Left in the Weimar Republic. from Caligari to Kuhle Wampe*. Austin: University of Texas Press.
Neergaard, Ebbe. 1963. *The Story of Danish Film*. Copenhagen: Danske Selskab.
Nørrested, Carl. 1991. 'Over de nordiske grænser.' *Kosmorama* 198, no. 37 (Winter 1991): 50–66.
——. 1996. 'Fy og Bi.' *Kosmorama* 215, no. 42 (Spring 1996): 32–5.
——. 1996a. 'Mellem stumfilm og lydfilm – overgangsfænomener.' *Kosmorama* 217, no. 42 (Spring 1996): 39–43.
Prawer, S. S. 2005. *Between Two Worlds. The Jewish Presence in German and Austrian Film, 1910–1933*. New York and Oxford: Berghahn Books.
Putz, Petra. 1996. *Waterloo in Geiselgasteig. Die Geschichte des Münchner Filmkonzerns Emelka (1919–1933) in Antagonismus zwischen Bayern und dem Reich*. Trier: WVT Wissenschaftlicher Verlag Trier.
Rössler, Patrick. 2017. *Filmfieber. Deutsche Kinopublizistik 1917–1937*. Erfurt: Universität Erfurt.
Saunders, Thomas J. 1999. 'Germany and Film Europe.' In *'Film Europe' and 'Film America'. Cinema, Commerce and Cultural Exchange 1920–1939*, edited by Andrew Higson and Richard Maltby. Devon: University of Exeter Press, 157–80.
——. 2011. 'Film and Finance in Weimar Germany: the Rise and Fall of David Schratter's Trianon-Film, 1923–1925.' *Film History* 23, 38–56.
Stratenwerth, Irene and Hermann Simon, eds. 2004. *Pioniere in Celluloid. Juden in der frühen Filmwelt*. Berlin: Henschel.
Thompson, C. Claire, Isak Thorsen and Pei-Sze Chow, eds. 2021. *A History of Danish Cinema*. Edinburgh: Edinburgh University Press.
Thompson, Kristin. 1985. *Exporting Entertainment. America in the World Film Market 1907–34*. London: British Film Institute.
——. 1996. 'National or International Films? The European Debate During the 1920s.' *Film History* 8 (1996): 281–96.

———. 1999. 'The Rise and Fall of Film Europe.' In *'Film Europe' and 'Film America'. Cinema, Commerce and Cultural Exchange 1920–1939*, edited by Andrew Higson and Richard Maltby. Devon: University of Exeter Press, 56–81.

Tybjerg, Casper. 2001. 'Et lille lands vagabonder.' In *100 års dansk film*, edited by Peter Schepelern. Copenhagen: Rosinante, 63–89.

———. 2015. 'On the Periphery of the "National Film": Danish Cinematic Border Crossings, 1918–1929.' *European Journal of Scandinavian Studies* 45, no. 2 (2015): 168–87.

———. 2021a. 'The European Principle: Art and Border-Crossing in Carl Theodor Dreyer's Career.' In *A History of Danish Cinema*, edited by C. Claire Thompson, Isak Thorsen and Pei-Sze Chow. Edinburgh: Edinburgh University Press, 41–50.

———. 2021b. '*Jokeren*.' Le Giornate del Cinema Muto, online catalogue. Accessed 14 February 2023. http://www.giornatedelcinemamuto.it/en/jokeren-der-faschingskonig-the-joker/

Vonderau, Patrick. 2007. *Bilder vom Norden. Schwedisch-deutsche Filmbeziehungen 1914–1939*. Marburg: Schüren.

Ward, Ken. 1989. *Mass Communications and the Modern World*. London: Palgrave Macmillan.

Wedel, Michael. 1999. 'Messter's "Silent" Heirs: Sync Systems of the German Music Film 1914–1929.' *Film History* 11, no. 4 (1999): 464–76.

Weniger, Kay. 2011. '*Es wird im Leben dir mehr genommen als gegeben....*' *Lexikon der aus Deutschland und Österreich emigrierten Filmschaffenden 1933 bis 1945: eine Gesamtübersicht*. Hamburg: Acabus Verlag.

Index

1000 Worte Deutsch ('1000 Words in German'), 219, 222–3, 224, 225, 227

Aarhus, Denmark, 80, 94
Abel, Richard, 165
Abwege (*The Devious Path*), 150
Adventures of Maya, The, 195
Afgrunden (*The Abyss*), 59, 64, 86, 164
Albani, Marcella, 202
Alf's Carpet, 219, 222
Algol, 177–8
Allen, Julie, 12, 62, 63, 133
Allianz-Tonfilm, 225
Alraune (*A Daughter of Destiny*), 150
Altenloh, Emilie, 168
Andersen, Valdemar, 199
Anderson, Benedict, 52, 71, 88
Ankerstjerne, Johan, 167
Anna Boleyn, 4, 99, 100
art films, European, 161, 165–6
art films, German, 166–7
Assmann, Aleida, 35
Atlantis (1913), 11, 60, 94, 167, 170–1
Austria/Austrian
  Anschluss to German Reich, 227
  Palladium and, 208, 227–30
  Pat and Patachon, 208–9, 210, 211–22
  Sascha-Film, 232
'Autorenfilm' (the author's film), 9, 11, 167

Bachmann, Anne, 212–13
Balázs, Béla, 51
Bang, Herman, 8
Basch, Felix, 202
Baskerville film series, 119–24
bateau de verre, Le, 202
Bauder, Carl, 198, 199
Baxandall, Michael, 28
Becker, Rudolph, 198, 199
Behn, Manfred, 9, 12
Bella Donna, 146
Bencard, Christian, 192, 198
Bergfelder, Tim, 32
Bergkatze, Die (*The Wild Cat*), 146
Berlin, 33, 56–7, 82, 89, 186; *see also* Nordisk Films Kompagni
'Berlin Letters', 89
Berliner Illustrierte Zeitung, 55
Berlingske Aften (Copenhagen daily), 87
Berlingske Tidende, 97–8, 120, 226, 231
Berne Convention, 114

Biene Maja und ihre Abenteuer, Die (*The Adventures of Maya*), 195
Billig, Michal, 90
Biltereyst, Daniel, 130
Biografteaterbladet, 94
Blinde Passagiere (*Stowaways*), 222, 224, 226–7
Bloch, Harriet, 101, 193
Blom, August, 11, 115, 167, 171, 178
Bock, Hans-Michael, 188-9
Boese, Carl, 211, 219, 224
Bonn, Ferdinand, 108, 113, 114–15
Bordwell, David, 27, 160, 161
Børge, Vagn, 10
bourgeois realism, 161, 162
Brandes, Georg, 7, 62, 88, 163
British Association of Sound Film Industries, 199
B.T. (Danish daily), 136, 141, 223
Bushidô: Das eiserne Gesetz (*Bushido: The Iron Law*), 200–1

Cabinet des Dr. Caligari, Das, 166, 176
Calvino, Italo, 25
cartoons, Holmes, 109
celebrity portraits *see Klokken 5*; *Vore Damer*
celebrity portrait(s), definition, 132–3
celebrity terrain, 58–60, 66
censorship, 15, 102, 131, 133, 138, 143
Chaplin, Charles, 135
child actors, 89–90
Chmara, Gregorij, 143
Christensen, Benjamin, 13, 90, 193
Christensen, Thomas C., 15
Cinéa, 176
Cine-Allianz Tonfilm, 212, 219, 220
CineFest, 33

CineGraph, Hamburg, 9, 32–3
Ciné-Journal, 161
CiNéMAS (Canadian film studies journal), 27, 36
cinematographers, 170, 171, 179; *see also individual cinematographers by name*
Claus, Horst, 212, 217
Claussen, Sophus, 64
Clever Cannibals, 219
Comédie Française, La, 161
comparative approach, 27–8, 40
Conrad, Sebastian, 31
consumer culture, Danish stars and narrative of Germanic heritage, 60–1
Copenhagen, 5, 84, 110, 113, 137
Copenhagen Region Cinema Owners Association, 85; *see also Filmen* ('The Film')
Crazy Night, A, 201–2
Cronqvist, Maria, 37
cultural transfer approach, 27, 28–9, 31

Da hält die Welt den Atem an (*Make Up*), 202
Danish American Film Corporation (DAFCO), 190–1, 204
Danish cinema
first Golden Age (1910s), 159
see also individual films by name
Danish Film Institute
digitisation initiative, 13–16
fan mail collections, 53, 66–71
Graatkjær special collection, 172
Kosmorama.org, 13
Nordisk Special Collection, 198
Palladium collection, 213

Danish media/newspapers
  'Berlin Letters', 89
  Ferslew group, 100
  film journalism in 1910s, 93–4
  Holmes novel serialisation, 109–10
  and official neutrality in WWI, 92, 96
  post-war German historical film, 97–8
  see also newspapers, Danish; *individual names of newspapers*
Danish nationalism, 6–7, 24, 90
Danish Royal Library, newspaper collection, 84
Danish trade press
  on German films, 84, 86–8, 92–3
  see also fan magazines; *Filmen* ('The Film'); *individual names of publications*
Danish-German War (1864), 5, 6
Dassanowsky, Robert, 210
Daughter of Destiny, A, 150
daylight cinematography, 173–4
Denmark
  and Schleswig, 28
  see also Copenhagen
detective films, Danish *see* Holmes films
detective films, German, 85
Deutsch Nordischen Film-Union, 223
Deutsch-Amerikanische-Films-Union (DAFU), 193–4; *see also* DNFU
Deutsche Bioscop, 62–3, 166
Deutsche Digitale Bibliothek, 111
Deutsche Lichtspiel Gesellschaft (DLG), 190
Deutsche Universal, 34

Deutsches Lichtspiel-Syndikat AG (DLS), 222
Deutsch-Nordische-Films-Union (DNFU), 194–203
Deutsch-Nordische-Film-Union (DNFU), 183
Devious Path, The, 150
Dickens film adaptations, 195, 202
Dieterle, Wilhelm, 202
Dinesen, Robert, 2, 51–2, 193
Distelmeyer, Jan, 219
distribution, film, 185, 187, 189
DNFU, 194–8, 199–203
Dogme 95, 158
Doll's House, A, 163–4
Don Quixote, 218
Doppelgänger, Der, 221
Doyle, Arthur Conan, 106, 108, 114
Dreyer, Carl Theodor, 2, 13, 42, 131, 141, 193
Droop, Maire Luise, 56–7
Druk (*Another Round*), 158
Dukkehjem, Et (*A Doll's House*), 163–4
Dupont, E. A., 32–3, 192
Dydsdragonen (*The Plaster Saint*), 203
Dyer, Richard, 52, 132–3

Edison, Thomas, 174
Eibye, Poul, 203
Ekman, Gösta, 202
Ekspeditricen (*In the Prime of Life*), 170
Ekstra Bladet, 109
Ekstrabladet, 229
Elegante Welt (ladies' journal), 53, 54
Elsaesser, Thomas, 36, 165

Emo, E. W., 210, 220
Engberg, Marguerite, 9, 11, 15, 167, 175, 210
Engelein, 83, 175–6
Enhver ('Everyman'), 11
entangled history approach, 24–5, 26, 35, 38–9, 41, 42–3, 185
Entangled Media Histories (EMHIS), 36–8
Erdgeist (*Earth Spirit*), 174
European art (house) films, 161
Expressionist movement, 32, 165–6, 176–7
EYE Film Museum, 175

Famous Players (US company), 191
fan magazines, 53, 55, 59–61
fan mail/fandom, 16, 62
  DFI archive, 53–4, 66–70
  imagined communities, 70–1
  press coverage on, 65
  stars on, 65–6
Fardon, Richard, 25
feature films, 161–2, 195
Federal Archive, Germany, 16
Féraudy, Maurice de, 202
Ferslew group (Danish press), 100
Film, Der, 224
Film d'Art, Le, 161
'Film Europe' movement, 184, 199–203
film palaces, 137, 161
film propaganda *see* propaganda
film trade journals *see* Danish trade press; German trade press
Filmen ('The Film'), 88–9, 97
  'Berlin Letters', 89–90
  'Clips and Flicks', 89
  on Danish stars, 88
  on the Reinwald family, 89–90
Film-Kurier, 209
Filmprimadonna, Die (*The Film Primadonna*), 175
Fiske, John, 132, 136, 141
Fiskerliv i Norden, 175
Flamme, Die, 146
Folkets Avis, 121
Fønss, Olaf, 61, 101
  cosmopolitan self-representation, 52
  fan magazines, 55, 61, 74
  fan mail, 16, 54–4, 63, 68–71
  German press's Germanic image of, 63–4
  Homunculus series, 61
  memoirs, 66
  Tysk Skuespilkunst ('German Art of Acting'), 59
Forbidden Paradise, 149
Fotorama, 80, 200
France, film settings, 202
Frandsen, Steen Bo, 80
Frau Sopherl vom Naschmarkt, 217
Fräulein Julie ('Miss Julie'), 102
Frelst fra den vaade Grav ('Saved from a watery Grave'), 93
freudlose Gasse, Die (*The Joyless Street*), 136, 137–8, 139, 142, 143
Freund, Karl, 83, 159, 175–4
Froelich, Carl, 159
Frost, Harald, 167
Fuglsang, Frederik, 2, 125, 193, 219
Fuhrman, Wolfgang, 33
Fuller, Kathryn, 53
Funkzauber, 201
Fyrtaarnet & Bivognen *see* Pat and Patachon (films)

Gad, Urban, 13, 87, 138, 159, 166
  Babelsberg studio, 179
  images, 83, 175–6
  move to Germany, 86, 170
Garbo, Greta, 137–8, 139
Garncarz, Joseph, 32, 209, 212
Geheimnis des Abbé X, Das, 202
German cinema
  1910s, 166
  on Danish screens, 4–5
  dominance of, 32
  and import ban, 1916–1921, 100, 165, 168, 176, 191
  international breakthrough, 84
  Pat and Patachon, 208–9, 210, 222–7
  pre-war style, 165
  Weimar 'Expressionism', 32, 165–6, 176–7
  see also individual films by name
German Cinema Reform Movement, 3
German Digital Library, 16
German film actors' union, and child actors, 70
German language area
  fandom and fan magazines, 72, 73
  see also fan magazines; fan mail/fandom
German newspapers *see* newspapers, German; *individual names of newspapers*
German propaganda films, 126, 177, 189
  German trade press, 86; *see also Kinematograph, Der*; *individual names of publications*
German-Danish War, 5, 6
Germany
  and Nazism, 177, 226
  Weimar. *see* Weimar Germany
Gestrich, Constanze, 12
Gezeichneten, Die, 13
Gillette, William, 110, 113
Girl Kidnappers, 222, 224, 225, 226
Glenthøj, Rasmus, 7
Glück, Oscar, 220
Golden Clown, The, 202
Gómez Muriel, Emilio, 33–4
Gottschalk, Ludwig, 59
Graatkjær, Axel, 2, 82–3, 159–60, 162, 169–79
Graf, Heinrich, 198
Great Northern Film Company, 162–4
Gregory, Arthur G., 219–20, 228, 231–2
Griffithiana (journal), 9
Gunning, Tom, 183–4

Hagener, Malte, 38–9, 40, 184
Hallo! Afrika forude! (*Clever Cannibals*), 219
Hamlet, 121
Han, Hun og Hamlet (*He, She and Hamlet*), 222
Harris, Sue, 32
Hauptmann, Gerhard, 94, 167
Heiland, Heinz Karl, 200–1
Heinke, Ralf Heiner, 32, 33–4
Helm, Brigitte, 220
  celebrity portrait, 149–52
  Metropolis, 130, 135, 136, 139–40, 153
  New Woman, 130, 134
  and UFA, 151, 152
Helt fra 64, En ('A Hero from 64'), 80–1

Hending, Arnold, 116, 120
Herder, Johann Gottfried, 57
Herms, Edmund, 194, 195–6
Hero from 64, A, 80–1
Herr des Todes, Der (*The Master of Death*), 217
Higson, Andrew, 32, 183, 184, 199, 200, 204
Hilgert, Christoph, 37
Himmel über Berlin, Der (*Wings of Desire*), 158
Himmelskibet (*A Trip to Mars*), 92
histoire croisée, 25–7, 29, 31, 33, 36, 39–42, 58–9
historical films, German, 85, 98–9, 100
Hitchcock, Alfred, 179
Hjort, Mette, 34–5
Hollmann, Anton, 7
Hollywood movies, 35, 135, 164
  1910s, 187
  1920s, 131
  Danish press on, 99–100
  and German screens, 32
Holmes films, 104, 107–8
  Bonn and Nordisk Films, 114–17
  German, 120–24
  Larsen's Danish, 118–20
Holmes stories/novels, 106, 114, 121–3
  in Denmark, 108, 109–10
  in Germany, 108–9, 110–13
Homunculus series, 60, 61, 65
Honey-Moon Island, 202
Horney, Oscar, 194, 195
horror films, 175
Horwa-Goron (German company), 203
Hound of the Baskervilles, The, 110

Hr. Tell og Søn (*William Tell and Son*), 212
Hugenberg, Alfred, 199
Hugo Engel-Film, 213, 214, 217
Hund von Baskerville, Der (*Hound of the Baskervilles*), 106, 107
  film adaptation, 125
  stage play, 113–14
  see also Baskerville film series
hvide Slavehandel, Den (*The White Slave Trade*), 161–2

I Once Had a Beautiful Fatherland, 201
Ibsen, Henrik, 163–4
Ich habe im Mai von Liebe geträumt, 201
Ich hatte einst ein schönes Vaterland, 201
Illustrierte Film-Woche, 53, 54, 57
Illustrierte Kino-Woche, 53, 54
imagined communities, 52, 71–2
import ban on foreign films, 1916–1921, 73, 100, 165, 168, 176, 191
individual agency, and interactive processes, 42
Internationale Arbeitershilfe (IAH), 193
intertextuality, 132

Jacobsen, Wolfgang, 10
Jacoby, Georg, 202–3, 222, 223, 224
Jannings, Emil, 98, 99, 177–8
Japan, 200
Joan the Woman, 98
Jokeren/Der Faschingskönig (*The Joker*), 202–3, 223

Joyless Street, The see freudlose Gasse, Die (*The Joyless Street*)
Jyllandsposten, 99–100

Kærligheds-Øen (*Honey-Moon Island*), 202
Kalbus, Oskar, 8
Kallmann, Felix, 192
Kiepura, Jan, 220
Kinder des Generals, Die (*Falsely Accused*), 63–4
Kinematograph, Der, 61, 86, 161, 194, 196, 201, 224
on DNFU films, 200–1, 202
Kinografen, 80
Kino-Palæet, Copenhagen, 137, 138
Kladd und Datsch, die Pechvögel, 212
Klieg lights, 174
Klokken 5, 149–52, 210
Klovnen (*The Golden Clown*), 202
København, 123, 124
Kohner, Paul, 34
Kosmorama.org, 13
KoWo company, 109
Kracauer, Siegfried, 10, 166, 195
Krauss, Werner, 202
Kubler, George, 160
Kurrent, 70–1
Kvinde af Folket, En (*A Woman of the People*), 162

Ladies' magazines, 136; *see also Vore Damer*
Lamac, Carl, 210, 221
Landsvägsriddare (*Love and Burglars*), 208
Lang, Fritz, 136, 139, 176, 192
Lange, Sven, 167

Lange-Fuchs, Hauke, 210
Langen, Ulrich, 36
Lani, Lili, 214–16
Larsen, Lisbeth Richter, 13
Larsen, Viggo, 15, 82, 93
  German film titles, 2, 15
  Holmes films, 107–8, 118–20
  at Nordisk Films Kompagni, 2, 166, 167
Lauritzen, Jr, Lau, 219
Lauritzen, Lau, 209, 210, 212, 213, 223, 228–9, 231
letze Mann, Der (*The Last Laugh*), 192
Lichtbild-Bühne (film trade journal), 24, 115, 166, 191, 198, 221
lighting, 173–5
Lille Dorrit (*Little Dorrit*), 195
lille Hornblæser, Den ('The Little Trumpeter'), 80, 81
Linder, Max, 86
Lindqvist, Ursula, 34–5
Locher, Jens, 100
Loiperdinger and Jung anthology, 61
London, 108, 186, 199
lookalike contests, 142
Love and Burglars, 208
Løvejagten (*Lion Hunting*), 82
Lubitsch, Ernst
  Anne Boleyn, 4, 100
  Forbidden Paradise, 149
  and Graatkjær, 159
  Madame Dubarry, 98–9, 100, 136
Lumpenkavaliere, 2010–11, 212, 219, 225
Lund University Library, Sweden, 54
Lutz, Stuttgart, 111

Macht des Goldes, *Die* (*The Might of Gold*), 87
Mack, Max, 201
Mad Love, 146
Madame Dubarry, 98–9, 100, 135, 137
　and Germanness, 142
　reviews, 136, 138
　success of, 138, 146
Mädchenräuber (*Girl Kidnappers*), 222, 224, 225, 226
Madsen, Harald, 208, 209, 213–22, 229; *see also* Pat and Patachon (films)
Maharajahens Yndlingshustru (1926) (*Oriental Love*/*The Favourite Wife of the Maharadja*), 195
Maharadjahens Yndlingshustru (1917) (*A Prince of Bharata*), 12
Maharadjahens Yndlingshustru II (*A Daughter of Brahma*), 12
Majestic Film, 225, 227
Make Up, 202
Mann ohne Namen, *Der* (*The Man Without Name*), 192–3
marketing, Danish stars and narrative of Germanic heritage, 60–1
Marshall, P. David, 59, 60, 61
Martyrium, *Das*, 146
May, Joe, 32–3, 98, 100–1
Med fuld Musik ('With Full Music'), 208
Meers, Phillip, 130
Meinert, Rudolf, 125
melodramas, Danish, 131
Messtro-Film, 224–5
Metropolis, 130, 135, 136
　1927 production, 199
　Helm's double role, 138, 150, 151, 153

popular success, 142
　reviews, 139–40
Mexico, 34
Meyer, Leo, 223
Mikkelsen, Mads, 158
Mit Fædreland, min Kærlighed! (*Through the Enemy's Lines*), 92
Morena, Erna, 90, 92
Moretti, Franco, 108
Moser, Hans, 220
Moving Picture News, 164
Moving Picture World, 161, 162–3, 164
Mülleneisen Jr, Christoph, 225
Müller, Corinna, 212
multiple-reel films, 186, 187
Murnau, F. W., 173–4, 192
Mysteries of India, Part I: Truth, 100–1

Nansen, Betty, 51–2, 57, 164
National Filmography, 2
nationalism, 6, 24, 51, 90
nationality, and Danish-German relations, 184
Nazism, propaganda, 177, 226
Ned med Vaabnene! (*Lay Down Your Arms!*), 92
Negri, Pola, 98
　cast as exotic vamp, 146
　Madame Dubarry, 137, 138
　New Woman, 130
　transnational star image, 133–5
　Vore Damer portrait, 140, 147–9, 153–4
Neorealism, Italian, 38
Neuss, Alwin, as Holmes, 108, 120–24
New Cinema History, 27, 53, 132

New Woman, 135–6, 154
New York, 186, 192
newspapers, Danish, 227
  digital archives, 16
  on German films (post-WWI), 97–8
  on German films (pre-war and WWI), 87, 92
  on Nazi propaganda film, 226
  on Pat and Patachon, 223, 224, 225–6
  on Westi-Palladium plan, 230–1, 232
  see also Danish media/newspapers; *individual names of newspapers*
newspapers, German, 63–4, 108–9, 111–12; *see also individual names of newspapers*
Nibelungen, Die, 192
Nielsen, Asta, 10, 86, 142
  1920s, 133, 134, 141
  Afgrunden (*The Abyss*), 164
  art films, 131
  'Asta' subsidiary, 166
  Babelsberg studio, 179
  cosmopolitan self-representation, 51–2, 74
  and Danish trade press, 87
  Engelein, 83, 175–6
  Erdgeist (*Earth Spirit*), 174
  fan magazines, 54–5, 62
  fan mail, 16, 54, 63, 73
  film censorship, 138, 143
  Filmen ('The Film'), 88
  'Germanisation' of, 64–5, 101–2
  and Graatkjær, 159
  The Joyless Street, 137–8, 139, 142, 143
  marketing of, 61
  memoirs, 67
  and negotiations of nationality, 65–6
  New Woman, 130, 135
  perfume, 62
  Vore Damer portrait, 143–6, 152, 154
  works on, 12, 39
Nielsen, Jan, 11
Nielsen, Svend, 209, 214, 228, 229
Nordic Film Cultures and Cinemas of Elsewhere, 39
Nordification of Scandinavian stars, 56–8, 63–4, 69
Nordisk Biograf-Tidende, 84
Nordisk Films Kompagni, 5, 16, 82, 101, 198
  and *Atlantis*, 94–5, 170–1
  and 'Autorenfilm'/art films, 9, 11, 167
  bankruptcy, 223
  Berlin, 56–7
  Bonn at, 114–17
  break with UFA, 192–3, 194
  collection at DFI, 198
  co-productions with DNFU, 200–1
  DAFCO deal, 190–1, 192, 204
  and DAFU/DNFU, 193–6
  Danish-German-British co-production, 223
  expansion during WWI, 165, 186–7
  Film Europe, 202
  financial decline, 193, 194, 198
  focus on international markets, 190
  forced sale of assets in Germany, 97, 100
  Graatkjær at, 159, 169

INDEX

Holmes films, 110, 114–16, 118–20, 125
  Larsen at, 2, 15, 119
  and narrative feature films, 161–2
  orientation towards foreign markets, 160
  Reinwald family at, 90
  rules for directors and cinematographers, 170
  and Scandinavian theatre, 163–4
  transition to longer films, 169, 186
  and UFA, 3, 96–7, 168, 187–92
  in US, 162, 163
  Valby studios, 171–2
  see also Olsen, Ole
Nordisk Tonefilm, 223
Nørrested, Carl, 210
North Schleswig, 85, 89, 103
Norwegian playwrights, 163

Oehlenschläger, Adam, 6
Oes, Ingvald C., 162, 163
O'Fredericks, Alice, 219
Olsen, Ole, 82, 96, 159, 178, 188, 199
  co-writer of *A Trip to Mars*, 92
  DAFCO deal, 191
  feature films, 161
  founded Nordisk Film, 186
  and Graatkjær, 169
  and UFA, 188, 192
One Arabian Night, 146
Opium, 173
Oriental Love/The Favourite Wife of the Maharadja, 195
Oswald, Richard, 32–3, 113, 124–5, 201

Pabst, Georg Wilhelm, 136
Palads-Teatret, Copenhagen, 137
Palladium, 3, 16, 207, 209, 210, 212, 219
  transnational entanglements, 227–30
  and Westi Film, 230–2
Parufamet agreement, 196–7
Passion de Jeanne d'Arc, La (*The Passion of Joan of Arc*), 131
Pat and Patachon (films), 3, 13, 14–15, 131, 208–37
  Palladium and, 227–30
  produced in Austria, 213–22
  produced in Germany, 222–7
  and Westi-Palladium plan, 230–2
  see also Palladium
Pat und Patachon im Paradies, 221
Pathé, 167, 186, 232
penny dreadfuls, 107, 110, 112
Petro, Patrice, 135
Phantom, 173–4
photo cards, 141–2
Pickford, Mary, 51
Pictorial movement, 174
Plaster Saint, The, 203
Polis Paulus påskasmäll (*The Smugglers*), 213–14
Politiken, 16, 120, 123, 138, 139
Pommer, Eric, 192
Pordenone Silent Film Festival, 9–10
Porten, Henny, 87, 90–1, 99, 102
portrait genre, celebrity, 132–3
pragmatic induction, 30–1
Pressburger, Arnold, 212, 219–20
production, film, 185, 187
Projectograph-Film, 220
Prometheus, 212
propaganda, 103–4, 177, 189, 226
Prussians, in Danish film, 80–1
Psilander, Valdemar, 54–5, 67, 88

Rabinowitsch, Gregor, 212, 219
race ideals and Nordification, 56–8, 62–3, 68–9
Raske Riviera Rejsende (*At the Mediterranean*), 214
Rätsel von Borobudur, Das, 200–1
Redes, 33–4
reflexivity, 42–3
Reinert, Robert, 173
Reinwald, Otto, 90–1
Rekrut fra 64, En (*A Recruit from 64*), 80, 81
Richard Oswald Film, 228
Richard Wagner (*The Life and Works of Richard Wagner*), 94
Riddle of Borobudur, The, 200–1
Riese, Hilde, 72
Riget (Copenhagen daily), 86
romantic nationalism, 6
Ross, Michael, 113
Rung, Otto, 167
Ruppert, Sophie, 66
Rye, Stellan, 93, 166

Sacchetto, Rita, 54
Salt, Barry, 170
Sandberg, A. W., 131, 161, 193
Sappho (*Mad Love*), 146
Sascha Goron (French company), 202
Sauer, Fred, 225, 226
Säugetier, Das ('The Mammal'), 103
Scandinavian Modern Breakthrough, 56
Schaefer, Eric, 41
Schatten des Lebens ('Shadow of Life'), 87
Schenstrøm, Carl, 208, 209, 213–22, 229; *see also* Pat and Patachon (films)

Schleswig
  Danish minority, 7, 80
  division of, 1920, 7–8, 28
  Prussian rule and Germanisation, 6–7
  see also North Schleswig
Schleswig wars
  First, 1848–1850, 6, 80
  Second, 1864, 5, 6
Schleswig-Holstein, 6
Schmidt, Heike, 25
Schrøder, Kim, 107
Schröder, Stephan Michael, 3, 4, 11–12, 13, 183
Schünzel, Reinhold, 32–3
Schwarzer Traum und weiße Sklavin, 9, 74
Schwiegersöhne ('Sons-in-Law'), 210, 211, 212, 217–18
scriptwriters, 2, 219, 224
Sealed Orders, 90–1
Second Schleswig War (1864), 5, 6
Seeber, Guido, 166, 175
Shaw, Deborah, 31–2
Sherlock Holmes films *see* Holmes films
Sherlock Holmes (play), 110; *see also* stage plays
Sherlock Holmes stories *see* Holmes stories/novels
shooting ratios, 171
singende Stadt, Die (*The Singing City*), 220
Skandinavisk Films Union, 189
Smugglers, The, 213–14
Social-Demokraten, 93–4, 100–1, 227
  1920s films, 139
  on Holmes films, 120, 121, 122

on Pat and Patachon/Palladium, 215, 216–17
Søland, Brigitte, 135
Song of Death, 172
Sørensen, Axel *see* Graatkjær, Axel
sørgmuntre Barber, Den (*The Tragi-Comic Barber*), 203
sound films
　advent of, 178
　Pat and Patachon, 208, 210–11, 212, 219, 222
Soviet Russia, 36, 193
Sport Cigarette cards, 141–2
stage plays
　Hound of the Baskervilles, 113–14
　Sherlock Holmes, 110
Stanziani, Alessandro, 40
Stark, Else, 228
Stark, Lothar, 190, 202, 209, 228–30, 231
state censorship, 133, 136
Steinhoff, Hans, 212, 217, 224
Stiller, Mauritz, 150
Stinnes, Hugo, 230
Stowaways, 222, 224, 226–7
Strand, Paul, 34
Street, Sarah, 32
Student von Prag, Der (*The Student of Prague*), 93, 166
Suffragette, Die, 138
Sumurun (*One Arabian Night*), 146
Sweden, 11, 33, 213

tableau-style film, 161, 170, 175, 178–9
Talmadge, Norma, 141
Tatjana, 101
tertiary texts, 132, 136, 141
theatre industry, Nordisk's relationship with, 163–4
theatrical unions, 167
Theunissen, Michael, *Der Andere*, 42
Thompson, Kristin, 4, 187
Thorsen, Isak, 11, 168, 169–70
Toa Tojin, 200
Tobis Klangfilm sound system, 225, 226
tolle Nacht, Eine, 201–2
Tolnæs, Gunnar, 54, 56–7, 193
Töteberg, Michael, 188
Totentanz, Der (*Song of Death*), 172
Trade Information Bulletins, US Department of Commerce, 4
trade press
　articles on film, 1910s, 87–8
　see also Copenhagen Region Cinema Owners Association; Danish trade press; German trade press; *specific names of publications*
Tragödie der Macht, Eine (*Power*), 177
Traitress, The, 86–7
translators/translations, and Doyle's Holmes stories, 108–9
transnational film history, 25, 30–5, 183–4, 185, 204
Transnational Screens (journal; previously *Transnational Cinemas*), 31
transnationality *see* transnational film history
Trenker, Luis, 33–4
Treumann, Wanda, 93, 98
Trier, Lars von, 158
Trip to Mars, A, 92
Trocadero café, Friedrichstrasse, 89–90

Tryde, Wilhelm, 112–13
Tunnel, Der, 177

Ufa international (anthology), 33
United States of America
   Great Northern Film Company, 162–4
   Nordisk Films, 163
   and Parufamet agreement, 196–7
   post-WWI, films screened in Denmark and Germany, 199
Universum Film Aktien-Gesellschaft (UFA), 168–9, 179
   1924–1925 film releases, 24
   break with Nordisk Films, 192–3, 194
   DAFCO deal, 190–1
   Expressionist movement, 176
   formed (1917), 3
   German archive, 16
   Helm and, 135, 151, 152
   and Parufamet agreement, 196–7
   Pressburger and Rabinowitsch at, 219
   role post-war, 100, 101
   takeover and collaboration with Nordisk Film, 187–92
   and the US film industry, 200
US Department of Commerce, Trade Information Bulletins, 4

Valentino, Rudolph, 135, 141
Varieté, 192
Veritas Vincit ('Truth Triumphs'), 98
Verlagshaus für Volksliteratur und Kunst, 112
verlorene Sohn, Der, 33–4
Verräterin, Die (*The Traitress*), 86–7

Vienna, 186, 211, 216
   Listo studio, 217
   Pat and Patachon, 217
   Projectograph-Film, 220
   Tobis-Sascha studio, 220
Vinding, Andreas, 215
Vinterberg, Thomas, 158
Vonderau, Patrick, 11, 33
Vore Damer, 136, 137, 141
   Negri portrait, 140, 147–9, 153–4
   Nielsen portrait, 143–6, 152, 154

war films, Danish, 80–1, 92
Warm, Hermann, 177
Waxworks, 166
Wedel, Michael, 167
Wegener, Paul, 93, 166
Weimar Germany, 'Expressionism', 32, 165–6
Weisse Geisha, Die (*The White Geisha*), 200
Wenders, Wim, 158
Wengeroff, Vladimir, 230, 231
Werner, Michael, 40, 185–6
   histoire croisée, 25–7, 28, 29–30, 41–2, 58–9
Westi Film, 230–2
White Geisha, The, 200
White Slave Trade, The, 161–2
Wiene, Conrad, 98
Wiene, Robert, 159, 176, 179
Wieth, Carlo, 56
Wieth, Clara, fan mail, 53–4, 62, 66, 68
Wild Cat, The, 146
Wilhelminian discourses on 'Northernness', 56–7
William Tell and Son, 212
Wings of Desire, 158

Woman of the People, A, 162
World War I
   Danish neutrality, 7, 85, 92, 165
   film import ban, 100, 165, 168
Wulff, Emil, 113, 114

Zanmu Kako, 200
Ziener, Cristoph, 32, 33–4
Zimmerman, Bénédicte, 185–6

histoire croisée, 25–7, 28, 29–30,
   41–2, 58–9
research on unemployment, 40–1
Zinnemann, Fred, 33–4
Zirkus Saran ('Circus Saran'), 210, 220
Zukor, Adolph, 191
Zwei Vagabunden im Prater ('Two
   Vagabonds in the Prater'), 210,
   214–15, 227, 230

EU representative:
Easy Access System Europe
Mustamäe tee 50, 10621 Tallinn, Estonia
Gpsr.requests@easproject.com

www.ingramcontent.com/pod-product-compliance
Lightning Source LLC
Chambersburg PA
CBHW051120160426
43195CB00014B/2271